Focus on
LITERACY

Teacher's Resource Book 6

John McIlwain

 COLLINS

Author: John McIlwain

Design: Grasshopper Design Company

Editor: James Ryan

Cover image: Michael Scott, Tony Stone Images

Illustrations: Brian Walker

Published by Collins Educational
An imprint of HarperCollins*Publishers* Ltd
77–85 Fulham Palace Road
Hammersmith
London W6 8JB

Telephone ordering and information:
0870 0100 441

The HarperCollins website address is:
www.**fire**and**water**.com

First published 1999

Reprinted 2000

ISBN 0 00 302522 5

British Library Cataloguing in Publication Data
A catalogue record for this book is available from the British Library.

Printed in Great Britain by Martins the Printers, Berwick-upon-Tweed

Acknowledgements
The author and publishers wish to thank the following for permission
to use copyright material:
Unit 14: "The bee is a merchant" by Peter Kelso from *Junior Voices*,
edited by Geoffrey Summerfield (Penguin Education); Doubleday, a
division of Random House Inc. for "Sudden Shower" by Basho from
An Introduction to Haiku by Harold Henderson, © 1958 by Harold
G. Henderson; "In a Station of the Metro" by Ezra Pound from *Personae*,
© 1926 by Ezra Pound; "Across I travel" by Christian Tatteresfield from
Does it Have to Rhyme? by Sandy Brownjohn (Hodder & Stoughton,
1982); Unit 17: Marian Reiner for "Mean Song" by Eve Merriam, © Eve
Merriam; Unit 20: Pearson Education Ltd for extracts from *Grandfather
Singh Stories* by Pratima Mitchell (Longman, 1985); Unit 24: from
"Naming of Parts" by Henry Reed from *Collected Poems*, edited by Jon
Stallworthy (Oxford University Press, 1991); Ewan Macnaughton
Associates on behalf of the Telegraph Group Ltd for "I wandered lonely
as a cat" by Brian Aldiss from *The Book of Mini-Sagas II* (Alan Sutton,
1988), © Sunday Telegraph Colour Magazine; Unit 27: Doubleday, a
division of Transworld Publishers Ltd for "D is for Dad" from *The
Suitcase Kid* by Jacqueline Wilson, © 1992 by Jacqueline Wilson.

Every effort has been made to trace copyright holders and to obtain
their permission for the use of copyright material. The author and
publishers will gladly receive any information enabling them to rectify
any error or omission in subsequent editions.

Contents

Focus on Literacy and the National Literacy Strategy

You will find in *Focus on Literacy* a strong support in the teaching of reading and writing within the context of a literacy hour. All the literacy objectives of the National Literary Strategy for each term may be covered by using the Big Book anthologies together with the Pupil's Book, the Homework Book, the Copymasters and the Teacher's Resource Book. Here, in one grand design, are sufficient teaching materials for five full literacy hours per week throughout the entire school year.

The aims of *Focus on Literacy*

The aims of *Focus on Literacy* are identical to those of the National Literacy Strategy: to develop each child's ability to read and write. It promotes their development by honing the literary skills necessary to meet the Range, Key Skills, and Standard English and Language Study of the National Curriculum Programmes of Study.

These skills are wide-ranging and specific, and worthy of review:

- to read and write with confidence, fluency and understanding

- to use a full range of reading cues (phonic, graphic, syntactic, contextual) to self-monitor their reading and correct their own mistakes

- to understand the sound and spelling system and use this to read and spell accurately

- to acquire fluent and legible handwriting

- to have an interest in words and word meanings, and to increase vocabulary

- to know, understand and be able to write in a range of genres in fiction and poetry, and understand and be familiar with some of the ways that narratives are structured through basic literary ideas of setting, character and plot

- to understand and be able to use a range of non-fiction texts

- to plan, draft, revise and edit their own writing

- to have a suitable technical vocabulary through which to understand and discuss their reading and writing

- to be interested in books, read with enjoyment and evaluate and justify preferences

- to develop their powers of imagination, inventiveness and critical awareness through reading and writing.

The NLS framework and *Focus on Literacy*

The NLS teaching objectives for reading and writing are set out in termly units to ensure progression. Each term's work focuses on specific reading genres and related writing activities. *Focus on Literacy* offers carefully selected examples of these reading genres and stimulating activities relating to them.

The overall structure is the same for each term and is divided into three strands: text, sentence and word levels. Text level refers to comprehension and composition, sentence level to grammar and punctuation and word level to phonics, spelling and vocabulary. The activities in *Focus on Literacy* offer many opportunities for the development of handwriting, while leaving you free to follow your school's own writing policy.

The Literacy Hour and *Focus on Literacy*

The NLS framework requires a literacy hour as part of school work each day. The literacy hour is designed to establish a common pattern for all classes and is carefully structured to ensure a balance between whole class and group teaching, as the diagram below shows.

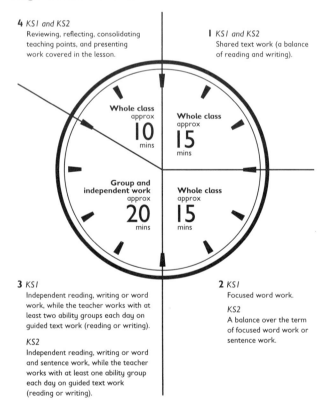

4 *KS1 and KS2*
Reviewing, reflecting, consolidating teaching points, and presenting work covered in the lesson.

1 *KS1 and KS2*
Shared text work (a balance of reading and writing).

Whole class approx **10** mins

Whole class approx **15** mins

Group and independent work approx **20** mins

Whole class approx **15** mins

3 *KS1*
Independent reading, writing or word work, while the teacher works with at least two ability groups each day on guided text work (reading or writing).

KS2
Independent reading, writing or word and sentence work, while the teacher works with at least one ability group each day on guided text work (reading or writing).

2 *KS1*
Focused word work.

KS2
A balance over the term of focused word work or sentence work.

This structure enables you to spend up to 100 per cent of your time in direct teaching. Children work in a direct teaching relationship for approximately 60 per cent of the time and independently for the remaining 40 per cent.

The high-quality texts of *Focus on Literacy* and the related activities directly meet the NLS objectives, and so relieve you of the burden of deciding *what* to teach. The teacher's notes support you in planning *how* to use the materials in your teaching.

Shared whole class time

Shared whole class time takes place during the first half of the literacy hour. It is generally divided into 15 minutes of shared text work (a balance of reading and writing) and 15 minutes of focused word and sentence work. This is the time when you can effectively model the reading/writing process with the children.

In shared reading you can help to extend reading skills in line with the NLS objectives, teaching and reinforcing grammar, punctuation and vocabulary.

The reading texts also provide ideas and structures for shared writing. Working with the whole class, you create the opportunity to teach grammar and spelling skills, to demonstrate features of layout and presentation, and to focus on editing and refining work. The shared writing will also be the starting point for independent writing.

Independent activities

The shared whole class time of the literacy hour is usually followed by 20 minutes of independent activities. During this time you will probably work with a guided reading or writing group, while the children will be working independently, but within a group organised by ability to cater for differentiation.

To help you with this, the word and sentence work in the Pupil's Book is divided into two, three or four sections identified as A, B, C and D; A is the easiest and D is the hardest. It is important to match carefully these activities to the children's ability, and to explain them thoroughly before the children begin. This leaves you free to work with your group without interruptions from children seeking your further support.

Each section is short so that children will be able to complete the activities you select in the time available. The Homework Book is available for those who finish early and wish to keep busy, as well as for work outside the classroom. Other activities which the children may do during this time are independent reading and preparing presentations for the class.

It is suggested that you aim to work with each guided reading and writing group for two sessions per week, organised so that you see each child in the class at least once.

Plenary

The final 10 minutes of the literacy hour is a plenary session for reviewing, reflecting upon and consolidating teaching points, and presenting work covered in the lesson. This is an essential element of the hour. It is important to plan this activity so that every child has the opportunity to feed back once as part of their group during the course of a week. A different objective will be featured each day so that each objective is reinforced in turn. This will allow you to monitor each group's progress and highlight the teaching/learning points as necessary.

Using *Focus on Literacy*

The Big Book anthologies

There are three Big Book anthologies. These consist of carefully chosen texts for shared work on word, sentence and text levels. The extracts also provide the context for the independent activities. Each unit provides texts for a week's shared reading.

Each extract in the anthology begins with a short introduction, placing the text that follows in context. The extract is accompanied by a *To think and talk about* section to prompt and stimulate the children's responses.

Further teaching points and suggestions are given in the Teacher's Resource Book.

The Pupil's Book

The Pupil's Book is made up of 30 units. Each unit begins with the main text and is followed by the independent activities for the week.

To help you with differentiation, the independent activities are identified for level of difficulty, section A being the easiest and D the hardest. Each section is scaled to a workable size. By matching the level of difficulty to a group's ability level, you can help assure that children can complete the activities in the time available.

The five-day spread

Each unit provides work for five days. The spread of work is typically organised as follows (though the pattern is varied, especially in later units, to allow for extended SATs-type work):

The independent activity for **Day 1** is text-based. Section A has questions for literal recall, while those in section B are inferential. These independent questions are in addition to those in the *To think and talk about* section, which are intended as shared reading questions in order for you to help the children to explore the text at greater depth.

Day 2 independent activities focus on word, sentence or text work.

Day 3 begins with shared writing, followed by independent writing.

Day 4 is the same as Day 3.

Day 5 completes the word, sentence or text work.

'Stickers' provide the children with the facts they need to complete the work and make the most of the activities.

The Homework Book

The Homework Book contains activities which consolidate and extend the work in the Pupil's Book. This book is equally useful in the classroom outside the literacy hour and out of the classroom for work at home.

The Teacher's Resource Book

The Teacher's Resource Book comprises notes, copymasters, record sheets and NLS charts. It also outlines a basic approach to each unit in the Big Books and Pupil's Book and includes two award certificates.

The teacher's notes and you

The teacher's notes help you use the *Focus on Literacy* material to the best advantage. The notes are arranged in five sections, each covering one literacy hour. These are further subdivided according to the literacy format: shared text/shared writing work, focused word/sentence work, independent work, and plenary.

A termly planning chart introduces each term's group of units. This chart lists the range of texts for that term, the text, sentence and word work which is explicitly covered, and the continuous work which will be part of your teaching throughout the term, such as practising reading and spelling strategies.

The teacher's notes for each text are organised to facilitate the literacy hour.

A *Key Learning Objectives* box lists the key literacy objectives covered in that week's work, and a *Resources* box identifies the range of texts covered, details of the extracts and the page references of all the components used in the unit.

Details are given of any special preparation you need to do for the unit, for example, providing dictionaries.

The *Shared reading* section lists teaching points and suggestions on how to explore the meaning of the text, in line with the literacy framework objectives. In fiction and poetry this entails exploring genres, settings, characters, plots, themes, figurative language, authorship and the way different texts are organised. In non-fiction text this involves genres, structures and presentation, identifying main points, skimming and scanning, following an argument, exploring steps in a process, comparing different sources and differentiating fact, opinion and persuasion.

The texts often provide both structure and content for writing activities, and the context for many of the activities at sentence and word level on the copymasters.

The *Shared writing* section reflects the increased emphasis placed on writing in Year 6, offering guidance on how texts are composed. The main text studied in earlier shared reading sessions will provide the ideas and structure for this writing. Each shared writing activity is the starting point for subsequent independent writing.

The *Focused word/sentence work* section offers appropriate teaching points and suggestions for investigating text in detail to explore how its message is influenced by style: language, grammar, choice of vocabulary and presentation. The Pupil's Book supports independent consolidation of the work.

The *Independent work* section introduces the independent reading, writing or word and sentence activities which may be found in the Pupil's Book, the Homework Book or on Copymasters.

The *Plenary* section has suggestions for reviewing and reflecting upon the work covered, consolidating teaching points and presenting work.

A *Consolidation and extension* section has ideas and suggestions for follow-up activities.

The *Homework* section describes the related activity in the Homework Book.

Copymasters

The Copymasters offer a range of support material among which are book reviews, planning sheets, charts for collecting and classifying words, and consolidation and extension work.

Assessment

Year 6 materials include a wide range of SATs-style tests in all units from 15 to 27, linked to the material in the Big Books and designed to give teacher and pupil maximum practice and support in reading, writing and spelling during the run-up to the "real thing". There is also a revision page on the last page of Homework Book 6.

Record keeping

Record sheets are provided at the back of the Teacher's Resource Book. They feature a summary of the term's objectives, each with a space for your comments.

Award certificates

Photocopiable award certificates are provided to reward significant individual achievements in literacy.

NLS charts

A chart listing all literacy objectives for the year, and showing how these are covered by *Focus on Literacy* materials, is included in the back of the Teacher's Resource Book.

Basic approach to each unit

The basic approach to each unit in *Focus on Literacy* is as follows:

Day 1

Shared **reading** of the week's main text in the Big Book.

Focused word/sentence work based on the main text.

Independent text work on the main text, which is reproduced in the Pupil's Book.

Plenary session for which there are suggestions in the teacher's notes.

Day 2

Further shared **reading** of the main text.

Further focused word/sentence work based on the main text.

Independent word, sentence or text work in the Pupil's Book.

Plenary suggestions in the teacher's notes.

Day 3

Shared **writing**, using the main text as a model or stimulus.

Focused word/sentence work, appropriate to the shared writing task.

Independent writing, using guidance in the Pupil's Book.

Plenary suggestions in the teacher's notes.

Day 4

Shared **reading** of the second text in the Big Book.

Focused word/sentence work based on the second text.

Continuation of the independent writing from Day 3.

Plenary suggestions in the teacher's notes.

Day 5

Further shared **reading** of the second text.

Focused word/sentence work based on the second text.

Independent word, sentence or text work in the Pupil's Book.

Plenary suggestions in the teacher's notes.

This approach is flexible, and is sometimes varied to make the most of the week's activities. For example, the shared reading for Day 4 might be replaced by shared writing when more extended written work is being developed; shared writing might begin on Day 2; or the second text might be shared on Day 2.

Work outside the literacy hour

The Copymasters and Homework Book provide activities for outside the literacy hour and outside the classroom.

The extracts in *Focus on Literacy* are only part of the genre coverage. You will need time outside of the literacy hour to read aloud to your class, giving children the opportunity to hear complete stories, novels and poems. You will also need to show them complete non-fiction texts, so that features such as covers, blurbs, information about authors, contents, indexes and chapter headings can be discussed and appreciated. Children will need further time for their own independent reading for interest and pleasure, and older pupils will need time for extended writing.

You can help to reinforce genre features when children choose books for independent reading, or during guided reading sessions when you are working with a group.

Big Book contents

TERM 1

BIG BOOK 6A

BIG BOOK 6B

TERM 2

BIG BOOK 6B

TERM 3

BIG BOOK 6C

Pupil's Book contents

TERM 1

TERM 2

TERM 3

Homework Book contents

Copymaster checklist

TERM 1

Unit 1	1	Describing an event
Unit 2	2	Play scripts
Unit 3	3	Journal of a Russian gunner
Unit 4	4	Comparing accounts
Unit 5	5	Planning a biography
Unit 6	6	Creating a glossary
Unit 7	7	The Seven Ages of Man
Unit 8	8	A newspaper report
Unit 9	9	Personification
Unit 10	10	Our region
Unit 11	11	Changing moods
Unit 12	12	Good King Wenceslas – the page's story

TERM 2

Unit 13	13	A sudden change of scene
Unit 14	14	Planning a haiku
Unit 15	15	Zulema Menem
Unit 17	16	Jabberwocky
	17	An animal that can talk
Unit 18	18	A person who makes me laugh
Unit 19	19	A glossary of terms
Unit 20	20	A farewell letter
Unit 21	21	The birth of a poem
Unit 22	22	Main and subordinate clauses

TERM 3

Unit 23	23	The killer spelling test
Unit 24	24	Naming of Parts
Unit 25	25	Signs, symbols and abbreviations for taking notes
Unit 26	26	Dictionary definitions
Unit 27	27	D is for Dad
Unit 28	28	An extended story
Unit 29	29	Crossword
Unit 30	30	Books by Anne Fine

Teacher's Notes

Year 6 • Terms 1–3

HALF-TERMLY PLANNER

Year 6 • Term 1 • Weeks 1–6

TERM 1

SCHOOL _____   CLASS _____   TEACHER _____

		Phonetics, spelling and vocabulary	Grammar and punctuation	Comprehension and composition	Texts
Continuous work **Weeks 1–6**		WL 1, 2, 3	SL 1	TL 1, 18	**Range** Classic fiction, diaries, journals, classic poetry, letters, notes, anecdotes, autobiography and biography, classic drama – Shakespeare, non-chronological reports
Blocked work					
Week	**Unit**				**Titles**
1	1	WL 4	SL 4, 5, 6	TL 3, 5, 7, 8	From *The Call of the Wild*, Jack London
2	2	WL 4	SL 4	TL 2, 3, 6, 9	From *The Growing Pains of Adrian Mole*, Sue Townsend
3	3		SL 2, 3, 5	TL 3, 8, 12, 14	From *A Victorian RSM*, George Loy Smith
4	4	WL 7, 10	SL 3	TL 2, 3, 6, 8, 11, 12, 14	*The Charge of the Light Brigade*, Alfred, Lord Tennyson; From *Letters from the Crimea*, Florence Nightingale, edited by Sue M. Goldie
5	5	WL 5	SL 6	TL 11, 14	From *Boy*, Roald Dahl; From *Roald Dahl: A Biography*, Jeremy Treglown
6	6	WL 7, 9, 10	SL 4, 6	TL 3, 4, 5, 6, 10	From *Macbeth*, William Shakespeare; From *Dungeons and Torture*, John McIlwain

Focus on Literacy Teacher's Resource Book 6 © John McIlwain, HarperCollins*Publishers* Ltd 1999

SCHOOL _____   CLASS _____   TEACHER _____

		Phonetics, spelling and vocabulary	Grammar and punctuation	Comprehension and composition	Texts
Continuous work **Weeks 7–12**		WL 1, 2, 3	SL 1	TL 1, 18	**Range** Classic drama, Shakespeare, non-fiction, journalistic writing, poetry by long-established authors, non-chronological reports, classic fiction, classic poetry
Blocked work **Week**	**Unit**				**Titles**
7	7	WL 5, 7	SL 4, 5, 6	TL 3, 4, 5, 6, 8, 12	From *As You Like It*, William Shakespeare; "London Bound", John McIlwain
8	8	WL 9	SL 4	TL 12, 15, 16	"Den 'n' dusted", *Sun*; "Scholes steals the thunder", *Independent*; "Teddy bears' picnic", *The Week*
9	9		SL 6	TL 3, 10	"Xmas", Wes Magee; "Silver", Walter de la Mare; "The Poet Takes a Walk in the Country", Roger McGough
10	10	WL 8	SL 4, 5	TL 8, 12, 13, 17	From *AA Discovering Britain*; From *The Cambridge Encyclopedia of Language*, David Crystal
11	11	WL 7, 10	SL 2, 4, 6	TL 2, 3, 4, 5	From *A Christmas Carol*, Charles Dickens
12	12	WL 6, 7		TL 6, 8	"Good King Wenceslas", J.M. Neale; The Lord's Prayer

Unit 1 Call of the Wild

Key Learning Objectives

TL3	to articulate personal responses to literature, identifying why and how a text affects the reader
TL5	to contribute constructively to shared discussion about literature, responding to and building on the views of others
TL7	to plan quickly and effectively the plot, characters and structure of their own narrative writing
TL8	to summarise a passage, chapter or text in a specified number of words
SL1	to revise from Y5: a) the different word classes b) re-expressing sentences in a different order c) the construction of complex sentences d) the conventions of Standard English
SL4	to investigate connecting words and phrases: a) collecting examples from reading and thesauruses b) study how points are typically connected in different kinds of text
SL5	to form complex sentences through, e.g.: a) using different connecting devices b) reading back complex sentences for clarity of meaning, and adjusting as necessary c) evaluating which links work best
SL6	to secure knowledge and understanding of more sophisticated punctuation marks – semi-colon, ellipses
WL3	to use independent spelling strategies, including ... applying knowledge of spelling rules and exceptions
WL4	revise and extend work on spelling patterns for unstressed vowels in polysyllabic words from Year 5 Term 3

Range:	Classic fiction
Texts:	From *The Call of the Wild*, Jack London (1903)
Resources:	Big Book 6A pp. 4–7 Pupil's Book 6 pp. 2–4 Homework Book 6 p. 2 Copymaster 1: Describing an event

DAY 1

Big Book pp. 4–6; Pupil's Book pp. 2–3

Shared reading

- Buck, a big St Bernard/collie cross, is a comfortable house dog in sunny California, stolen to be part of a dog team in frozen Alaska (60° below zero, we are told) in the gold rush of the 1870s and 1880s. Although the book is written in the third person, we see things from the dog's point of view. Despite harsh treatment and conditions, Buck adapts well, fighting his way up to be a great team leader. Thornton rescues him from cruel and stupid masters, in effect saving the dog's life; he and Buck therefore have a great bond of love. The passage describes how Buck shows his awesome strength, and his love for Thornton, by breaking out and pulling a huge sled, normally pulled by a team of at least eight dogs.

- Ask children if they can tell what Buck was.

- Where do they think the action takes place? Fill in some of the story background for them.

- What did they think about the story? Would they like to hear more of it? Why/why not?

- How did his weight compare with ours? 150 pounds = nearly 11 stone or 68 kg.

- Yards and inches: how do these compare with metres and centimetres?

- Discuss these meanings: *traces* (leather straps by which a dog team is harnessed to a sled), *arrested, duplicated the manoeuvre, unconscious, compactly, rapid succession, perceptibly diminished, momentum, babel* (Genesis Ch.10).

Focused word/sentence work

- Revision: Identify the first three verbs (*stepped, said, tightened*); nouns (*Thornton, Buck, traces*); adjectives (*several, sharp, sudden*).

- What part of speech are *pivoting, slipping* and *grating*? They are present participles of verbs.

- What part of speech are *crackling* and *snapping* as used in the passage? Verbal nouns, i.e. nouns made from verb participles.

- Count the number of words in each of the first eight sentences. Why is varying the length of sentences an important feature of most good writing?

- Why does the writer use *unaware* not *unconscious* in the second sentence about the men breathing? Good writers avoid repetition unless deliberately for effect.

- Where in the passage do we learn how much Buck weighs? Note that good writers often impart information without a bald statement.

Independent work

- Comprehension.

Plenary

- Discuss selected answers to the independent comprehension work.

- Revise parts of speech above, looking also at other parts of speech such as nouns, adverbs and conjunctions.

DAY 2

Shared reading

- Look at the paragraph after *"Now MUSH!"* The second, third, fourth and fifth sentences are all good examples of complex sentences in which several ideas are combined effectively. Discuss each in turn, identifying the separate ideas and the way they are joined. How does using these techniques improve the sentences and the piece as a whole? Two techniques in particular should be mentioned: a) the use of the present participle, e.g. *tightening the traces*; b) the omission of verbs, e.g. *his head forward and down*.

- Together, practise combining ideas in sentences by omitting the verb, e.g. *His burden was huge. Buck strained with all his might.*

Focused word work

- Investigate the spelling of unstressed vowels in polysyllabic words:

  a) Identify unstressed sounds in these words: *unconscious, tremendous.* How is the sound spelled? Ask the children to name other examples of *-ous* words.

  b) Identify unstressed sounds in these words: *broken, sudden, tightened.* How is the sound spelled? Can children name other examples of *-en* words?

  c) Identify unstressed sounds in these words: *hundred, thousand.*

- Discuss the ellipsis and its use here: *... half an inch ... an inch ... two inches ...* Note that there are always three dots, used to indicate the passage of time or the omission of words. Mention the plural *ellipses*.

Independent work

- Children practise joining sentences a) by omitting verbs, b) by using any appropriate technique.

Plenary

- Discuss selected answers to the independent work on joining sentences, investigating alternative phraseology. Perhaps using children's examples, discuss the importance of agreement between the subject of the main sentence and its subsidiary clause. For instance, you could ask why this is wrong: *Having a bath one day, the window cleaner appeared at the window.* How do we avoid or correct this?

DAY 3

Shared reading

- Read the passage again, focusing particularly on how the writer builds up the tension of the scene, e.g. the reaction of the watching crowd, the meticulous build-up of small details, Buck's slip, the use of particular dramatic words, e.g. *tense, quivered, writhing*, the interjection of short sentences, e.g. *"Now, MUSH!"*, the alternation of "loud" and "soft" sentences.

Shared writing

- Plan a piece describing a dramatic event at school, e.g. the build-up to a test, exam, sports match, school play, a playground fight. Ask for examples corresponding to the elements of *The Call of the Wild* extract (e.g. the scene at the start, the atmosphere, other people involved, the event itself).

Independent work

- The children write a piece describing a dramatic event at school. Copymaster 1 provides a framework for planning this work.

Plenary

- Read a few selected pieces of independent work, discussing them constructively.

- Prepare for day 4 by reading aloud the first passage from *The Call of the Wild*, the aim being to savour and remember the emotion generated by the piece.

DAY 4

Shared reading

- Read the second passage from *The Call of the Wild*. What does the extract tell us about the relationship between Buck and Thornton? Why might it be so strong? Explain that Thornton had saved Buck's life.

- Why did the crowd withdraw to a respectful distance, rather than mobbing the man and his dog in celebration?

- Examine the meaning and use of: *back and forth, cursing, fervently, Gad* (by gad = by God), *frankly, animated by a common impulse, indiscreet*.

Focused word/sentence work

- *Head was against head.* Why does the writer use this abbreviated phrase, rather than *Buck's head was against Thornton's head*?

- Why does the Skookum Bench king repeat himself? What can we infer from the fact that the writer inserts a dash in this speech (presumably that Thornton gave him a very negative response).

- What does the persistent use of *sir* tell us about the country/period described?

- Examine the word *seized*. To what spelling rule is this an exception? Look at other examples which follow the "i before e" rule, emphasising that it only applies to words with the long "ee" sound, such as *believe* and *receive* as opposed to words like *weight* and *leisure*.

- There are many present participles in the piece. Identify some of them. Only a few have been used to join sentences together, e.g. *the muscles writhing and knotting ...* How might the three sentences beginning *Thornton rose to his feet* have been joined using participles?

Independent work

- Children continue the writing begun on day 3.

Plenary

- Read some more examples of independent work. Prepare for day 5's writing by inviting suggestions as to how they could be improved.

DAY 5

Big Book pp. 4–7; Pupil's Book p. 4

Shared reading

- Read the whole piece silently. Discuss its effect as a piece of writing and the reasons for this.

- Ask the children what writing, films, etc., move or have moved them. What elements cause this response in the audience?

- Ask the children to write a summary of the piece in 30 words. Then discuss why this is totally unsatisfactory as a description of what went on.

Focused word/sentence work

- Look at the first extract of the passage. Find the two similes in it: *like a pistol-shot, like live things*. (These were featured in the independent work on day 1.)

- Look at the word *babel*. It is like a simile, but not one. What is it? Discuss the difference between simile and metaphor. (A metaphor is also a non-literal image but is used directly rather than with *like* or *as*. Our language is packed with hidden metaphors, e.g. to *iron out problems*, *to attack someone in the newspapers*.)

- Talk about mixed metaphors and the need to avoid them, e.g. *We must keep our nose to the grindstone and put our best foot forward; to take part in the space project, we must get in on the ground floor; he said it was a piece of cake but he had to eat his words*.

- As an introduction to the word level work in the Homework Book, look at word endings. Distinguish between **endings**, e.g. *-ous* (*tremendous*), *-scious* (*unconscious*), and **suffixes**, which are added to the root, e.g. *-ment* (*movement*), *-ful* (*respectful*).

- Also look at the spelling of numbers.

Independent work

- Children work on prefixes and suffixes.

Consolidation and extension

- Ask children to discuss in detail an exciting event that happened to them.

- Ask them to discuss favourite exciting parts of other books they have read.

- Ask them to compile a list of similes, including those known to their parents or other adults.

Homework

- Page 2 of the Homework Book focuses on joining sentences by omitting verbs, on words ending in *-ous* and *-er* and beginning with *un-*, the spelling of number words, and *ie/ei*.

Unit 2 Adrian Mole's Diary

Key Learning Objectives

TL2	to take account of viewpoint in a novel through, e.g. a) identifying the narrator b) explaining how this influences the reader's view of events c) explaining how events might look from a different point of view
TL3	to articulate personal responses to literature, identifying why and how a text affects the reader
TL6	to manipulate narrative perspective by: a) writing in the voice and style of a text ... c) writing a story with two different narrators
TL9	to prepare a short section of the story as a script, e.g. using stage directions, location/setting
SL1	to revise from Y5: a) the different word classes ... e) adapting texts for particular readers and purposes
SL4	to investigate connecting words and phrases; ... study how points are typically connected in different kinds of text
WL2	to use known spellings as a basis for spelling other words with similar patterns or related meanings; ... building words from other known words, and from awareness of the meaning or derivations of words
WL4	revise and extend work on spelling patterns for unstressed vowels in polysyllabic words from Year 5 Term 3

Range:	Diaries
Text:	From *The Growing Pains of Adrian Mole*, Sue Townsend
Resources:	Big Book 6A pp. 8–11 Pupil's Book 6 pp. 5–7 Homework Book 6 p. 3 Copymaster 2: Play scripts

Preparation

- You will need etymological dictionaries (e.g. *Collins Shorter School Dictionary*) for day 5 word and sentence work.

DAY 1

Big Book pp. 8–9; Pupil's Book pp. 5–6

Shared reading

- Read the passage together. What type of writing is this?
- The introduction explains that Adrian is 15, but what clues are there in the passage?
- Discuss the children's initial reaction to the extract. What did they think was funny?
- Discuss on a literal level the meaning of these words and phrases: *nipper, restrict, Hindu Kush* (mountain range of Central Asia, partly in Afghanistan), *the Lake District* (the Lake Poets were William Wordsworth, Samuel Taylor Coleridge and Robert Southey), *Skegness* (a windswept seaside resort in Lincolnshire), *Greece, till roll, Tupperware, procedure, superior status, Worse luck!, wistfully, sari, downtrodden, sighed.*

Focused word/sentence work

- If you did not know from the title, what features of the writing identify it as a diary? (First person, several examples of non-formal word use, e.g. *got dead mad*, verbless sentence at start, comments such as *Worse luck!*)
- Note that there is no effort to write in any polished way, e.g. no sophisticated coupling of ideas. Each gets its own, often crude or truncated, sentence.
- Where is Mrs Singh likely to have come from originally? What is the evidence for this? (The name alone is not enough – she could have married an Indian.)

Independent work

- Comprehension.

Plenary

- Discuss selected answers to the comprehension questions.
- Set a task to investigate as homework: Why would the Lake District be likely to help Adrian's poetry? Caution the children that, if they know already, they should not say the answer out loud in class!

DAY 2

Big Book pp. 8–9; Pupil's Book pp. 6–7

Shared reading

- Reread the passage.
- Ask the children whether it necessarily reflects the truth of the situation. How might it be distorted?
- What features identify it as likely to be a piece of comic writing? Point out the cruel remarks, for example about the bus stop, the obvious contrast of Skegness and Greece, how the characters are exaggerated (although no doubt there are many such people out there!), details and inappropriateness: scrap of old till roll, Tupperware gravy maker.
- Why would the Lake District be likely to help Adrian Mole's poetry?
- From this part of his diary, what sort of person do the children think Adrian is? You might mention that he is intelligent, critical, takes himself seriously.

Focused word/sentence work

- Identify the difference between two pieces of speech in the passage. Direct: *My father said, "It'll probably be our last ..."* Reported: *She said that having a baby was not going to restrict her.*
- Change the first speech to reported speech (*My father said that it would probably have been ...*) and the second to direct (*She said, "Having a baby is not going to restrict me!"*)
- Change these over: *She said that if she felt like walking ...* and *Mrs Singh asked, "Why are you having this procedure, Mrs Mole?"*

- Explain that thoughts have to be treated like speech.
- Discuss how you would change *It* [the paper] *said "Skegness"* to reported speech, e.g. *The paper read that Skegness was our destination.*

Independent work

- Children change direct to reported speech, and vice versa.

Plenary

- Review answers to some of the questions from the independent work.
- Point out that *said* can often be overused in writing direct speech. Invite suggestions for words to replace *said* for:
  – statements (*put in, commented, remarked, snarled*, etc.)
  – questions (*asked, enquired, suggested*, etc.).

DAY 3

Big Book p. 10; Pupil's Book p. 7

Shared reading

- Read the second extract from Adrian Mole's diary on page 10 of the Big Book.
- How does this extract relate to the previous one?
- Discuss the meanings of: *"The Bridge on the River Kwai", knobbly knees competition, the Donkey Derby, humiliation.*
- Ask children to summarise the content of the two extracts in as few words as possible.

Shared writing

- In preparation for independent writing, involve the children in writing up the events at the holiday camp as if this were part of Mr Mole's diary.
- Make a brief writing plan: *entrance to camp; bar; Adrian outside; can't find Adrian*. It might be fun to make Mr Mole as self-centred and lacking in understanding of Adrian as possible.

Focused word/sentence work

- From the second extract, identify the parts of speech in the first few sentences. Here are some points to note:
  day tickets is a noun phrase, with *day* used as an adjective. *Holiday camp* is similar.
  today is an adverb of time in this case.
  all is an adjective (although the *Oxford Dictionary* calls it a "predeterminer" in this usage).
  inside is an adverb of place in this case.
  quite is an adverb of degree.

Independent work

- Children write the events of the first extract as part of either the father or the mother's diary.

Plenary

- Read selected extracts of the children's writing, and discuss whether they have the "feel" of a diary. If not, what could be done to improve this? Do they reflect adequately the father or mother's point of view?

DAY 4

Big Book pp. 8–10; Pupil's Book p. 7

Shared writing

- Write the first events of the first extract, i.e. up to the writing down of holiday choices, as a play script.
- Discuss how all the main ideas are communicated. For instance, how do we communicate to the "audience" that it is the "usual last-minute discussion"?

Focused word/sentence work

- Look at the second word of the second extract, *bought*. What other words are spelled with the same ending? Examples are *brought, sought, ought, nought*. What are the root words? *Ought* comes originally from Old English *ahte*, from *agan = to owe*; *nought* comes from Old English *not + aught = not anything*.
- What words have an *aught* ending?
- Look at *would* (OE *wolde*, past tense of *willan*). What other words have the same endings? They are *could, should*. Investigate their origins.
- Examine the punctuation and meaning of *p.m.* (*post meridiem* = after noon).
- Mention the punctuation of 2.30, etc.
- Look at *-tion* in *competition* (and ask for other *-tion* words); *-ant* in *attendant* (and ask for other *-ant* words).
- Ask the children to find other unstressed vowels in polysyllabic words, such as par*e*nt, list*le*ss, child*re*n, each time looking for words that work in the same way.

Independent work

- Children continue their writing from day 3.

Plenary

- Read some of the day's independent writing. Invite constructive feedback. Introduce tomorrow's shared writing task, seeking to agree on a reason why someone might have to report on the Mole family.

DAY 5

Big Book pp. 8–10; Pupil's Book p. 7

Shared writing

- Plan and begin a report by a social worker, policeman, witness or other suitable person, based on the first extract. It is important to establish why they might have been called in. In the light of this, discuss the important points to cover, in what way the writing style would be different from the original, and what details would be omitted. Also invite conclusions at the end of the report.

Focused word/sentence work

- Choose words from the second Mole extract, and where possible find others from the same root, naming the correct part of speech, e.g. *starved – to starve* (infinitive), *starving* (present participle; also adjective), *starvation* (noun); *humiliation – humiliate* (verb), *humble* (adjective), *humility* (noun).

- Using etymological dictionaries, look up the origin of these words that appear in the two extracts, seeking to cultivate a "feel" for the likely origins:
  restrict (look up *strict*); *superior*; *status*; *explain*; *kitchen*; *paper*; *bottle* (Latin origins)
  pathetic (Greek origin)
  holiday; *snarled*; *tug* (Old/Middle English origins)
  attendant (*-ant* always = *-ing*); *barbed*; *prisoner*; *torture* (French origins)
  sari (Hindi origin)
- Seek to draw out some of the main principles of identifying word origins. Words with prefixes usually come from Latin or Greek; "ugly" short words are usually Old English; many French words have been transferred directly into English via the Normans, e.g. *attendant* = *waiting*.

Independent work

- Children write a report on the events in the Mole household of June 29th.

Plenary

- Share a selection of the children's reports on the Mole household, discussing the appropriateness of style, suggesting improvements.

Consolidation and extension

- Write as a play script a short scene with no more than three characters from a story you are reading. Copymaster 2 can be used to help with this task.
- Ask children to keep a week's personal or class diary.
- Ask children to discuss or write about the worst holiday they ever had.

Homework

- Page 3 in the Homework Book focuses on direct and reported speech, and on words ending in *-tion* and *-ant*.

Unit 3   The Crimean War (1)

Key Learning Objectives

TL3	to articulate personal responses to literature, identifying why and how a text affects the reader
TL8	to summarise a passage, chapter or text in a specified number of words
TL12	to comment critically on the language, style, success of examples of non-fiction
TL14	to develop the skills of biographical and autobiographical writing in role, adopting distinctive voices
SL2	to revise earlier work on verbs and to understand the terms *active* and *passive*, being able to transform a sentence from active to passive, and vice versa
SL3	to note and discuss how changes from active to passive affect the word order and sense of a sentence
SL5	to form complex sentences through ... using different connecting devices
WL2	to use known spellings as a basis for spelling other words with similar patterns or related meanings

Range:	Journals
Texts:	From *A Victorian RSM*, George Loy Smith
Resources:	Big Book 6A pp. 12–14
	Pupil's Book 6 pp. 8–10
	Homework Book 6 p. 4
	Copymaster 3: Journal of a Russian gunner

Preparation

- In 1854 Russia invaded part of Turkey's large empire (today's Romania). Turkey ("the sick man of Europe", according to Tsar Nicholas I) declared war. Britain and France joined in, invading the Crimean Peninsula with the aim of capturing the port of Sebastopol. The invasion was a disaster. The Charge of the Light Brigade took place during the Battle of Balaclava. Communications broke down and the British light cavalry were ordered to charge into a valley at the end of which the Russian artillery was dug in. The brigade was cut to ribbons and over one third of Lord Cardigan's 673 cavalrymen were killed. George Loy Smith was a sergeant in the 11th Hussars.

- The Tony Richardson film *The Charge of the Light Brigade* (1968), starring Trevor Howard and John Gielgud, is very effective in depicting the battle, and the pride, harshness and discipline behind the Charge.

DAY 1

Big Book pp. 12–13; Pupil's Book pp. 8–9

Shared reading

- Read the first extract together. Ask the children what facts tell us this is not a modern battle (trumpets, horses, cannonballs, etc.).
- Ask the children to estimate the date. Then give brief facts of the event, the war and the date.
- Discuss the meaning of the military vocabulary in the passage: *regiment, batteries, in flank*.
- Ask the children who might have written it. What type of writing is it? How can they tell? (There are facts only, lack of emotion, comment or criticism.)
- What does this tell us about the character of the writer? (That he was cool, brave, tough, etc.)
- How does the writing make the children feel?

Focused word/sentence work

- Discuss what elements of the writing style identify the text as not being of modern style. For example, *bespattered, to such a nicety were* (sentence order), *mortally*.
- Identify the first five verbs, nouns, adjectives and adverbs in the passage.
- Write down several of the verbs in the past tense ending in -*ed*, e.g. *sounded, moved, fancied*. What other part of the verb can these be (past participles)? Discuss a definition of past participle: a word that is used with an auxiliary verb to form other forms of the past tense, e.g. *We had moved, The trumpets have sounded*.

Independent work

- Comprehension.

Plenary

- Recap the facts of the event described, the war and the date.
- Recap the meanings of words in the passage. Are there any phrases that children still do not fully understand?

DAY 2

Big Book pp. 12–13; Pupil's Book p. 9

Shared writing

- Together, write a summary of the passage in 100 words, using varied contributions from the whole class, pairs or individuals working on sentences.
- If time permits, summarise again in 50 words, then in 25 words.

Focused word/sentence work

- In the first paragraph, identify the verbs in each sentence and whether they are active or passive. Which "active verb" sentences can be changed to passive? Which "passive verb" sentences can be changed to active? Discuss ways of doing this. Why are some sentences unsuitable? What effect does the change have?

- Active verb sentences are those in which the subject of the sentence performs the action, e.g. *The dog bites the man*. Passive verb sentences are those in which the action is done to the subject, e.g. *The man is bitten by the dog*. It is generally held that active verb sentences are more "punchy" than their passive equivalents: compare the academic style of *It is thought that ...* with the more populist *People think that ...*

Independent work

- Children work on changing active sentences to passive, and vice versa.

Plenary

- Discuss answers to the independent work on active and passive verb sentences.

DAY 3

Big Book p. 14; Pupil's Book p. 10

Shared reading

- Read the second extract.
- Invite children to imagine and describe the scene: as the Light Brigade approached the guns, as they passed through the guns, at the end of the charge (smoke, dust, horses and men lying dead and wounded; some dazed survivors walking or riding, occasional shots, groans, cries for help).
- In terms of style, which phrases might have been different in a more modern account?

Shared writing

- Plan the first paragraph of an account of the Charge by a Russian gunner.
- It is important that children understand the elements of Loy Smith's account and have adequate information about the circumstances. Questions you might ask to elicit this information include:
  - How were orders passed? By horse messenger from generals on neighbouring hilltops; very muddled command.
  - What was the situation? Because their orders were confused, the British charged 2.4 km down the wrong valley into the mouths of Russian guns while artillery batteries raked them from either side.
  - What weapons did they have? The British had rifles and swords; the Russians had 30 cannons firing round shot (cannonballs) and shells (hollow cases containing explosives).
  - What protection did soldiers wear then? Apart from helmets, virtually nothing.
  - What were conditions like? Unbearably hot at the time of the Charge in October 1854, but it was bitterly cold in winter, disease was rife, rations were limited, medical facilities were poor, and nearly 750,000 died.

Independent work

- Children write a chronological account of the Charge by a Russian gunner.
- Copymaster 3 can be used to plan this work.

Plenary

- Read aloud samples of work that the children have produced, and compare them for style against Loy Smith's account. Style points that might be raised include:
  - What was the purpose of the account?
  - Is it chronological? Do you believe it? Why?
  - Was it written to make people admire the soldiers or feel sorry for them?
  - How does it differ from the diaries that most people write?

DAY 4

Big Book pp. 12–14; Pupil's Book p. 10

Shared writing

- Plan and experiment with writing paragraphs 2 and 3 of a Russian gunner's account: the scene as the Light Brigade approached the guns and passed through them; after the charge.

Focused word/sentence work

- Identify any adverbs in the passage that end in *-ly*: *actually, consequently, coolly, mortally, scarcely*.
- Note that most *-ly* adverbs are adverbs of manner, answering the question how the action was performed. (Other adverbs in the passage include *now*, *soon*, *afterwards*, which are adverbs of time.)
- Point out that adding *-ly* to the adjective means in some cases doubling the *l*.
- Draw attention to a common mistake: no adverbs end in *-ley*. Only nouns such as *valley* are spelled that way.

Independent work

- Children continue with their account of the Charge by a Russian gunner begun on day 3.

Plenary

- Read aloud samples of work that the children have produced, and compare them for style against Loy Smith's account. Style points that might be raised include:
  - How does the passage make you feel?
  - How does the style of writing indicate the character of the writer?

DAY 5

Big Book pp. 12–14; Pupil's Book p. 10

Shared reading

- Read the extracts again. As you do so, draw the children's attention to the different ways that complex sentences are constructed. You might also look at *consequently* (in the third sentence of the first paragraph), which technically should be at the start of a new sentence.

Focused sentence work

- Introduce the technique of joining clauses with present participles. The present participle of a verb consists of the root + *ing*.

- Examine sentences in the passage where participles are used to join sentences. For instance, the sentence *We moved off, soon breaking into a gallop* is a blend of two ideas: *We moved off* and *We soon broke into a gallop*. Look at other examples, isolating the ideas that are amalgamated, for instance: *I, being close on his right rear, fancied I felt ...; Happening at this moment to look to the rear, I saw ...; In another moment we passed the guns, our right flank brushing them.*

- When is it appropriate to use participles in this way? (When one thing happens as a result of another, or when two things happen simultaneously.)

- Ask the children to join sentences in the same way. Choose pairs of ideas such as these:
  The trumpets sounded the advance. We moved off.
  He turned his horse. He galloped to the back of the regiment.
  I looked down. I saw my cuff had been blackened.
  In each case, discuss which clause would be better suited to take the participle replacement, and why.

Independent work

- Children work at identifying the two ideas in complex sentences.

- Children work at joining sentences using present participles.

Plenary

- Recap briefly on some of the examples the children have used for independent work.

- Recap on agreement. Why are the following sentences wrong?
  Having carved legs, the lady wanted to buy the table.
  Being rainy, I wore my mac.
  Discuss the necessity for agreement of subject and verb when two sentences are joined. How should the examples be phrased correctly?

- Other examples to try:
  I looked down. An ugly face stared up at me. Avoid the incorrect *Looking down, an ugly face stared up at me.*
  It was sunny. David felt good. Avoid the incorrect *Being sunny, David felt good.*

Consolidation and extension

- Suggest children search for and then discuss examples of complex sentences from their own reading, class story, etc., in particular identifying how these sentences are joined, then trying to imitate them in other examples.

- Ask children to discuss other examples of "howler" sentences, such as those quoted for the day 5 plenary session above.

Homework

- Page 4 of the Homework Book focuses on joining sentences with participles, and on active and passive verb sentences.

Unit 4 The Crimean War (2)

Key Learning Objectives

TL2	to take account of viewpoint through, e.g. a) identifying the narrator b) explaining how this influences the reader's view of events c) explaining how events might look from a different point of view
TL3	to articulate personal responses to literature, identifying why and how a text affects the reader
TL6	to manipulate narrative perspective by: a) writing in the voice and style of a text b) producing a modern retelling c) writing a story with two different narrators
TL8	to summarise a passage, chapter or text in a specified number of words
TL11	distinguishing between fact, opinion and fiction
TL12	to comment critically on the language, style, success of examples of non-fiction
TL14	to develop the skills of biographical and autobiographical writing in role, adopting distinctive voices
SL3	to form complex sentences
WL2	to use known spellings as a basis for spelling other words with similar patterns or related meanings
WL7	to understand how words and expressions have changed over time
WL10	to understand the function of the etymological dictionary and use it to study words of interest and significance

Range:	Classic poetry; letters, notes, anecdotes
Texts:	"The Charge of the Light Brigade", Alfred, Lord Tennyson From *Letters from the Crimea*, Florence Nightingale, edited by Sue M. Goldie
Resources:	Big Book 6A pp. 15–21 Pupil's Book 6 pp. 11–14 Homework Book 6 p. 5 Copymaster 4: Comparing accounts

Preparation

- Note that the writing activity is on days 4 and 5 in this unit.

- Alfred, Lord Tennyson (1809–92) was Britain's most popular poet of Victorian times, succeeding Wordsworth as Poet Laureate from 1850 to 1892. He gave the role its greatest ever influence. He was famous for the rhythm of his poetry; he also wrote "The Lady of Shalott" (see Unit 29), which makes for a useful comparison. "The Charge of the Light Brigade" was perhaps written within the constraints of his role as Laureate; the Laureate's duty is and was to write verse on important royal or national occasions, so it had to be uncritical and patriotic in tone. "The Charge of the Light Brigade" is indeed a little corny and jingoistic, and is by no means regarded as his best work.

- The second text is a letter to a friend in England from Florence Nightingale in Scutari in 1855. Florence Nightingale (1820–1910) came from a privileged and wealthy Hampshire family. Having trained as a nurse and become a hospital superintendent, she volunteered to help in the Crimea, taking 38 nurses with her. She encountered appalling conditions and inadequate resources and launched a ferocious tirade against the medical authorities. However, she was greatly impressed by the courage of the soldiers. By introducing strict discipline and better sanitation she reduced the mortality rate drastically. Returning to England in 1856, she became a prime mover in the drive to improve standards of nursing and public health. Her influence lasts to this day. Sir John McNeill was a British diplomat working in the Middle East.

DAY 1

Big Book pp. 15–18; Pupil's Book pp. 11–12

Shared reading

- Read together the poem "The Charge of the Light Brigade".

- Discuss these word meanings: *dismay'd, to reason why, blunder'd, sabres*.

- What is a *league*? (3 miles) And *half a league*?

- The sergeant in the prose account (explain "prose", if necessary) described the same event. In what ways are the two accounts similar? In what ways different? Which phrases from the poem would never have been found in the sergeant's account? Examples include *jaws of Death, mouth of Hell*.

- The sergeant's aim (in the extract reproduced in Unit 3) was to give a factual account of his experience in the Charge. What was Tennyson's aim?

- Ask the children to summarise the events of the Charge in as few words as possible.

Focused word/sentence work

- Ask the children whether they can identify the main characteristic of the poem, which is the use of repetition. Why did Tennyson do this?

- Find several examples of the old-fashioned use of apostrophes in verb endings, e.g. *dismay'd*. Ask the children to discuss why Tennyson might have used these (presumably to avoid confusion with the archaic/poetic *-ed* pronunciation, e.g. *blessed, wretched, ragged* and many Shakespearean pronunciations.

- In the original version *Theirs* was written *Their's*. Why would this now be thought wrong? (*Men's* means *of men*; *theirs* means *of them* not *of their*.)

- Ask the children to consider whether *Was there a man dismay'd?* is a genuine question. Discuss the meaning and use of rhetorical questions (questions posed for effect that do not invite an answer).

Independent work

- Comprehension.

Plenary

- Ask the children if they can spot which metaphor Tennyson uses twice in the third verse (*mouth/jaws*). Why is this appropriate? (It emphasises the narrowness of the valley.)
- What effect does Tennyson's deliberate repetition have? (It evokes determination and bravery.)

DAY 2

Big Book pp. 15–18; Pupil's Book pp. 12–13

Shared reading

- Reread some or all of "The Charge of the Light Brigade".
- Ask the children how they feel about the poem, and to compare this with their feelings after reading the sergeant's account. Which is more effective? Why?
- Was Tennyson at the battle? What makes the children think that he wasn't? If he **had** been there, would he have wanted to write a poem at all? In what ways might his poem have been different?
- Compare the two accounts of the Charge of the Light Brigade. You can use Copymaster 4 to help with this.

Focused word/sentence work

- Introduce the concept of metre. Metre is the rhythm of a poem, most simply analysed in terms of the number of syllables in each line.
- Use clapping to count the syllables in each line of the first two verses, recording the result at the end of each line. What is unusual about the metre of this poem, compared with many others? Is there a line which doesn't fit too well? (*Into the Valley of Death* has seven syllables.)
- What does it mean if two words rhyme? Ask the children to try to define the concept of rhyme exactly.
- Examine the rhyme scheme of the first verse (ABCBDDCB). (In a rhyme scheme, the first line is designated A, and all rhyming lines in a verse are given the same letter.) Are the rhymes exact? Does this matter? Why not? What is the rhyme scheme for verse 2?

Independent work

- Children work at finding pairs of rhyming words in the poem; recording the metre of verses 4, 5 and 6 of the poem; and recording the rhyme scheme of verses 3 to 6.
- They record the rhyme and metre of a limerick.
- They plan and write their own limerick.

Plenary

- Look at the metre and rhyming scheme of the last verse.
- Bearing in mind the irregular syllable count and rhyme in the rest of the poem, analyse what holds the poem together. Point to the repetition of phrases, particularly *six hundred*, and the six-syllable/five-syllable combination of lines.

DAY 3

Big Book pp. 19–21; Pupil's Book pp. 13–14

Shared reading

- Ask the children to read Florence Nightingale's account silently.
- Discuss the author of the extract. What was Florence Nightingale doing in the Crimea? (See **Preparation** on page 29.)
- What are the three main things Florence Nightingale feels most strongly about? She emphasises the soldiers' conditions, their courage and their poor treatment.
- What type of writing is this? Is it fact, opinion or fiction? Even if it is not proven fact, do the children believe it? Why?
- Ask the children to discuss how they would feel about being a soldier or a nurse in the Crimean War.

Focused word/sentence work

- What features identify this extract as a letter? Draw attention to the use of many dashes, ampersands (&), numbers, informal phrases, sentence beginning with *And*, use of the second person, abbreviations. Discuss why many of these are not found in formal writing.
- Discuss the meaning of these words: *hardship, sublime, spectacle, disgust, expression.*

Independent work

- Comprehension.

Plenary

- Recap on the difference between fact, opinion and fiction.
- Look at selected answers to the independent work set in the Pupil's Book.

DAY 4

Big Book pp. 15–21; Pupil's Book p. 14

Shared writing

- Introduce the writing task, which is to write a letter from a soldier or nurse in Scutari Hospital to a relative or friend back in England, if possible imitating Victorian style.
- Identify from Florence Nightingale's letter, and make notes on, the things that a nurse writing from the hospital would mention (e.g. the suffering and bravery of the soldiers, her long hours, the poor food, the hard work and strict discipline imposed by Florence Nightingale, the poor level of care provided by the doctors). Are there any other things found in Tennyson's poem or the sergeant's account of the Charge in Unit 3 that a nurse might mention?
- Identify the things that an ordinary soldier writing from the hospital would mention. How might a soldier's letter differ from a nurse's letter? (The former would have a lower standard of education, he would talk less about wounds, be more concerned to reassure his loved ones, have more information about the battle, greater admiration for Florence Nightingale, and so on.)

Focused word/sentence work

- Identify elements of Nightingale's letter that give it a Victorian style. Mention the formality of the style by today's standards, the lack of apostrophes of omission, the use of participles in sentences (e.g. *preserving*, *being*), the use of &, the impersonal use of the name Florence Nightingale, the phrase *three times three*, faith in God, vocabulary (*consider, sublime, Serjt, nosegay*).

- Discuss ways in which the letter might have begun and ended.

Independent work

- Children write a letter home from a soldier or nurse in Scutari Hospital.

Plenary

- Ask children to read out their writing and invite comment on how successfully they have achieved the Victorian style. Seek examples of how they might develop such a style.

DAY 5

Big Book pp. 15–21; Pupil's Book p. 14

Shared reading

- Select and read aloud some of the children's work from day 4. Invite constructive criticism, and in particular discuss how well or otherwise they have captured the spirit of the Victorian letter. Invite suggestions for improvement.

Focused word/sentence work

- Examine the complex sentences of Florence Nightingale's letter. Identify the main and subsidiary ideas in each, then look at how the subsidiary ideas have been interwoven. Do sentences tend to be longer in a letter or not? Why is this?

- Look at particular examples of Victorian phraseology which may provide ideas for the children's writing:
what the work has been, what the hardships makes economical use of words by omitting an unnecessary verb.
There was nothing empty ... nor in the heart ... makes interesting use of *nor*.
which "The Times" has said ... of hardship uses the now rare expression to say or talk *of* something.

Independent work

- Children continue day 4's writing.

Plenary

- Ask children to read out parts of their writing and invite comment on how successfully they have described conditions in the Crimea. Find examples in which a modern nurse or soldier might have used different words or phrases.

Consolidation and extension

- Ask the children to learn and/or write out neatly part of Tennyson's poem.

- Ask the children to plan and write a letter from Florence Nightingale to Field Marshal Lord Raglan (Baron Raglan of Raglan), Commander-in-Chief, British Army in the Crimea. The letter should list the problems she faces, and her very firm suggestions for improvement. The letter should maintain Victorian dignity and style at all times. For instance, the salutation might read: *I have the honour to remain your obedient servant.*

- Children could read "The Charge of the Mouse Brigade" (see Unit 17), and then write their own parody of Tennyson's poem.

Homework

- Page 5 of the Homework Book focuses on rhyming words and word origins.

Unit 5 Roald Dahl at Repton

Key Learning Objectives

TL11 to distinguish between biography and autobiography:
a) recognising the effect on the reader of the choice between first and third person
b) distinguishing between fact, opinion and fiction
c) distinguishing between implicit and explicit points of view, and how these can differ

TL14 to develop the skills of biographical and autobiographical writing in role, adopting distinctive voices:
a) preparing a CV
b) composing a biographical account based on research

SL6 to secure knowledge and understanding of ... parenthetic commas, dashes, brackets

WL5 to use word roots, prefixes and suffixes as a support for spelling

Range:	Autobiography, biography
Texts:	From *Boy*, Roald Dahl From *Roald Dahl: A Biography*, Jeremy Treglown
Resources:	Big Book 6A pp. 22–24 Pupil's Book 6 pp. 15–17 Homework Book 6 p. 6 Copymaster 5: Planning a biography Sample CV in large format (see **Preparation**)

Preparation

- Some or all children could be invited, a few days previously, to bring along a few favourite lines from a Roald Dahl book for discussion.

- Decide on an interesting personality from a topic being studied, or a character from a book being read to the class. Prepare a sample CV of this person that illustrates the important features.

- Children need to be warned well in advance that they are going to be writing about their own history, and will need to have gleaned some details of their origins, ancestry, earliest memories, happiest and saddest recollections – anything that might go into an autobiography.

- Prepare a small selection of appropriate biographies and autobiographies from the school or local library or both.

- *Roald Dahl* by Chris Powling is a children's biography of Dahl, written for the Y3 or Y4 age group, which may be more appropriate for less able Y6 children. It gives little of the flavour of true biographical writing, being written in a chatty style echoing Dahl's own, concentrating solely on the facts of Dahl's life and offering no assessment of his character. You may, however, find it useful to invite children to compare it with the Treglown extract.

DAY 1

Big Book pp. 22–23; Pupil's Book pp. 15–16

Shared reading

- Read the extract from *Boy* together. Ask the children to discuss what type of writing this is. What is the difference between autobiography and biography? How does this show itself on the page? The extract is written in the first person: *I am sure ...* It expresses intimate thoughts and feelings, and is written in his own style.

- Ask the children what they think about the corporal punishment. Does it surprise them that this went on?

- Ask them to identify the main features of Roald Dahl's style of writing – that it is addressed personally to reader, and is very conversational (e.g. using *wasn't, weren't*; and a variety of sentence lengths including very short ones).

- What do children think about Roald Dahl's books in general? Why is his style successful – if, in their eyes, it is successful? If not, why not? Stress the importance in a lot of writing, particularly personal writing, of writing as one thinks and speaks.

- Ask children to cite favourite short examples of Dahl's style.

Focused word/sentence work

- Discuss the derivation of the words *biography* and *autobiography* (Greek: *autos* = self; *bios* = life; *graphe* = writing). Make a list of other words of related origin, e.g. *automatic, biology, geography*.

- Discuss these words from the passage: *to lay emphasis on, appalled, literally, impression* (its physical and metaphorical meaning), *Lamb of God* (= Jesus). What parts of speech are they? What do they mean?

- What is the difference between smacking and flogging/ beating?

- Why does Dahl use capital letters for Mercy and Forgiveness?

Independent work

- Comprehension.

Plenary

- Introduce the word "explicit" in describing Dahl's views as expressed in the piece. Explain that the opposite is "implicit", something which is taken for granted within a text but not stated explicitly, e.g. that it was not a good thing to confuse pupils.

- Recap on the answers to the independent comprehension work, particularly checking on the response to C, Dahl's views on corporal punishment. Check that they were aware of his limited degree of approval in certain circumstances.

- If time allows, children could share their own views on this.

DAY 2

Big Book pp. 22–23; Pupil's Book p. 16

Shared writing

- Plan and make notes for a mini-autobiography. What should it include? Mention details of birth, earliest memories, brothers and sisters, friends and how you first met them, happiest moments, saddest moments. The planning example could use your own experiences, a character from fiction or history, or an imaginary child in the class made up from spontaneous contributions.

- If time permits, begin to expand the notes into a draft text.

Focused word/sentence work

- Recall the meaning of rhetorical questions. Can the children spot the one in the passage? It is very typical of Dahl's style. Ask them to think of rhetorical questions from everyday life. (Who cares? How should I know? What's it got to do with you? Do you think I'm made of money?)

- Discuss the use of the word *tickles*. Is this literally true? Introduce the word *euphemism* (Greek: *eu-* = well/easy; *pheme* = speaking) and reach a definition by quoting some examples (*pass away* = die, *rub out* = kill, *trots/runs* = diarrhoea, *the Big C* = cancer). Can the children spot another one in the passage (*rump* = buttocks)? What other examples can they think of? Why do people use euphemisms?

Independent work

- Children plan and write a mini-autobiography. Ask them when they redraft to keep previous versions for comparison.

Plenary

- Discuss the problems the children have experienced in writing, and read out samples of work.

- Invite constructive criticism on the style, interest, etc.

DAY 3

Big Book pp. 22–24; Pupil's Book p. 17

Shared reading

- Reread the first passage together.

- Recap on the definition of *autobiography* and *biography*.

- Ask the children what might prompt someone to write an autobiography or biography. The answers could include: an interesting life; fame; an important position; or self-justification.

- Do they believe what Roald Dahl has written? Why is this?

- Which is more likely to offer facts rather than opinions: biography or autobiography? Explain that things may not be quite as simple as they seem. You would expect an autobiography to tell the truth, but in Dahl's case a) it was written many years later, and b) the author had perhaps too strong feelings about the issues raised.

- Ask children if they have read any auto/biographies.

- Ask them to visit their library in the next few days and write down the names of five auto/biographies of people they are interested in.

Focused word/sentence work

- Look at the parenthetic use of commas in the sentences beginning *It would, of course, ...* and *Even today, whenever ...* Explain that we use commas a) to isolate the intervening words from the main sentence (identify the main sentence in each case), and b) to ensure that the sentence is read with appropriate pauses. Ask the children to consider why we do not use dashes or brackets in such cases. Use the word *parenthesis* (= the additional part to the sentence) and its plural, explaining that brackets are often called *parentheses*. Point out that, for style and continuity, it is important not to make the parenthetic part of a sentence too long.

- Ask the whole class to make up three more examples of this use of commas. These could include speeches, e.g. *"The time has come," the walrus said, "to talk of many things."*

- Look at the use of *neither/nor*. Explain that *nor* is normally used only with *neither*.

- Identify as many parts of speech from the passage as possible in the remaining time. Ask the children to look for the first five verbs, then five nouns, adjectives, adverbs and so on.

Independent work

- Children plan and write a short biography of a character being studied elsewhere in the curriculum. Copymaster 5 can be used to help plan this work.

Plenary

- Read the last few lines from the first extract, then continue with the extract from Jeremy Treglown's biography.

- Did Roald Dahl write the second extract? How can the children tell?

- Therefore what sort of writing is it?

- What error does it appear that Dahl had made when he wrote that chapter of *Boy*?

- What does the author mean when he writes, *Perhaps Dahl didn't have to look far to understand a bully*? Why does he say this?

DAY 4

Big Book pp. 22–24; Pupil's Book p. 17

Shared reading

- Reread the second extract if necessary.

- Which writer do the children trust more to accurately report the incidents described? Why is this? Does this mean we can trust all biographies more than autobiographies? The answer to this question may be that it depends on a) how detached from the issues the writer is, b) how conceited or defensive autobiographers are about their lives, and c) the pedigree of a biographer – the Kitty Kelley, Albert Goldman style of sensational biography has little credibility, whereas Treglown and many other biographers are interested only in the truth. Many autobiographies have been exercises in self-justification in defiance of the known facts.

Shared writing

- Have the children plan for and write part of a biography about a character central to a topic being studied elsewhere in the curriculum, using either the formula developed during shared writing on day 2, or alternatively relevant parts of Copymaster 5.

Focused word/sentence work

- Read the second extract again.
- Discuss the following words: *successor* (and its opposite, *predecessor*), *sadists, arbitrary, contemporary, persisting.*
- Recap on the evidence that shows this is a biography.
- Ask the children how we may conclude that the biography has been carefully researched. Treglown appears to have talked to several people who knew Roald Dahl at that age.

Independent work

- Children continue writing their biography.

Plenary

- Discuss samples of independent work, inviting constructive criticism on content and style.

DAY 5

Big Book p. 24; Pupil's Book p. 17

Shared reading

- Read the second text again, discussing what is explicit (that Dahl got his facts wrong) and what is implicit (e.g. that the truth is important in writing auto/biography, that bullying is wrong).

Shared writing

- Ask the children to prepare a CV of a person central to a topic being studied. Explain that *curriculum vitae* is Latin for *the course of life.* The layout of a CV should be clear, with bold headings and use of indents. It should include the place and date of birth, nationality, education with approximate dates, career experience with approximate dates, hobbies and interests.

Focused word/sentence work

- Ask the children to find an example of commas used parenthetically in the second extract (around the phrase *then or later*).

Independent work

- Children practise the use of parenthetic commas.
- Children explore word classes with the help of a dictionary.

Plenary

- Discuss what potentially interesting biographies or autobiographies children found in the library. Show them the selection you made, and if possible talk about them or read from them.
- Discuss samples of independent work, inviting constructive criticism on content and style.

Consolidation and extension

- Ask children to discuss auto/biographies they have previously read.
- Ask them to prepare imaginary CVs for themselves in twenty years' time.

Homework

- Page 6 of the Homework Book focuses on parenthetic commas, *neither/nor,* and forming parts of speech from others in the same family.

Unit 6 Witches

Key Learning Objectives

TL1	to compare and evaluate a novel or play in print and the film/TV version, e.g. treatment of the plot and characters, the differences in the two forms, e.g. in seeing the setting, in losing the narrator
TL3	to articulate personal responses to literature, identifying why and how a text affects the reader
TL4	to be familiar with the work of some established authors, to know what is special about their work
TL5	to contribute constructively to shared discussion about literature, responding to and building on the views of others
TL6	to manipulate narrative perspective by: a) writing in the voice and style of a text b) producing a modern retelling
TL10	to write own poems experimenting with active verbs and personification; produce revised poems for reading out individually
SL4	to investigate connecting words and phrases; ... study how points are typically connected in different kinds of text
SL6	to secure knowledge and understanding of more sophisticated punctuation marks: a) colon b) semi-colon
WL7	to understand how words and expressions have changed over time, e.g. old verb endings -st and -th, and how some words have fallen out of use, e.g. yonder, thither
WL9	to understand how new words have been added to the language
WL10	to understand the function of the etymological dictionary and use it to study words of interest and significance

Range:	Classic drama: Shakespeare; non-chronological reports
Texts:	From *Macbeth*, William Shakespeare From *Dungeons and Torture*, John McIlwain
Resources:	Big Book 6A pp. 25–30 Pupil's Book 6 pp. 18–21 Homework Book 6 p. 7 Copymaster 6: Creating a glossary

Preparation

• Familiarise yourself with the plot of *Macbeth*, a brief version of which follows. A fuller summary is available in *Tales from Shakespeare* by Charles and Mary Lamb, or from the BBC Animated Tales series, abridged by Leon Garfield. In NLS pilot schools the latter has been successfully used as the basis for fulfilling the requirements of TL1.

• Macbeth, Thane (Lord) of Glamis, is a successful general and kinsman of the Scots king, Duncan the Meek. With fellow general Banquo, he meets three witches who predict to his amazement that Macbeth will be first Thane of Cawdor and later king, but that Banquo's sons will succeed him. Immediately messengers arrive telling him he has been made Thane of Cawdor. Amazed at this, he is convinced that the prophecy is correct. When the king comes to stay, Macbeth, urged by his wicked wife, resolves to hasten its fulfilment by murdering the king. He stabs Duncan in his sleep, and is duly made king, but is then assailed by bloody visions and nightmares. Macbeth and his wife then seek to dismiss the rest of the prediction by murdering Banquo's sons. On his way to dine with Macbeth, Banquo is killed, but his son escapes. Banquo's ghost, however, attends the dinner, and Macbeth is indeed a tormented soul. He revisits the witches to know the worst about the future. After conjuring the infernal spirits (hence the spell), they tell him he is safe until Birnam Wood shall come to Dunsinane. This is so absurd a notion that Macbeth is calmed. Yet the queen dies and the other lords turn against him, Macduff and Malcolm, the rightful king, besieging him in his castle. Beyond saving himself, Macbeth sallies forth bravely and is eventually beaten in combat by Macduff, who cuts off his head, and presents it to the new king, Malcolm. Birnam Wood comes to Dunsinane because the enemy army moved forward camouflaged as trees!

• William Shakespeare (1564–1616) was the greatest English dramatist, as well as being an actor and a poet. After his marriage to Anne Hathaway and the birth of three children, he left Stratford-upon-Avon for London to work as an actor and playwright with one of the touring companies that had visited his home town. Despite success in the capital, he owned property in Stratford and maintained his interest in the place. Between 1592 and 1594 the theatres were closed by plague, and Shakespeare wrote sonnets. After that his plays took London by storm; their language and characters captured people's imagination and entered their daily conversation. The Globe Theatre was built in 1599, bigger and better than anything before, opening in triumph with a production of Shakespeare's *Henry V*. King James I was an even bigger fan than Elizabeth had been. He gave the company royal patronage and doubled their pay. Performances at court were regular. After 1608 Shakespeare sought to return to Stratford, and by 1612 he had freed himself of active commitments in London. He died in 1616 and is buried in Stratford parish church.

DAY 1

Big Book pp. 25–28; Pupil's Book pp. 18–20

Shared reading

• Before you read the first extract, introduce it briefly by putting it in the context of the play.

• Discuss Shakespeare's origins, his status as England's greatest dramatist and his lasting appeal. Ask children what other plays he wrote, using the terms "comedy" and "tragedy".

• Read the Witches' spell, perhaps twice, placing the accent on enjoying the vocabulary even if many meanings are unclear to the children at present.

- After the reading, ask children to go through the text (perhaps using photocopies to highlight, underline, etc.) and identify the words and phrases they do not understand.

Focused word/sentence work

- Discuss the meanings of these words from the first part of the poem, asking the children to take notes with the help of Copymaster 6, prior to creating a glossary of terms:

cauldron: Check that everyone understands this word.

thrice: three times

thrice and once: There has been much debate about this in the commentaries. a) Did it mean three times, a gap, then once more? b) Were even numbers thought inappropriate to magical spells? c) Was it just a device to fill out the rhythm?

brinded: brindled, i.e. streaked (derives from *branded*). Refers to the first witch's familiar Graymalkin. A *familiar* was a demon in animal form acting as a witch's assistant.

hedge-pig: hedgehog

Harpier: the third witch's familiar. This could be a harpy (a monster from mythology with a woman's head and body and a bird's wings and claws) or it could be an owl.

'tis: it is. Ask the children why this is a useful device for poets.

entrails: intestines

Swelter'd: sweated. Toads were thought to be very popular with witches. They do secrete an acrid substance in their skin glands for protection.

sleeping got: Presumably the toad was captured while it was sleeping, i.e. at the dead of night.

i'the: Why the apostrophe?

fillet of a fenny snake: a slice of a snake from the fens (flat, marshy land)

wool: downy hair

adder's fork: double tongue of an adder

blind-worm: a slow worm – which, like newts, were once thought to be dangerous

howlet: owlet

- Why has *brinded* got an *e* and *mew'd*, etc., not?

- Why is there a dash after *throw* in line 5?

- Why does Shakespeare use *sleeping got*? He presumably wanted to impart an air of mystery (at the dead of night), and also to rhyme with *pot*.

Independent work

- Comprehension.

Plenary

- Invite selected answers to questions A and B, and particularly C, in the Pupil's Book.

- Recap on the words most likely to be found elsewhere in Shakespeare, e.g. *thrice, hath, 'tis, thou*.

DAY 2

Big Book pp. 25–28; Pupil's Book p. 20

Shared reading

- In the whole class, ask children to read the spell again aloud, perhaps taking turns at a line or section, aiming for maximum expressiveness.

- Discuss the features of the layout of plays, set instructions, stage directions, the use of a colon after the speaker's name (Shakespeare used a dash, in fact). Point out the lack of speech marks.

- What is a witch? Discuss the medieval preoccupation with witchcraft. (The extract "The Witch Report" in the Big Book, pages 29–30, has further information.)

- Why were the witches so influential in the story of Macbeth?

- Why might witches be useful in terms of producing and performing the play? They helped to establish a dark, menacing tone for the dark deeds that the play describes. They permitted a completely different type of scene, which added variety to the play. They also needed very little scenery, which possibly helped stage managers to change major scenery at the back of the stage while the cauldron scene was playing.

Focused word/sentence work

- Discuss the meanings of these words from the second part of the extract, asking the children to take notes prior to creating a glossary of terms. As necessary, discuss the importance of clarity and brevity in note-taking. In the interests of speed, you could ask children to take notes in pairs, each child being responsible for noting the details of every other word mentioned.

mummy: a powder made from the dried flesh of a body

maw: throat

gulf: stomach

ravin'd ... shark: a shark that has glutted itself on its prey. Why does Shakespeare say *salt-sea*, not *sea*?

hemlock: a poisonous plant

digg'd i'the dark: Plants were supposed to be at their strongest if gathered at night.

blaspheming Jew: Jews were much maligned in the Middle Ages – heavily taxed, often persecuted, often restricted in movement, and occasionally massacred.

Sliver'd in the moon's eclipse: cut/sliced off at a time considered unlucky for lawful enterprises and therefore excellent for evil deeds. Make sure that the concept of an eclipse is understood.

Turks, Tartars: unchristened people valued by witches. Tartars come from Uzbekistan in the former USSR.

birth-strangled babe: once more an unchristened person. Why does Shakespeare use *babe*, not *baby*?

drab: prostitute

gruel: a porridge-like mixture (mention Oliver Twist asking for more?)

slab: another word for thick

thereto: to it

chaudron: entrails

- Examine the use of the semi-colon in the spell. Why are there not more full stops? Presumably to indicate that the spell continues.
- Explain the use of the colon in writing a glossary. This is a more modern use than Shakespeare's. Normally today the colon is used as an introduction to further details, speech, etc.

Independent work
- Children create a glossary based on the notes taken using Copymaster 6.

Plenary
- Recap on a few of the meanings mentioned, particularly those that recur in the work of Shakespeare and others: 'Tis; thrice.
- Recap the use of the apostrophe in whin'd, i'the, etc.

DAY 3

Big Book pp. 25–28; Pupil's Book p. 20

Shared reading/writing
- Establish the metre (seven syllables per line, eight in the chorus) and rhyming scheme (AABBCCDD, etc.) of the spell.
- Plan a class spell together, in the same manner as Shakespeare's spell. Decide on what the spell is supposed to do. Choose various suitable ingredients and make a word bank for less able children to draw on in their independent writing.
- If time permits, start to write a poem together.

Focused word/sentence work
- Discuss how poets are trying to express ideas in an imaginative, exciting way. Look for examples of the expressive and exciting use of words in the extract:
  Harpier cries: – 'tis time, 'tis time – a haunting line
  Gall of goat; and slips of yew,/ Sliver'd in the moon's eclipse;/ Nose of Turk and tartar's lips – consonant sounds. Where is the alliteration in this?
  How now, you secret, black and midnight hags – Macbeth's greeting to the witches elsewhere in the play, a good example of Shakespeare's special way with words
  sleeping got, birth-strangled babe, ditch-deliver'd by a drab, – compactness of phrase, and more alliteration
- How important is rhyme in the piece? Is rhyme always important in poetry? Look for examples where lines have been reversed to accommodate the rhyme, e.g. *Days and nights has thirty-one / Swelter'd venom.*

Independent work
- Children write their own spell.

Plenary
- Read selected examples of children's spells, inviting constructive comment on effective use of language, choice of ingredients, metre.

DAY 4

Big Book pp. 25–28; Pupil's Book p. 20

Shared writing
- You may wish to do the shared writing after the focused word work.
- The class writes the start of a script of a TV cookery programme, in which the TV chef or chefs are making up the recipe of the witches' spell. The script could feature the witches or alternatively well-known TV chefs. It can include stage directions (*Enter right*, etc.). The aim is to capture an appropriate style for the chef(s) concerned.

Focused word work
- Examine the use of *thereto*. Discuss other archaic words such as *thereabouts*, *thereafter* (after that; e.g. *Thereafter they lived in peace*), *thereby* (by that, e.g. *He drew his sword, thereby making a duel inevitable*), *thereupon* (as a consequence of that, immediately after that, e.g. *Hansel cried out. Thereupon the witch seized the boy ...*), *thereof* (of that, e.g. *You, sir, are the owner thereof!*), *hereafter* (after this: e.g. in a legal document: *Fred Bloggs, hereafter called the owner*), *hereby* (by this: e.g. *I hereby swear to tell the truth, the whole truth ...*).

Independent work
- Children continue with writing the spell begun in day 3.

Plenary
- Read further selected examples of children's spells.

DAY 5

Big Book pp. 29–30; Pupil's Book p. 21

Shared reading
- Read the second extract in the Big Book.
- Invite the children to discuss the purpose for which it was written. Was it intended for children, for an academic audience, for ordinary adults? Ask them to give reasons for their choice. In fact the title is a pun on *The Which? Report*. The extract comes from a small, mainly pictorial, book on dungeons and torture written by the author of these notes for the average visitor to places like Madame Tussaud's and the London Dungeon. Pictures take up more space than text, so the writing must be accurate and authoritative, but very economical. Often the original draft for these small pictorial guides has to be cut substantially to fit the picture design.
- Discuss use of *inquisitor monks* rather than *the monks who carried out the Inquisition*.
- Discuss *The hunt was on*. Sentence length must vary for interesting reading.
- Why is a dash used before *witches*? The purpose is to create a pause and thereby add drama to the sentence. In academic essay writing, dashes are best avoided.
- What other instances of a non-academic style can the children find, e.g. *Result: no reaction, ...*

Focused word/sentence work

- Discuss these words: *crones*; *purveyors*; *Papal Bull* (*papal* = adjective of Pope; *Bull* = edict, instruction); *desecrate* (use of *de* [away from] + *sacred*); *conjure* (*con* = with + *jurare* [Latin: to swear]); *peasant*; *hysteria*; *misfortune* (negative prefix *mis* = badly, wrongly); *denounce* (prefix *de* [from] + *nuntius* [Latin: messenger]).

- Discuss the use of the term *awful machinery*. There is a double meaning here: the figurative meaning of *awful* is something unthinking, uncaring, inevitable and unstoppable; literally, it refers to the instruments of torture (rack, thumbscrews, etc.) used to get witches and other "heretics" to confess.

- Introduce the writing task: to write simple notes on the passage "The Witch Report".

Independent work

- Children write notes on the extract about witches.

Plenary

- Starting with suggestions from the children's independent work, write a set of notes on witches with the class.

Consolidation and extension

- Ask the children to write out their spell as a modern recipe.
- Discuss other Shakespearean plays known to the children (and important ones that they do not know).
- Make a class display of spells, illustrating their ingredients.

Homework

- Page 7 of the Homework Book focuses on these forms of the verb: infinitive, past and present participles, and on well-known archaic forms of English.

Unit 7 Shakespeare's World

Key Learning Objectives

TL3	to articulate personal responses to literature, identifying why and how a text affects the reader
TL4	to be familiar with the work of some established authors, to know what is special about their work, and to explain their preferences in terms of authors, styles and themes
TL5	to contribute constructively to shared discussion about literature, responding to and building on the views of others
TL6	to manipulate narrative perspective by ... producing a modern retelling
TL8	to summarise a passage, chapter or text in a specified number of words
TL12	to comment critically on the language, style, success of examples of non-fiction, such as periodicals, reviews, reports, leaflets
SL4	to investigate connecting words and phrases
SL5	to form complex sentences through, e.g. ... exploring how meaning is affected by the sequence and structure of clauses
SL6	to secure knowledge and understanding of more sophisticated punctuation marks; ... parenthetic commas, dashes, brackets
WL3	to use independent spelling strategies, including: a) building up spellings by syllabic parts, using known prefixes, suffixes and common letter strings b) applying knowledge of spelling rules and exceptions c) building words from other known words, and from awareness of the meaning or derivations of words
WL5	to use word roots, prefixes and suffixes as a support for spelling
WL7	to understand how words and expressions have changed over time

Range:	Classic drama; non-fiction
Texts:	From *As You Like It*, William Shakespeare "London Bound", John McIlwain
Resources:	Big Book 6A pp. 31–35 Pupil's Book 6 pp. 22–24 Homework Book 6 p. 8 Copymaster 7: The Seven Ages of Man

DAY 1

Big Book pp. 31–33; Pupil's Book pp. 22–23

Shared reading

- Before reading the first extract together, introduce it. Explain that it comes from Shakespeare's comedy *As You Like It*, written around 1599. The words "All the World's a Stage" were the motto of the Globe Theatre which opened in that year (the idea isn't an original of Shakespeare's).

- The plot of *As You Like It* is complex, and the extract is self-contained, but this brief storyline may be helpful: Duke Frederick seizes the lands and castle of his brother, Duke Senior, who is banished to live a Robin Hood style life in the forest. Senior's daughter, Rosalind, stays on at the castle as companion for Frederick's daughter, Celia. A young wrestler, Orlando, visits the castle and wins Rosalind's heart, but Duke Frederick discovers that Orlando's father was one of his banished brother's greatest friends. The Duke turns sour and Rosalind is banished for her affections; Celia leaves with her. To survive in the outside world they pretend to be brother and sister, Ganymede and Aliena. Orlando is also adrift on life's ocean. With his faithful manservant, Adam, he wanders in the forest seeking food. The aged retainer is exhausted and starving by the time they come across Duke Senior's camp in the forest. Around at the time is Jaques, who is peripheral to the plot but acts as a melancholy commentator on the action. Orlando says his manservant is oppressed with the twin evils of age and hunger. Duke Senior offers them food and, in an optimistic frame of mind, says to Jaques that there are many more *woeful pageants* being played out in the *wide and universal theatre* of life. Jaques replies with the speech. Naturally there is a happy outcome to the play.

- Read the passage (or perhaps listen to a professional tape) together. Ask the children to identify the first point that Shakespeare is making – that we all act different roles in life. How does this tie up with the plot of *As You Like It*?

- Repeat the first couplet, and ask the children to say what figure of speech is represented here. It is a metaphor, more than a comparison or simile, a direct statement: *All the world's a stage.*

- What word would we normally use today instead of *players*?

- What is the second main point that Shakespeare makes, the substance of most of the speech (that our lives are divided into seven ages)?

- Check the children's understanding of what an act of a play is – a section between intervals, made up of several scenes.

- When Jaques says *man*, does he mean only males?

Focused word/sentence work

- How would children rate their level of understanding of the speech, say in marks out of 10? What about their level of enjoyment?

- To boost these scores, explain some of the meanings more clearly. Like most of Shakespeare's work, this is a very clever piece of writing – which is why he is still so popular 400 years later. (You could use the analogy of an ice lolly with several layers: you can enjoy and understand it superficially, but it often gets better as you get through to the layers underneath.) Have the children read the text again together, or take it in turns, but this time stop the process to question them on individual meanings:

merely players: players and nothing else

exits and entrances: Does this mean we have doors built into us? Explain the theatrical meaning.

infant: baby, rather than infant as in school terms

mewling: crying gently like a baby, originally linked with a cat's *mewing*

puking: being sick

satchel: Check understanding of this.

furnace: Check understanding again, but leave room for children to deduce why the word is used (there is a question in the comprehension work).

mistress: girlfriend, in modern terms

oaths: swear words or, more likely, muttered vows to do this, that or the other

pard: leopard

jealous in honour: proud, defensive, quick to rise. Discuss what having a sense of honour would mean. A code of honour was a strict code of conduct, implying deep self-respect, so if anybody dared to question one's honour one would be very quick to defend it. A knight's code of honour was a very serious matter in medieval times.

the justice: What does *justice* normally mean today? Here it means a magistrate. (Magistrates are still formally called the justices; in paying a fine one writes to the Clerk to the Justices.)

in fair round belly: This probably means it was a fair size!

with good capon lin'd: stuffed with chicken. A capon is a domestic cockerel, neutered and fattened for eating. They were often given as presents to magistrates.

saw: a proverb or maxim, e.g. *More haste less speed; marry in haste, repent at leisure*

instances: examples of personal experience (perhaps a hint that these are rather tedious)

Pantaloon: a traditional character from Italian comedy (in the same sense as the pantomime dame or Punch and Judy), a thin, foolish old man with slippers, pantaloons (long johns) and spectacles

youthful hose: the leggings he had as a young man (link with modern word *hosiery*)

shank: leg

childish treble: high voice, as in treble recorder, treble clef

whistles in his sound: Why might an old person whistle in speaking? (Because s/he has no or few teeth.)

mere: petty, unimportant, inconsequential (e.g. *mere words not deeds*)

oblivion: presumably not death but that sad state of being distant from what is going on

sans: French for *without*. Refer to the huge influence of Norman French on today's English. In the Middle Ages Aquitaine, Calais and other areas were part of the English kingdom. Does *sans eyes* mean having no eyes?

sans everything: What might this mean? Is there a deliberate order to the last line? Why might this be?

Independent work

• Comprehension.

Plenary

• Discuss answers to sections A and B of the children's independent work.

• If time permits, recap on the more obscure vocabulary.

DAY 2

Big Book pp. 31–33; Pupil's Book p. 23

Shared reading

• Ask the children to read the piece again together, looking for greater expressiveness this time.

• Discuss question C from day 1's independent work.

Focused word/sentence work

• Draw attention to the following meanings in the extract:

one man in his time plays many parts,/ His acts being seven: Note the use of the present participle to join the subsidiary clause to the main sentence. Ask children to make up two modern examples, e.g. *I walked to school this morning, my bike being broken.* This exercise is taken further in the day's independent work.

like snail: This is an example of a simile. Compare with the metaphor: *All the world's a stage.*

whining, shining, morning, creeping: In poetry there are often rhymes, assonances or patterns within lines. Often we don't notice them but they add to the effectiveness of the poem, e.g. *soldier/oaths; severe/beard.*

woeful: This is a wonderful, almost onomatopoeic, word.

his mistress' eyebrow: There are two possibilities here: a) Shakespeare is making fun of a ballad that praises every silly detail; b) Shakespeare imagines the lover's head tilted back in rapture as he recites his ballad.

seeking the bubble reputation: A metaphor. Why is reputation like a bubble? This is a brilliant encapsulation of a big idea in a single simple word.

even in the cannon's mouth: A metaphor within a metaphor: a) *mouth* is itself a metaphor; b) *in the cannon's mouth* = in the heart of the battle (*heart* is also a metaphor!).

With eyes severe and beard of formal cut: Note the ponderous sound which this line makes. Compare it with *Jealous in honour, sudden and quick in quarrel.* (Also notice alliteration here: *quick in quarrel.*)

And so he plays his part: Shakespeare recaps to remind us of his metaphor. A gentle reminder is a useful technique if you are sustaining some sort of literary convention for a considerable time.

sixth age shifts into the lean and slipper'd: An example of assonance – it sounds thin!

a world too wide: Another fine expression; also alliteration.

shrunk shank: How much better than saying *thin legs!*

Independent work

• Children work at joining clauses with participles.

Plenary

• Go through the answers to the children's independent work, in particular pointing out:

a) the necessity for agreement: *Having comfy cushions, I wanted to buy the sofa* – wrong; *Its having comfy cushions, I wanted to buy the sofa* – correct.

b) the logical order of clauses. The above would be better as: *I wanted to buy the sofa, its having comfy cushions*, or better still: *I wanted to buy the sofa as it had comfy cushions.*

c) the necessity to use the possessive pronoun: *My having returned early, Mum was able to relax* is correct; *Me/I having returned early …* is wrong.

DAY 3

Shared writing/preparation for independent writing

- Prepare for a modern retelling by writing collectively a set of notes on the passage. Mention the need in notes for clear headings, numbering and lettering where necessary to clarify the structure, indents to distinguish notes from headings, etc.

- Introduce Copymaster 7, which provides a starting point.

- Then discuss various possibilities for a first sentence or two, setting the guidelines in terms of style. For instance: *The world is like the stage of a theatre, our lives being a play performed there. Shakespeare compares our lives to a play in seven acts, with the world as the stage we perform on.*

Focused word/sentence work

- Point out that there are three words ending with -*ly* in the extract. What parts of speech are they? *Belly* is a noun; *merely* and *unwillingly* are adverbs. However, *manly* is an adjective, as are *leisurely* and *comely*.

- *Whining, shining, puking*: Identify the infinitives: *to whine, to shine, to puke*. What is the spelling rule when -*ing* is added? (Drop the *e*.) Ask the children to name some more examples. Are there any exceptions? (Yes: *singeing, canoeing*.) The same rule applies to other extensions (e.g. *shine – shiny, dodge – dodgy*).

- *Bubble, spectacles, whistles*: Ask children to name twenty more words that end in -*le* (e.g. *battle, thistle*).

- *Woeful*: All -*ful* adjectives have one *l* at the end. Ask for ten more examples.

- Why did Shakespeare write *mistress'*, not *mistress's*? Presumably to suit the metre of the poem; the latter is also rather ugly, as are *Jesus's, Julius's*. You could also examine the other apostrophes in the passage (*the world's a stage, nurse's arms, lin'd, cannon's mouth*).

Independent work

- Children are asked to translate Shakespeare's speech into their own words.

Plenary

- Discuss the children's independent work of rewriting. Invite constructive criticism on clarity, effectiveness of expression.

- Compare the children's writing with Shakespeare's, showing how economical and mellifluous Shakespeare's expressions are.

DAY 4

Shared reading

- Read "London Bound". What does *London bound* mean?

- What does *life must have had its frustrations* mean?

- Hide the text and ask the children to try to remember:
  a) the basic details of Shakespeare's life: Whom did he marry? Where did he live at first? How many children did he have? Shakespeare's children were Susanna and the twins Hamnet and Judith. Hamnet died in 1595, aged 11. Shakespeare wrote in *King John* (1595): *Grief fills the room up of my absent child, lies in his bed, walks up and down with me*. As Shakespeare was one of eight children, there may have been other childhood deaths in Shakespeare senior's house as well.
  b) some of the differences between the Shakespearean theatre and that of today.

Focused word/sentence work

- Examine the use of brackets, sometimes called parentheses. They are preferable to commas or dashes when the rest of the sentence is grammatically complete **and** the words in brackets are additional and might otherwise impede the flow of the sentence.

- In the second paragraph, look at the way *in the first place, secondly*, etc., are used to develop a list of points. Write together, in this way, the method for making a cup of tea. Use the impersonal approach, e.g. *Firstly one must fill the kettle with water*.

Independent work

- Children complete the writing assignment begun in day 3.

- If time permits, ask them to make simple, clear notes on Shakespeare's life before he went to London.

Plenary

- *London bound* is an example of a double-barrelled adjectival phrase. In the witches' spell (Unit 6) we had *ditch-deliver'd*. In the *As You Like It* speech Shakespeare might have said that the justice was *capon lin'd*, i.e. stuffed with chicken. What other similar phrases do the children know? E.g. *panic-stricken, house-bound, foot-weary*. Invent others: e.g. the headteacher could be *rage-swollen*, or *care-broken* (!); children could be *car-carried* or *lunchtime-longing*. (*Under Milk Wood* is packed with imaginative examples.)

- Many people do not realise how important Shakespeare is to today's English language. These are just a **few** of the words and phrases he coined personally: *gust* (of wind), *savage* (uncivilised), *restraint, unwillingness, uncomfortable, in one fell swoop* (**not** *foul swoop*), *pound of flesh, to have seen better days, the be-all and end-all, brave new world, a blinking idiot, to not budge an inch, to be cruel to be kind, to eat someone out of house and home, fair play, for goodness' sake, a foregone conclusion, good riddance, in my heart of hearts, knock knock who's there, method in one's madness, in my mind's eye, pomp and circumstance, a sorry sight, too much of a good thing, tower of strength, what the dickens, the world is my oyster.*

DAY 5

Big Book pp. 34–35; Pupil's Book p. 24

Shared writing

• Read "London Bound" again. Look at as many sentences as you can, discussing whether the order of information can be changed. What changes to the wording would be needed? Do they affect the meaning or the effectiveness of the sentence?

Focused word/sentence work

• Look at the way some of the sentences are joined. There are several words (*as, therefore, consequently, so*) that are useful when developing an argument, i.e. when one point leads to another. Try these out together on a simple proposition, e.g. *3 + 3 = 6, 3 × 2 = 6: As three add three makes six, we can say two threes make six.* Do the same for *therefore, consequently* and *so.* Try out other pairs of connected sentences, e.g. *Mexico City is the most heavily populated city in the world. Therefore Mexico City must be the most heavily populated city in Central America.*

Independent work

• Children practise the use of *as, so, therefore* and *consequently* to link ideas.

• Children practise forming adverbs from adjectives by adding *-ly.*

Plenary

• Discuss answers to the children's independent work.

Consolidation and extension

• Ask children to learn as much as they can of the *All the world's a stage* speech.

• Ask children to look up Shakespeare in a reference book and try to memorise ten important facts about him.

Homework

• Page 8 of the Homework Book focuses on the spelling rules associated with forming adverbs, on adjectives with a *-y* ending, and on using different conjunctions.

Newspaper Reports

Key Learning Objectives

TL12 to comment critically on the language, style, success of examples of non-fiction, such as periodicals, reviews, reports, leaflets

TL15 to develop a journalistic style through considering:
a) balanced and ethical reporting
b) what is of public interest in events
c) the interest of the reader
d) selection and presentation of information

TL16 to use the styles and conventions of journalism to report on, e.g. real or imagined events

SL1 to revise from Y5: ...
c) the construction of complex sentences
d) the conventions of standard English
e) adapting texts for particular readers and purposes

SL4 to investigate connecting words and phrases; ... study how points are typically connected in different kinds of text

WL3 to use independent spelling strategies, including:
a) building up spellings by syllabic parts, using known prefixes, suffixes and common letter strings; ...
c) building words from other known words, and from awareness of the meaning or derivations of words

WL9 to understand how new words have been added to the language.

Range:	Journalistic writing
Texts:	From the *Sun* and the *Independent* From *The Week*
Resources:	Big Book 6A pp. 36–38 Pupil's Book 6 pp. 25–28 Homework Book 6 p. 9 Copymaster 8: A newspaper report (planning sheet) Copy of the *Sun*; copy of the *Independent*

Preparation

- Write headings on board or large paper: *4 syllables, 3 syllables, 2 syllables, 1 syllable*.
- Ask children to bring in a daily newspaper for day 2 (one between two will be adequate).

DAY 1

Big Book pp. 36–37; Pupil's Book pp. 25–26

Shared reading

- Read the extracts of reports on the Manchester United *v.* Liverpool match. Which newspapers might the extracts have come from? Explain the **physical** difference between tabloid and broadsheet newspapers.

- Which extract is easier to read?

- Divide the class into two groups, and allocate each group to one of the extracts. Then ask them to find the 50th word, but excluding all headlines and proper nouns e.g. *Premiership*, names of people, ground name or figures. (These don't reflect the style of the newspaper, but will just confuse the issue.) Count hyphenated words as two words in terms of readability. The 50th word in the *Independent* extract is *penalty* (in *penalty by Denis Irwin*); the *Sun*'s 50th word is *hopes* (in *hopes of a comeback*).

- Now ask each group to count the number of syllables in the first 50 words of their extract and record the results by tallying: How many words are there of one syllable? How many of two syllables? And so on. In this way, find out which paper has more long words. What does that tell us about the writing and the target audience?

- What other differences in style are there? What differences exist between tabloids and broadsheets in terms of content (topics covered, amount written and subject priorities), headline size, layout? Why are there such differences?

Focused word/sentence work

- Examine the meaning of potentially difficult vocabulary, using dictionaries as appropriate, e.g. *supine, resilience, verve*.

- Draw attention to the headlines. Ask the children what *Den'n'dusted* might mean. It is a pun on the phrase *Done and dusted*, linking Denis Irwin with the notion of Liverpool being finished off by his penalty. What does *to steal someone's thunder* mean? Why has the *Independent* sub-editor chosen a reference to thunder? He is picking up on the reporter's mention of Scholes's thunderous shot. Explain that headlines are not normally written by the reporter.

- There are examples of alliteration in both extracts. What are they? E.g. *Scholes smashed a stunning second, raw rugged*.

- How would you expect *raw rugged* to be punctuated in a novel or other book? Why is there no comma here? The reason could be to increase speed and impact of reading; it could be because there is a shortage of space in the column, or it may be just newspaper style to minimise usage of commas.

Independent work

- Comprehension.

Plenary

- Select answers from children's comprehension work. Be sure to include answers to question B5; the answer is no, the clue being the phrase *if not all their verve* in the *Independent* report.

DAY 2

Big Book pp. 36–37; Pupil's Book pp. 26–27

Shared reading

- Read the reports again, looking for examples of metaphor. For the first two or three, point out how they are not literally true, and invite a more conventional alternative. For subsequent ones, invite children to analyse them in the same way:
  fired: Irwin didn't use a gun or set fire to anything.
  wrecked: There was no debris left on the pitch or in the stands.
  drilled: No Black & Deckers are allowed on the pitch.
  Other examples include: *spot-king, rocket-shot, to power, stunning, fortress, killed off, smashed, supine, thunderous*.

- In which type of newspaper is metaphor more heavily used? Why is this? Brevity and excitement are both necessary where reading abilities may not be high.

Focused word/sentence work

- Draw attention to the language of journalism. Newspapers, especially tabloids, have a "shorthand" language all their own. Give examples of this from the two reports and ask why they get the name:
  e.g. *spot-kick* (= penalty kick from the spot); *to book someone* (= to caution them by writing their name in a notebook); *Kop* = the Liverpool fans (who have a stand at their ground called the Kop). Why do the tabloids use these short words?

- Discuss these examples of favourite tabloid words, inviting children to translate: *drama* (e.g. clifftop drama); *bid* (bid to save town hall); *blow* (blow to town's jobs); *shock* (star in booze shock); *plea* (girl in transplant plea); *to flee* (to escape); *horror* (fire horror); *scare* (BSE scare hits sheep); *to dub* (PM dubbed "smiler" by his pals); *to hit* (TB hits city). Leave the examples visible during the independent work that follows.

- Give children two minutes to find their own examples from their newspapers. Write their suggestions down.

Independent work

- Children work at "translating" tabloid headlines into ordinary English, and invent some headlines of their own.

Plenary

- Pick out the key "tabloid" words and recap on their meaning.

- What are the possible dangers of tabloid journalism? Answers could include over-simplification, sensationalism, unethical reporting, an aggressive attitude (as in witch-hunts, character assassination).

DAY 3

Big Book pp. 36–38; Pupil's Book p. 28

Shared reading

- Read together the extract in the Big Book about the ruined teddy bears' picnic. Check on any words that are not understood. There should not be too many.

- What does this extract reveal about the type of paper it comes from (an Australian tabloid)?

Focused word/sentence work

- Look at the football report from the *Independent*. How many ideas does the first sentence contain? There are six: rediscovered resilience; weak in previous game; didn't have their former verve; beat Liverpool; drew level in Premiership; have 11 points.

- Identify the main sentence in the *Independent* report: *Manchester United rediscovered their resilience at Old Trafford last night to defeat Liverpool.* Point out how the *supine* and the *verve* ideas are interwoven in the main sentence, and a subsidiary clause about the league position is tacked on at the end.

- Examine the second and third sentences of this extract in the same way. Why does the reporter say *at United*, then *at Old Trafford*? (To avoid repetition.)

- Examine the *Sun* football report for the number of ideas per sentence. Identify the main part of the sentence in each case. Discuss the complexity or otherwise of the sentence construction.

Shared writing

- Prepare the children for writing independently a newspaper report on a subject (or subjects) of their choice connected with a topic being studied, as appropriate.

- Ask children what they notice about the first few sentences of the teddy bear article and the two football reports. Most news stories begin with a summary of the report, and journalists are taught to make this interesting enough to "hook" the reader into reading the rest of the article. The children's "news" stories should begin in this way.

- Mention also that most news stories include words from a person who has been interviewed. These are very often quoted as direct speech. Children's writing should include at least one piece of direct speech, with full details of who is talking and their relevance to the subject.

- Plan the writing together, perhaps by choosing a sample subject and showing the different angles that could be explored. For example, if they are studying the Tudors you could plan a story on the sudden arrest of Anne Boleyn on 2 May 1536. Henry VIII had abruptly ridden off from a Greenwich tournament on 1 May, leaving Anne behind. The next day she was taken to the Tower. The headline could be *KING DUMPS QUEEN. ANNE IN TOWER SHOCK* or something similar. An eyewitness at the tournament could be "interviewed"; a member of the

Hampton Court staff could be suitably non-committal; Anne's parlourmaid could feature. Earlier in the year, she had given birth to a stillborn son, which would lead to speculation in the report about the reasons for her sudden arrest. On 19 May, Anne was executed, so the report could end with a prediction, perhaps expressing fear for the Queen's future safety.

Independent work

• Children write a newspaper story on a topic being studied. Copymaster 8 can be used to plan this work.

Plenary

• Select and discuss examples of children's writing.

DAY 4

Big Book pp. 36–37; Pupil's Book p. 28

Shared writing

• Either continue the collective writing of the sample topic-based story planned in day 3's shared writing session, or plan and begin to write a new topic-based story.

Focused word work

• Draw attention to common prefixes. Scan the *Sun* and *Independent* extracts for words beginning with *re* and list them on the board, OHP, etc. Explain that many *re* words come from a Latin prefix meaning *again* or *back*. Examine meanings in this context, starting with *rediscovered*. *Resilient* comes from Latin *re-silire* = to jump back again. *Republic*, however, is from *res publicus* = people's things. Think of other examples where *re* means *again* or *back*, e.g. *return*, *review*, *reverse*.

• Look at the word *Independent*. The *in* prefix means *not* in this case (i.e. not dependent). Think of other similar examples: *incorrect*, *insufficient*, *intolerant*, *insincere*. *In* is also a Latin word itself (meaning *in*!) and is used in many words such as *insert*, *input*, *inspect*, *invade*.

• Look at *defender* and *demand*. Think also about *defraud*, *descend*, *decode*. What might the Latin prefix *de* mean (away from)? It can also signify reversal of procedure, e.g. *defrost*, *defuse*, *decelerate*.

• Another prefix to look at is *dis* in *disputed* (*dis* = not; *puto* = to reckon; leads on to *compute*: *con* = with + *puto*; and *repute*: *re* = again + *puto*).

Independent work

• Children continue with their writing assignment from day 3.

Plenary

• Discuss examples of children's journalistic writing from days 3 and 4, inviting children to point out where expressions used are appropriate to the genre, or where the style could be improved.

DAY 5

Big Book p. 38; Pupil's Book p. 28

Shared reading

• Read the third extract in the Big Book again.

• Discuss the rules, written and unwritten, that govern what people write in newspapers. For instance, their writing must be accurate, fair and balanced; it must interest the reader; it must not give offence, so there should be no swearing (even if the teddy bear pilot had been swearing); it must not go against the public interest, e.g. it must not prejudice any court proceedings.

• How might the teddy bear story have been written if it was not fair and balanced?

Focused word work

• After guessing which language they may have come from, ask the children to find the origins of these words from the first and second extracts, using a dictionary: *United*, *penalty*, *rocket*, *title*, *demise*, *premiership*, *attempt*.

• Ask them to put these words in columns by origin.

• Draw out patterns of origin, e.g. words ending in *le* are usually French.

• Look separately at *smash*, which is an example of onomatopoeia (it was coined to imitate the sound it now describes).

Independent work

• Children write the story of the ruined teddy bear's picnic from a biased point of view – the pilot's.

Plenary

• Discuss examples of children's journalistic writing from day 5, inviting them to point out where the expressions used are appropriate to the genre, or where the style could be improved.

• Recap on the meaning of *onomatopoeia*.

Consolidation and extension

• Ask children to look in their own papers for examples of alliteration.

• Ask children to cut out and discuss interesting newspaper stories, particularly those which represent the styles of journalism discussed.

• Have children make a class newspaper on school affairs, on current events or connected with an area of study.

Homework

• Page 9 of the Homework Book focuses on important prefixes from Latin and Greek.

Unit 9 — Personification in Poetry

Key Learning Objectives

TL3   to articulate personal responses to literature, identifying why and how a text affects the reader

TL10   to write own poems experimenting with active verbs and personification; produce revised poems for reading out individually

SL1   to revise from Y5 ... the different word classes

SL6   to secure knowledge and understanding of more sophisticated punctuation marks: ... semi-colon

WL2   to use known spellings as a basis for spelling other words with similar patterns or related meanings

Range:	Poetry by long-established authors
Texts:	"Xmas", Wes Magee "Silver", Walter de la Mare "The Poet Takes a Walk in the Country", Roger McGough
Resources:	Big Book 6A pp. 39–43 Pupil's Book 6 pp. 29–31 Homework Book 6 p. 10 Copymaster 9: Personification

Preparation

- Walter de la Mare (1873–1956) worked for the Standard Oil Company (Esso) for 18 years before becoming a full-time writer. His most famous poem is "The Listeners", published in 1912. He is buried in St Paul's Cathedral.

- Make copies of Copymaster 9 for each child or pair of children on day 3, and perhaps reproduce the same headings on an OHP transparency.

DAY 1

Big Book pp. 39–41; Pupil's Book pp. 29–30

Shared reading

- Read the poem "Xmas". What metaphors and similes can the children find in it?

- Read the poem "Silver" together, emphasising the gentle, dignified plod of the verse, the clarity of consonants and the alliteration. Mention the importance of enjoying the consonants and the sounds of the words in the poem, then read it again slowly and expressively.

- The whole of "Silver" pursues a single metaphorical theme. What is a metaphor? What is the theme?

- What overall effect is Walter de la Mare trying to create by his use of language? Smooth, silent action of moonlight gently creeping over the village.

- What techniques does he use to achieve this? Ask the children to find examples of alliteration, e.g. *slowly/silently*, *couched/kennel*; assonance, e.g. *peers/sees/gleam/reeds/stream*; repetition of *silver*.

- What is the rhyme scheme of "Silver"? (AABBCCDDEEFFGG) In further explanation, introduce the phrase "rhyming couplet" (couplet = a pair of lines, usually rhyming and usually with the same number of

syllables). How does the rhyme scheme help the overall impression de la Mare is trying to create? The gently plodding rhythm echoes the quiet persistence of the moonlight.

- Which is the more recent of these two poems? What evidence is there for this? Suggest reasons why "Xmas" might have been paired with "Silver". (The answer will come on day 2, if it is not forthcoming now.)

Focused word/sentence work

- Discuss the following words in "Silver":
  shoon = shoes. What does this tell you about the likely time of writing (1912)?
  peers: How does this differ from *looks*? Why could the moon be said to peer rather than look?
  casement: a vertically hinged window
  couched: Why does the poet use this rather than, say, *asleep*? This is indicative of the thought that goes into poems.
  cote
  silver-feathered sleep: Note the compression of ideas into a single short phrase.
  moveless: Explain that this is not a normal word, but is a brilliant choice. Why didn't the poet choose, for example, *still* or *motionless*? The very word has a still quality about it.

- In "Silver" explain why the dog has only paws of silver.

- Why does De la Mare use the phrase *one by one* (to indicate the movement of the moon through the village)?

Independent work

- Comprehension.

Plenary

- Discuss selected answers to the children's independent comprehension work.

- Read "Xmas" again. Explain that the two poems are good examples of a particular technique, not so far mentioned. Ask children to consider what this might be (but don't tell them until day 2!).

DAY 2

Big Book pp. 39–41; Pupil's Book pp. 30–31

Shared reading

- Read the poems "Xmas" and "Silver" again. Examine in detail the stylistic differences between them, in terms of rhyme, metre, vocabulary (e.g. *shoon* is used to fit in with the rhyme whereas *electronic* is an uncompromisingly unpoetic word), sentence construction (e.g. *sleeps the dog* – few modern poets ever reverse subject and verb; also the *doves* lines have been turned around).

Focused word work

- Despite their differences, what technique do both poems have in common? Introduce the concept of *personification* (the investing of non-human subjects with human characteristics). Look for verbs which exemplify this, first in "Silver" (e.g. the moon *walks*, *peers*; casements *catch* the moonbeams; doves' breasts *peep*), then in "Xmas" (e.g. *stirs, huddles*).

- Prepare the children for independent work by thinking of possible examples of personification. Start with areas of human action, thinking of a non-human subject that might match it:
  1) looking: What non-human thing might look/stare/ glance at you? Perhaps a closed-circuit TV camera, a portrait on a wall, the trees in a forest at night.
  2) movement: What non-human thing might run/ dance/swallow/glide?
  3) sound: What non-human thing might scream/call/ whistle/whisper?

Independent work

- Children work on personification. There is a structured introduction to the use of active verbs in personification, requiring progressively more imagination.

Plenary

- Discuss possible answers to the independent work, encouraging children to be as imaginative in their ideas as possible, e.g. time yawning, a machine dreaming of freedom, a sudden thought snatching the attention.

DAY 3

Big Book p. 39; Pupil's Book p. 31

Shared reading

- Read "Xmas" again, then discuss the reasons behind the choice of words and the effect they have, e.g. *duvet, advent, warble, tipsy*.

Shared writing

- Recap on the concept of personification.
- Develop together a bank of verbs describing human actions and thoughts that could be applied in non-human contexts.
  1) Ask children to supply broad headings for human activity: sounds (differentiate between verbal and non-verbal), ways of looking, ways of moving, ways of not moving, ways of using the mouth, ways of thinking, ways of dealing with others.
  2) Give out Copymaster 9. Ask children to think of verbs that might go under each of these headings.
  3) Write the best of the children's ideas under the same headings on the board or an OHP transparency.
- Discuss how emotions could be employed in descriptions (e.g. anger, sadness, to sulk, to get upset).

Focused word/sentence work

- Ask children to employ six or so words from the word bank they have compiled to make exciting sentences. Subjects can vary.
- Examine ways of developing these sentences, perhaps by adding a related verb or by employing a second clause in a sophisticated way, e.g. *The wind moaned in the trees while the sky wept. The fruit machine hesitated for a moment, made its decision, then began to cough twopenny pieces from its gaping jaws.*

Independent work

- Children choose seven verbs which involve personification and use each of them to make simple, exciting sentences.
- Then they rewrite their sentences, adding other similar verbs, or other clauses, to make them even more effective and exciting.

Plenary

- Discuss selected examples from the independent work, inviting constructive criticism on their effectiveness and the level of imagination shown.

DAY 4

Big Book pp. 39–43; Pupil's Book p. 31

Shared reading

- Read "The Poet Takes a Walk in the Country" by Roger McGough.

Shared writing

- You may wish to introduce the shared writing after the focused sentence work.
- Choose a subject potentially rich in things to describe, e.g. a fire, a factory, a storm. Brainstorm ideas for turning as many of the "human" verbs and adjectives as possible into exciting sentences. E.g. *As the village slept, the barn lay defenceless. The raging fire ate into it, fingers of flame reaching to the sky; sparks spat in every direction.* (Don't worry about going over the top with the description; rather encourage an uninhibited approach.)
- Put these ideas together in a piece of communal blank verse (of no more than six lines) using personification, constantly seeking to improve and rework the lines. Emphasise that the quality of idea is the key thing and that, in this sort of verse, rhyme is unimportant (and often intrusive).
- Make a list of three other possible subjects for children to work on independently. (However, you may find it more productive for children to work in pairs, at least for the first five minutes or so of the allotted time.)

Independent work

- Children write a poem using personification, based on an idea of their own or one of those suggested.

Focused sentence work

- Examine all three sample poems, identifying the subject of each line. What is the normal relationship of subject and verb in a sentence (subject first, verb second)?
- Explain that in many poems this pattern, and other normal patterns, are reversed for the sake of the rhyme or the metre. What examples are there in the three poems? In "Silver": *sleeps the dog*; in "The Poet Takes a Walk in the Country": *Magical was the transformation.*
- You may wish to quote some more examples of subject/verb reversal, e.g. from "The Listeners" by Walter de la Mare: *Never the least stir made the listeners*; from "The Wreck of the Hesperus" by H.W. Longfellow: *Then the maiden clasped her hands, That savèd she might be*; from "Requiem" by R.L. Stevenson: *Home is the sailor, home from the sea, And the hunter home from the hill.*

- You could compare the style of Stevenson's "Requiem" with Wes Magee's "Xmas" poem:

Requiem

Under the wide and starry sky,
Dig the grave and let me lie.
Glad did I live and gladly die,
And I laid me down with a will.
This be the verse you grave for me:
Here he lies where he longed to be:
Home is the sailor, home from the sea,
And the hunter home from the hill.

What effect does this twisting of words have? You could suggest that it is old-fashioned, but dignified, less realistic, etc.

Plenary

- Listen to selected examples of "personification poetry" written as independent work. Encourage children to read good lines even if they have not finished drafting their poem.

DAY 5

Big Book pp. 39–43; Pupil's Book p. 31

Shared reading

- Read "The Poet Takes a Walk in the Country" again.

Focused word/sentence work

- Examine the use of the semi-colon in "Silver". Why has it been used rather than a full stop in many cases?

- Compare the punctuation of the three poems. What is noticeable about the punctuation of the modern poems?

- Challenge children, for any given word in the three poems, to identify the part of speech and then to find a specified type of word in the same family. You might choose *silently*. The response would be *adverb*. You (or a child) then nominate a part of speech, say, *adjective*. The response would be *silent*. This can easily be turned into a team game. Also the names of parts of speech could be written on cards and drawn at random.

Independent work

- Children finish the "personification poems" begun on day 4, if possible writing them out for display with a design that brings out the personification theme.

Plenary

- Read aloud several "personification poems", inviting constructive criticism.

Consolidation and extension

- Read other poems by Walter de la Mare (especially "The Travellers"), and A.E. Housman's "A Shropshire Lad" (*Loveliest of trees, the cherry now ...* in Unit 24).

- Ask children to learn the poem "Silver".

- Ask children to find and discuss examples of personification from their own reading.

Homework

- Page 10 of the Homework Book focuses on parts of speech (word classes) and the use of semi-colons.

Unit 10 Reports

Key Learning Objectives

TL8 to summarise a passage, chapter or text in a specified number of words

TL12 to comment critically on the language, style, success of examples of non-fiction, such as periodicals, reviews, reports, leaflets

TL13 to secure understanding of the features of non-chronological reports:
a) instructions to orientate reader
b) use of generalisations to categorise
c) language to describe and differentiate
d) impersonal language
e) mostly present tense

TL17 to write non-chronological reports linked to other subjects

SL1 to revise from Y5:
a) the different word classes
b) re-expressing sentences in a different order
c) the construction of complex sentences
d) the conventions of standard English
e) adapting texts for particular readers and purposes

SL4 to investigate connecting words and phrases:
a) collecting examples from reading and thesauruses
b) study how points are typically connected in different kinds of text
c) classify useful examples for different kinds of text, for example, by position (*besides, nearby, by*); sequence (*firstly, secondly ...*); logic (*therefore, so, consequently*)
d) identify connectives which have multiple purposes (e.g. *on, under, besides*)

SL5 to form complex sentences through, e.g.:
a) using different connecting devices
b) reading back complex sentences for clarity of meaning, and adjusting as necessary
c) evaluating which links work best
d) exploring how meaning is affected by the sequence and structure of clauses

WL8 to research the origins of proper names, e.g. place names, surnames, days of the week, months, names of products

Range:	Non-chronological reports
Texts:	From *Discovering Britain* (Automobile Association) From *The Cambridge Encyclopedia of Language*, David Crystal
Resources:	Big Book 6A pp. 44–48 Pupil's Book 6 pp. 32–35 Homework Book 6 p. 11 Copymaster 10: Our region (planning sheet)

Preparation

• It would be useful to familiarise yourself with the geography and history of your school's region, in order to introduce the topic for independent writing on day 3. The headings on Copymaster 10 give a possible structure for this.

DAY 1

Big Book pp. 44–45; Pupil's Book pp. 32–33

Shared reading

• Read the extract about Cornwall together.

• Is the passage fiction or non-fiction?

• What sort of book might it have come from? What evidence is there for this? Point to the use of the word *attractions* (and ask children to find examples of other "alluring" words), the use of dramatic vocabulary (again, ask children to find examples), economical writing covering a lot of ground in a short space, also tight phrases, e.g. *wave-lashed*.

• Go through the piece, asking children to put statements under the two headings *Fact* and *Opinion*. Some are obvious, but how do you prove, e.g., *Cornwall is most renowned for ...*? You may need a third *In-between* category.

• Discuss the vocabulary: *renowned, scenic, piskies* (= pixies), *legacy, huer*. Note that *huer* comes from Old French *huer* = to cry; *hue and cry* was when criminals were pursued by a posse of people; it is **not** connected with *to hew* = to quarry.

Focused word/sentence work

• Examine the economy of the writing. In the first sentence, what facts are communicated, and how are they shoehorned into one sentence? It is a common technique to put a clause in before the main sentence, leaving the writer free to make further points after the main statement without overloading the sentence. Think of another example (e.g. *The subject of much debate as to its value to society, television is nevertheless an accepted part of modern life and ...*).

• When using lists, it is unnecessary to restate the introduction to the sentence. So *Cornwall is renowned for ...* is not repeated for the harbours and creeks. The same technique is used with *land of giants and piskies, of saints and smugglers*. Think of other examples, e.g. *This school is known for its kindness and courtesy, for its wonderful teachers, for its brilliant children* (the continued inclusion of *for* here is not strictly necessary but helps the reader to understand the thrust of the sentence).

• Point out the omission of unnecessary words: *This is the land of King Arthur, [who was] among the greatest ...*

• Refer to connective words:
a) *yet*, an alternative to *but*. Think of other sentences using *yet*, e.g. *Durham is a remote county, yet its welcome is a warm one.*
b) *for*, a brief alternative to *because*: *She did not come prepared, for she had no mac with her.*

Independent work

- Comprehension.

Plenary

- Discuss selected answers to the children's independent comprehension work. Particularly check answers to question A5 for correctness, and show textual evidence for answer 5b.
- If time permits, ask children how they respond to the writing. Ask those who haven't been to Cornwall whether it attracts them now. (If you live in Cornwall, is it a fair reflection?)

DAY 2

Big Book pp. 44–45; Pupil's Book pp. 33–34

Shared reading

- Explain that the Cornwall extract is an example of non-chronological writing, specifically a report on things as they are at present. What do the children think *non-chronological* means? (Greek: *khronos* = time, so a non-chronological account does not describe a sequence of events, rather the state of things at any one time.)
- Examine the characteristics of non-chronological writing:
  a) What tense would it be written in?
  b) Would it be written in the same way as a letter? Explain that language in reports is impersonal (*There is ...* rather than *You will see ...*). Explain the use of the pronoun *one*.
  c) How would children expect non-chronological writing to start? Explain the need for instructions to orientate the reader – some sort of overall explanatory paragraph.
  d) Explain that it is normal to break down what is being described into sections, therefore necessary to draw out the differences between these. Look for examples in the piece (e.g. *rugged cliffs/sandy coves; saints and smugglers*). What other differences are drawn out?
- Can children find examples of generalisations, i.e. broad statements which are bound to have exceptions? For example, *dominated by its rocky, wave-lashed coastline* – there are many places in Cornwall completely out of sight of the sea, and in many ways uninfluenced by it; *the jagged heights of Tintagel* – this is true of the cliffs at Tintagel where King Arthur's castle is, but it certainly isn't true of the village or the area inland; *300-mile boundary* – almost certainly it isn't exactly 300 miles! Suggest that such generalisations are made in the interests of clarity and conciseness.

Focused word/sentence work

- Are there any "tricks" of literary style in evidence? Point out alliteration.
- Another element of economical writing is double-barrelled adjectives (if necessary explain *double-barrelled* – originally from a gun with two barrels). *Far-reaching* is a common one, but there are others invented just for this piece. Ask the children to find them (*wave-lashed, creek-cut, stone-walled*). What do they mean? Work out how many words are saved by using them.

- There is some hidden personification here, e.g. *friendly harbours*: can a harbour be friendly?; *brooding ... Bodmin Moor*: can a moor really brood?

Independent work

- Children work at joining sentences economically.

Plenary

- Discuss selected answers to the independent work.
- For questions C and D, discuss alternative methods of joining. Also, does *water and woods* in question B work better than *woods and water*?

DAY 3

Pupil's Book p. 34

Shared writing/preparation for independent writing

- Plan and begin to write a description of your own region with the aim of making it seem as attractive as possible. Copymaster 10 gives a possible structure, and children could jot down ideas under each heading before feeding them back to be assembled on OHP, board, etc. The heading *Brief history* means **very** brief – an outline only. If there are substantial and obvious things that visitors might not like, you will need to discuss at some stage how this is to be dealt with in your persuasive text.
- Remind children about the features of non-chronological writing. It might be useful to look at different ways of saying something impersonally. Start off with a personal example for your region: e.g. *I like walking by the River Severn.* How can this be put in impersonal terms? *Many visitors enjoy ...; One can walk ...; The River Severn is a popular ...; A walk along the Severn is ...*

Focused word/sentence work

- Return to the subject of agreement in sentences. Analyse what is wrong with these examples of incorrect usage:
  I reckon hippos are big. Having said that, there's a small hippo over there.
  [Spoken by a Liverpool supporter:] *Sadly, Manchester United won the cup.*
  Hopefully, the dead man will be identified.
  Next came a mother with a very small baby pushing a pram.
  The girl was followed by a small poodle wearing jeans.
- If time permits, you could discuss another unfortunate element of our language, the cliché (e.g. *At the end of the day, there's nothing like a proper breakfast*). What other overused phrases can the children think of (e.g. *sick as a parrot, over the moon, last but not least, the blushing bride*)?

Independent work

- Children write a description of your region.

Plenary

- Select examples of independent work, and examine whether they embody the techniques of joining sentences in an economical and sophisticated way. Discuss options with the children.

DAY 4

Big Book pp. 44–47; Pupil's Book p. 34

Shared reading

- Read the second extract, on dictionaries. Compare this piece with the piece about Cornwall. List similarities and differences.

- Recap on the criteria for non-chronological writing (discussed on day 2). How does this extract compare?
  - Does it use the present tense?
  - Is the language impersonal? E.g. *there is ... variation in the way this is used* is both passive and impersonal, as opposed to *in the way you might use it*, or *some people constantly use ... others ...*
  - Is there an explanatory/orientation paragraph to start?

Focused word/sentence work

- Discuss these word meanings: *status, drudges, arbiter, linguistically irrelevant, Preface, systematically, conclusion, inescapable.*

- Examine the ways ideas are joined or separated in the passage.
  Sentence 1 (*A dictionary is ...*): *That* is used as a conjunction (as opposed to *which*) because the clause that follows helps define what the dictionary is; *along with* is a very useful joining phrase. (*Also, in addition to, as well as* can be similarly useful; how would these sound if used instead?)
  Sentence 2 (*The process ...*): Why is a dash used before *harmless drudges*? (Because it is separate to the main idea of the sentence and could easily be left out.)
  Sentence 3 (*In literate societies ...*): *But* is the conjunction (used where the second clause contrasts in some way with the first).
  Sentence 4 (*Some people ...*): Note the use of the present participle *aiming* to add on an extra idea.
  Sentences 8 and 9 (*For a book ...; When people are asked ...*): Remember that sentences can start with a conjunction. It is often worth trying this for variety, and leaving the main statement to the end often adds punch to a sentence, e.g. *If you are good, you can go to the theme park.*
  Sentence 12 (*As a consequence ...*): This is a phrase to use where one sentence develops from the previous one (always a good thing). What other phrases could have been used? (*As a result, In consequence, Therefore, So ...*)

Independent work

- Children continue their day 3 work on regional descriptions.

Plenary

- Read selected examples of children's regional descriptions, inviting constructive criticism. Are they accurate? Would they tempt the prospective visitor?

DAY 5

Big Book pp. 46–47; Pupil's Book p. 35

Shared writing/reading

- What is the chief irony of people's behaviour regarding dictionaries?

- Check on children's knowledge of the word *irony* (a deliberate statement that contradicts what one is thinking or, as here, strangely contradictory behaviour; in this case it is said that people regard dictionaries as important, but neither choose them carefully nor know how to use them properly).

- Draw attention to the distinction between implicit and explicit statements. Ask children to find examples of explicit statements made in the text (e.g. *A dictionary is a reference book; In literate societies most homes have a dictionary*). There are also some implicit messages in the text – not hidden, but just taken for granted. What are they? You could suggest: people ought to think about the contents of a dictionary before they buy it; people ought to keep an up-to-date dictionary; people ought to read the Preface of a dictionary.

- Talk briefly about the independent work – a summary of the piece on dictionaries. Emphasise that in 100 words the children cannot put every detail in, and must ruthlessly discard what is unimportant. They must write in complete sentences, however. This is not to be a set of notes.

Focused word/sentence work

- Find a list in the passage (e.g. in the first sentence). Examine its punctuation (commas between each item). Explain that the last comma, before the *and*, is favoured by academics, but that most mainstream writers leave it out. It is sometimes known as the Oxford comma. Find another example in the passage. Write such a list on the board or OHP and get children to punctuate it.

- Look at the use of hyphens in *10- or 20-year-old*. Hyphens are especially to be used when a phrase is used as an adjective (e.g. *a 19th-century vase*, but *a vase from the 19th century*).

- Look at the phrase *is by no means uncommon*. It could have said *is quite common*. We often use a negative phrase to make a positive statement (*not bad* instead of *good*; *not unlikely* instead of *probable*; *not unusual* instead of *very possible*).

- Point out *inescapable*. What other *in-* opposites do the children know?

- Mention the colon (after *inescapable*). When do we use colons?

- Look at the last sentence. What metaphor is being used here? You might want to introduce the word *analogy*. It is probably more accurate in this case – the use of a parallel situation as an illustration of the point being made.

Independent work

- Children write a summary of the passage about dictionaries.

- Children who have not finished their regional description from days 3 and 4 could do that instead, although this is not presented as an option in the Pupil's Book.
- The following sample summary uses 79 words.

    A dictionary is an alphabetical book listing words, their meanings, spellings, derivations, etc. Dictionary compilers are called lexicographers.

    Most homes have a dictionary but often these are little used and out of date.

    Although people regard dictionaries as being important, many people choose them by looking at other factors rather than the words inside, do not know what dictionaries actually contain, do not understand how to use them fully and are not aware of how useful they can be.

Plenary

- Look at the passage together and write a joint summary, using ideas from the children's own summaries, and discussing the reasons for discarding or retaining various facts.

Consolidation and extension

- Ask children to make double-barrelled adjectives out of a selection of suitable phrases, e.g. *lashed by waves – wave-lashed*.
- Have the children make a display of the writing on your region, setting it round a map, and with suitable illustrations. Coloured strings could be used to link pictures with map locations.
- Ask children to write down and share details of the dictionaries they have at home, including their date of publication. (Useful learning: how to find this in a book.)

Homework

- Page 11 of the Homework Book focuses on joining sentences by omitting words and using different connecting devices.

Unit 11 A Christmas Carol

Key Learning Objectives

TL1	to compare and evaluate a novel or play in print and the film/TV version
TL2	to take account of viewpoint in a novel through, e.g. a) identifying the narrator b) explaining how this influences the reader's view of events c) explaining how events might look from a different point of view
TL3	to articulate personal responses to literature, identifying why and how a text affects the reader
TL4	to be familiar with the work of some established authors, to know what is special about their work
TL5	to contribute constructively to shared discussion about literature, responding to and building on the views of others
SL1	to revise from Y5: ... c) the construction of complex sentences d) the conventions of standard English
SL2	to understand the terms *active* and *passive*, being able to transform a sentence from active to passive, and vice versa
SL4	to investigate connecting words and phrases; ... study how points are typically connected in different kinds of text
SL6	to secure knowledge and understanding of more sophisticated punctuation marks: ... semi-colon; ... parenthetic commas, dashes, brackets
WL3	to use independent spelling strategies, including: ... building words from other known words, and from awareness of the meaning or derivations of words
WL7	to understand how words and expressions have changed over time, e.g. old verb endings -*st* and -*th*, and how some words have fallen out of use, e.g. *yonder, thither*
WL10	to understand the function of the etymological dictionary and use it to study words of interest and significance

Range:	Classic fiction by long-established authors
Texts:	From *A Christmas Carol*, Charles Dickens
Resources:	A complete copy of *A Christmas Carol* Big Book 6B pp. 4–7 Pupil's Book 6 pp. 36–38 Homework Book 6 p. 12 Copymaster 11: Changing moods (planning sheet)

Preparation

- *A Christmas Carol* is an ideal book to meet the NLS requirement for comparing and evaluating film and TV versions of a classic novel. There are several versions, straight and musical, most available cheaply on video and most repeated every Christmas on TV anyway. Our recommendation is the Alastair Sim version, *Scrooge*, of 1951 – in black and white, but a masterpiece nonetheless. You may therefore wish to have a video of this or another interpretation available for discussion.

DAY 1

Big Book pp. 4–5; Pupil's Book pp. 36–37

Shared reading

- Read the first extract from *A Christmas Carol* once, but before rereading it, discuss which points need vocal emphasis.
- What is the children's impression of or reaction to the character of Scrooge?
- What is their opinion of Dickens's writing?
- What part did they think was most effective? Ask them to give their reasons.
- Have children come across the story before? In what medium? How does the written form compare?

Focused word/sentence work

- Establish the meaning of words most likely not to be understood, e.g. *covetous, gait, shrewdly, rime, dog-days, bestow a trifle, courts, counting-house, palpable*. The archaic meaning of *shrewd* is *sharp, biting* (from the animal, shrew). *Dog-days* are the hottest weeks of the summer, so called because the Romans associated them with the rising of Sirius, the dog-star, in July and August. A *counting-house* was a place where a merchant kept his accounts, transacted business, etc.

Independent work

- Comprehension.

Plenary

- Discuss selected answers to the children's comprehension work.
- Also invite queries on any language used that has not been understood, or recap on the meaning of words previously discussed.

DAY 2

Big Book pp. 4–7; Pupil's Book p. 37

Shared reading

- Read the first passage again.
- Ask the children to consider what plan there is within this description: first, the person of Scrooge, then Scrooge's relationship with the outside world.

- Why does Dickens use *No beggars implored him* rather than *No beggars begged him*? Stress the importance in good style of not repeating similar words within several sentences of each other (unless for deliberate effect).
- Identify the technical devices Dickens uses to make his description so effective: rhythmic repetition; alliteration; assonance, e.g. *hard, sharp; nipped, shrivelled; thin lips; cold, froze, old*; the choice of words with an appropriate "feel", e.g. *hard and sharp as flint*.
- Then look through the extract, trying to find examples of each technique.

Focused word/sentence work

- Examine words that have changed meaning or gone out of use, e.g. *shrewd* (now means discerning, prudent), *gladsome, without* (formerly meaning outside), *courts* (for courtyards).
- What other phrases identify the story as Victorian? E.g. *what it was o'clock, to bestow a trifle* (How would we say these today?), *He carried his own low temperature always about with him* (The word order now seems unusual. How would we say this today?). What other examples are there of unusual word order in either extract?
- Examine the use of semi-colons to break up complex sentences with related parts. Discuss how we also use them in complex lists, e.g. *Two ham sandwiches – one with mustard; four cheese rolls – two with pickle; three fruit pies – two apple, one strawberry*.
- Point out the parenthetic use of dashes. Why is this done? The information within is important, but brackets would be inappropriate in this type of text, and the fact that the words within form a sentence in their own right demands something stronger than commas.

Independent work

- Children practise using writer's tricks – rhythmic repetition, alliteration, assonance.

Plenary

- Introduce the overall plot of *A Christmas Carol*, i.e. the visitation of the three ghosts. Then read the second extract.
- Why is the story set at Christmas time a) rather than in summer, b) rather than in February?
- Why do children think Dickens lays on so thickly his description of Scrooge's character? Presumably, as a contrast to his reformed character at the end.

DAY 3

Big Book pp. 4–7; Pupil's Book p. 38

Shared reading

- Read the second extract. Discuss the overall difference from the pre-Christmas Scrooge. What evidence is there that Scrooge is different?
- Remind children why he has changed (the ghosts and what they showed him – his own miserable childhood, the bountiful Mr Fezziwig, his transition to becoming a miser, the lonely friendless death that would be his if he did not change).

Focused word/sentence work

- What is different about the vocabulary and the sentences in the second extract, compared with the sonorous sentences of the first piece?
- Discuss the meaning of any potentially difficult words and phrases, e.g. *jovial, piping for the blood to dance to, loitered*.
- Why does Dickens repeat some of Scrooge's words and phrases?
- Why are some of the boy's answers in capital letters?

Shared writing

- Decide on a location and write brief descriptions about it that convey two contrasting situations or moods, e.g. the school hall during a disco, and the morning after; a sports match during and after; a seaside resort in and out of season. Look at the details of the scene, possible images and the type of words necessary to reflect the differing atmospheres. Discuss possibilities for children's own writing which will follow, and discuss ways in which the changed mood can be conveyed. You may wish to select a single topic for all the class to write about, or to let them choose their own subject.
- If you choose to use Copymaster 11, encourage children to pick details and adjectives which reflect the mood required, e.g. *damp litter blowing wearily along the prom, bright plastic ducks splashing happily between my soapy feet*.

Independent work

- Children work at writing sentences that convey a change of mood in a location. Copymaster 11 is available to help plan this work, if required.

Plenary

- Choose other paragraphs from *A Christmas Carol* that exemplify the contrast in moods between Scrooge's Christmas Eve and Christmas Day. This would perhaps work best if you alternate between pieces of different mood.

DAY 4

Big Book pp. 4–7; Pupil's Book p. 38

Shared writing

- Decide on a character who might undergo a significant change of mood – perhaps a fictional person, perhaps a person known to all. It could be the Head; it could even be you! Together, write a brief description of your person in both moods, looking at the details of behaviour, possible images and the type of words necessary to reflect the moods.
- Plan for children to write in the same way either about themselves or about someone they know well.

Focused word work

- Consolidate the children's understanding of active and passive. In the first extract, look at the sentences beginning *The cold within him ...* and *Nobody ever stopped him ...* Are they active verb or passive verb sentences? How would we change them to passive verb sentences? Are there any passive verb sentences in the extract? (There are none.)

- Read from a selection of children's writing from day 3. Invite constructive comment about how well they have achieved the contrast in moods. Point out the techniques used.

Independent work

- Children write sentences that convey a change of mood in a person.

Plenary

- Read further selected pieces of children's writing. Invite constructive comment about how well they have achieved the contrast in moods. Point out the techniques used.

- Recap on the meaning of alliteration.

DAY 5

Big Book pp. 4–7; Pupil's Book p. 38

Shared reading

- Read the first extract again, looking for examples of images (introduce the word *image* as necessary).

- Make a list of all the verbal comparisons Dickens draws (*tightfisted hand at the grindstone, oyster, cold within him, frosty rime ...*)

- Divide these up into similes and metaphors.

Focused word/sentence work

- What common similes do children know? List some of them.

- Ask the children to think of some original similes to complete sentences, e.g. *Scrooge had a heart as ...; The weather was as cold as ...*

- We use many metaphors without realising it, e.g. *to hammer on the door, the hard shoulder of a motorway, to hare after someone, don't be so soft*. Ask the children to use a dictionary to find at least ten examples.

Independent work

- Children work at completing standard examples of similes and inventing examples of their own.

Plenary

- Ask children to read out their own invented similes.

- Find a few more metaphors from the dictionary. Recap on the difference between a simile and a metaphor.

- Recap on the meaning of assonance.

Consolidation and extension

- Ask children to find and discuss examples of good description from their own reading. Share examples from **your** own reading.

- Discuss other well-known Dickens books.

Homework

- Page 12 of the Homework Book focuses on regular and irregular past and present participles.

Unit 12

Carols and Prayers

Key Learning Objectives

TL6	to manipulate narrative perspective by ... producing a modern retelling
TL8	to summarise a passage, chapter or text in a specified number of words
WL6	to investigate meanings and spellings of connectives
WL7	to understand how words and expressions have changed over time, e.g. old verb endings *-st* and *-th*, and how some words have fallen out of use, e.g. *yonder, thither*

Range:	Classic fiction/poetry
Texts:	"Good King Wenceslas", J.M. Neale The Lord's Prayer
Resources:	Big Book 6B pp. 8–11 Pupil's Book 6 pp. 39–41 Homework Book 6 p. 13 Copymaster 12: Good King Wenceslas – the page's story (planning sheet) Dictionaries (at least one between two) Authorised Version of the Bible (King James Bible) Shakespeare's complete works (or one or two sample plays) Good News Bible

Preparation

- Wenceslas (*c.* 907–29) was a Bohemian ruler (a Prince-Duke, not a king!) who was raised as a Christian by his grandmother, and resolved to promote Christianity and good order among his subjects; he also sought friendship with his German neighbours. His pagan brother Boleslaw opposed his plans, and picked a quarrel. In the fight Wenceslas was killed. He and his grandmother were acclaimed as martyrs, and he became patron saint of the old Czechoslovakia.

- The carol "Good King Wenceslas" by J.M. Neale (1818–66) is pure imagination. Although he was a famous writer of hymns, Neale himself was of very limited means.

DAY 1

Big Book pp. 8–10; Pupil's Book pp. 39–40

Shared reading

- During what period of history do the children think the events of the carol take place? Ask for their reasons. The carol **could** be medieval (1100–1500) or pre-medieval. Castles, pages and peasants all smack of this era. Christianity was established in Europe from AD 300 onwards, but was not widespread until the 9th and 10th centuries.

- Read the words of the carol. If the children didn't know already, how might they guess that these are the words of a carol, not poetry? Its jaunty, very rhythmical rhyme is not otherwise appropriate to the setting; winter in

poetry would otherwise call for a "bleaker" style – possibly blank verse.

- Ask the children to identify the rhyme scheme (ABABCDCD) and the metre (7,6,7,6,7,6).

- What type of poetry does lend itself to a strict rhyme and metre? Usually comic poems, e.g. limericks, Lear, or lighter poems such as Betjeman's. Perhaps ask children to give examples that illustrate this.

Focused word/sentence work

- Discuss the meaning of these "ordinary" words, and ask children to look them up as appropriate:
  Feast of Stephen: St Stephen's Day is Boxing Day; it honours the first Christian martyr, who was stoned to death.
  fuel: Does this mean petrol?!
  page
  peasant
  dwelling
  league: six miles, e.g. *Half a league, half a league, half a league onward*
  flesh
  to dine
  monarch: It would be possible to discuss gender here: masculine *king*, feminine *queen*, common *monarch*.
  rude: abrupt, startling, violent
  lament
  dinted
  Christian
  rank
  possessing

Independent work

- Comprehension.

Plenary

- Discuss selected answers to independent comprehension work, in particular the answers to sections B and C. The page, besides identifying the peasant, is a useful contrast to the strength and determination of Wenceslas. The fact that Wenceslas is wealthy and comfortable heightens the sacrifice he is making in going out on such a dreadful night.

DAY 2

Big Book pp. 8–10; Pupil's Book p. 40

Shared writing

- Begin to retell the events of the carol in modern English, as near to normal story style as possible. Discuss alternative possible beginnings:

It was one of the bitterest winters that Bohemia had known. Snow had been falling for several weeks, blanketing the land.

Wenceslas, prince-duke of Bohemia, stood at the casement, looking out at the black, swirling night. Behind him the roaring fire cast flickering shadows on the stone walls of his hall.

The blizzard roared over the castle battlements. Below, a hunched old man picked his way gingerly through the deep snow, a bunch of twigs on his back. The wind dropped momentarily and the sound of music and laughter reached his ears from a window high above.

Focused word/sentence work

- Examine the archaic words of the carol (perhaps citing other examples at random from Shakespeare or the King James Bible):
  thou = you nominative singular case, e.g. *thou art a rogue*;
  thee = you accusative singular, e.g. *What can ail thee, knight-at-arms?*; *thy = your* possessive singular, e.g. *Thy will be done.*
  ye = you nominative plural, e.g. *ye gods and little fishes.*
  Note that *Ye = The* as in *Ye Olde Tea Shoppe* is an artificially contrived usage.
  knowest: There are many other *-t* verb endings, e.g. *thou art, thou hast, thou dost, thou wilt, thou shalt; Lord now lettest thou thy servant depart in peace, according to thy word.*
  hither = to here, e.g. Kipling's "The Elephant's Child": *Come hither, little one.*
  thither = to there, e.g. *scattered hither and thither*
  forth = out from somewhere, e.g. *God told Moses to come forth; he came fifth and won a teapot* – an example of a pun.
  yonder: here used as an adjective = *over there*, e.g. *What light from yonder window breaks?* It is a useful poetic adjective, as it saves syllables; it is also used adverbially, e.g. *to go yonder.*
  the very sod: Note the emphatic use of *very*, e.g. *This is the very one I lost*. The carol writer has probably used it here to pad out the line!
  therefore: This offers a chance to remind children of the archaic/legal use of *thereby, thereto, thereafter, therefrom, therewith*, etc.; also *hereto, hereby*, etc.
  St Agnes' fountain: Why not St Agnes's?
  (If time runs out, any remaining words could be discussed on day 3.)

Independent work

- Children retell the story of Good King Wenceslas in modern English.

Plenary

- Read selected examples of the children's independent work. Invite constructive criticism on their quality as an opening. Do they make the reader want to read on? Do they bring out the contrast between the comfort of the castle and the blizzard outside?

DAY 3

Big Book pp. 8–10; Pupil's Book p. 40

Shared writing

- Plan and begin a retelling of the Good King Wenceslas story from the point of view of the page. Discuss the possible character of the page and his attitude to being ordered out on the mercy mission.
- Copymaster 12 could be used now or as part of the independent writing on day 4. It asks the pupil to explore systematically the page's background and what he might have thought before, during and after the journey.

Focused word/sentence work

- Discuss further archaic words from "Good King Wenceslas" as necessary.

- Show how in the English of the past many sentences had the ideas placed in a different order, e.g. *fails my heart I know not how; to thine own self be true* (Hamlet); *And the sons of Noah that went forth of the ark, were Shem, and Ham, and Japheth; A servant of servants shall he be unto his brethren*. Can the children find examples of their own? Many examples are to be found by dipping into the Bible or Shakespeare.

- Discuss other patterns in archaic words, perhaps by dipping into familar stories of the Old Testament (e.g. Abraham and Isaac, Noah, Cain and Abel) or Shakespeare. Include the verb endings *-eth* and *-est*, and commmon words such as *saith, spake, smote.*

- And Abraham was *an hundred years old*. The archaic use of *an* is very interesting. The word *newt* comes from the old *an ewt*; the word nickname comes from *an eke name*, meaning *a similar name.*

- Mention *mine = my, thine = your*, e.g. *mine host; Drink to me only with thine eyes; I will lift up mine eyes unto the hills, whence cometh mine aid.*

- Discuss the two meanings of the word *good* in the carol.

Independent work

- Children continue their retelling of the Good King Wenceslas story from day 2.

Plenary

- Read selected examples of independent work. Invite constructive criticism on the description of the journey and, in particular, the dialogue between king and page.

DAY 4

Big Book pp. 8–10; Pupil's Book p. 41

Shared writing

- Plan and start a retelling of the Good King Wenceslas story from the point of view of the king. Discuss his likely character (a curious combination of proud king and saintly figure). How would a king think? How would a saint think? How would he approach ordering his servant out on the mercy mission? How did his attitude to the journey differ from that of the page?

- Explain to the children that in their independent work for today they can choose between taking either the king's or the page's point of view.

Focused word/sentence work

- Discuss the meanings of these archaic words that are still used in legal English and occasionally elsewhere: *aforesaid; thenceforth; henceforth; said* (as an adjective, e.g. *the said Frederick Bloggs*), *hereinafter, forthwith.*

- Discuss these words, which have changed their meaning over time:
  naughty: literally means *worth nothing*
  treacle: from the Greek *therion = wild beast*; evolved as an antidote to the poison of a wild beast
  villain: A *villein* was a farm labourer in the feudal times of the Middle Ages.
  taxation: used to mean *fault-finding* (*taxing* still means *physically trying* or *testing*)
  crane: used to refer just to the bird with a long neck
  navigator: once used only for ships
  bonnet: once a hat for men!

furniture: used to mean *equipment*. We still say *street furniture* (lampposts, etc.) and *door furniture* (knobs, knockers, letterboxes).

pretty: used to mean *ingenious*

cheater: once was a *rent collector*

vulgar: meant *ordinary*. We still say *vulgar fraction*.

meat: Old English *mete* used to mean food in general (as in *sweetmeat, mincemeat*).

Independent work

- Children retell the Good King Wenceslas story from the king's or the page's point of view.

Plenary

- Consolidate the meaning and usage of any archaic words previously discussed.

DAY 5

Big Book p. 11; Pupil's Book p. 41

Shared reading

- The Lord's Prayer is the prayer that Jesus taught the disciples, shortly after he had delivered the Sermon on the Mount (*Matthew* 6:9; *Luke* 11:2). The version as we know it dates from the Authorized Version, ordered by King James I, the year after his accession in 1603, and published amazingly by 1611. It was the work of a number of committees set up especially for the task. Although the language is archaic, it is linguistically superb, and has proved immensely popular. The survival of the 1611 version of the Lord's Prayer against all the revised versions is proof of this.

- Read the Lord's Prayer together (or have children recite it from memory). Why is it called the Lord's Prayer?

- How old or new do the children think the language of the prayer is? What evidence is there for their guess? Draw their attention to words like *art, thy, this day*, and the reversal of sentences e.g. not *Thy name be hallowed*.

Focused word work

- Consolidate the meaning of these archaic words: *art, hallowed* (note the sentence reversal here), *thy, trespasses, deliver, thine*.

- Go through the prayer, identifying parts of speech, and for each word, if appropriate, try to find another part of speech from the same family, e.g. *our* (possessive adjective) – *ours* (possessive pronoun); *Father* (noun) – *fatherly* (adjective); *who* (relative pronoun) – *whose* (possessive pronoun).

Shared writing

- Rewrite the Lord's prayer in modern English, not attempting a poetic feel but just "translating" the meaning.

- You could compare the class's attempt with the version in the Good News Bible.

Independent work

- Children finish off at least one of their versions of Good King Wenceslas and write it up in their best handwriting. You may wish to ensure that there is a cross-section of different narrators (king, page, third person narrative).

Plenary

- Encourage children to talk about the process of writing the different narratives. Was one more difficult than another? What other differences were there?

- Read selected examples, inviting constructive criticism on their effectiveness.

Consolidation and extension

- Ask children to write e.g. the Highway Code or treasure map instructions in antique English.

- Discuss the meaning of the word *therefore* as in the Wenceslas carol, going on to talk about the usage and meaning of other more formal or archaic connectives, such as *furthermore, notwithstanding, nonetheless*, etc.

- Ask children to create a dramatised version of the Good King Wenceslas story.

- Ask children to learn a prayer.

Homework

- Page 13 of the Homework Book focuses on important archaic words and phrases.

HALF-TERMLY PLANNER

Year 6 • Term 2 • Weeks 1–5

SCHOOL _____ CLASS _____ TEACHER _____

	Phonetics, spelling and vocabulary	Grammar and punctuation	Comprehension and composition	Texts
Continuous work **Weeks 1–5**	WL 1, 2, 3, 4, 5			**Range** Science fiction, different poetic forms, discussion texts, longer-established stories and novels from more than one genre

Blocked work					
Week	**Unit**				**Titles**
1	13		SL 1, 5	TL 1, 2, 8, 11	*Living Fire and Other SF Stories*, Nicholas Fisk
2	14	WL 6		TL 3, 4, 5, 6	"Overheard on a Saltmarsh", Harold Monro; "Arithmetic", Gavin Ewart; "The Little Man with Wooden Hair", Kenneth Patchen; "View of Rabbit", Mark Richard; "Trout Haiku", Onitsura, trans. Harold G. Henderson; "Tanka Tanka", John McIlwain; "Poem on the Devonshire Grave of William H. Pedrick"
3	15	WL 8	SL 1, 4	TL 15, 16, 18, 19	"Are supermarkets a blessing or a curse?", *The Week*
4	16		SL 5	TL 1, 2, 8, 10, 11, 12	*Clockwork or All Wound Up*, Philip Pullman
5	17			TL 3, 4	"The Charge of the Mouse Brigade", Bernard Stone; "The Scorpion", Hilaire Belloc; "The Fly", Ogden Nash; "Well, Hardly Ever", Anon; "All Things Dull and Ugly", Monty Python; "OIC", Anon; "There Was a Young Lady from Ickenham", Anon; "Give Up Slimming, Mum", Kit Wright

HALF-TERMLY PLANNER

Year 6 • Term 2 • Weeks 6–10

SCHOOL _____   CLASS _____   TEACHER _____

	Phonetics, spelling and vocabulary	Grammar and punctuation	Comprehension and composition	Texts
Continuous work **Weeks 6–10**	WL 1, 2, 3, 4, 5			**Range** Humorous poems, non-fiction texts, historical novels, non-chronological reports, domestic ethnic fiction, various poetic forms, descriptive writing, longer-established stories and novels from more than one genre: adventure

Blocked work					
Week	**Unit**				**Titles**
6	18		SL 2	TL 17, 18, 20	"The Prevention of Head Lice" (DOH)
7	19	WL 7	SL 4	TL 1, 2, 7, 18	*Eagle's Honour*, Rosemary Sutcliff; *Everyday Life in Ancient Greece*, C.E. Robinson
8	20			TL 1, 2, 10	*Grandfather Singh Stories*, Pratima Mitchell
9	21			TL 3, 4, 5, 6, 9, 14	"After Prévert", Alan Brownjohn; "I Saw a Jolly Hunter", Charles Causley; "Good Hope", Benjamin Zephaniah
10	22		SL 3, 5	TL 7, 9, 10, 11, 13	*Goldfinger*, Ian Fleming; *The Adventures of Sherlock Holmes*, Sir Arthur Conan Doyle

   Focus on Literacy Teacher's Resource Book 6 © John McIlwain, HarperCollins*Publishers* Ltd 1999

Unit 13　Living Fire

Key Learning Objectives

TL1　to understand aspects of narrative structures, e.g.:
a) how chapters in a book (or paragraphs in a short story or chapter) are linked together
b) how authors handle time, e.g. flashbacks, stories within stories, dreams

TL2　to analyse how individual paragraphs are structured in writing

TL8　to analyse the success of texts and writers in evoking particular responses in the reader, e.g. where suspense is well-built

TL11　to write own story using, e.g. flashbacks or a story written within a story to convey the passing of time

SL1　to investigate further the use of active and passive verbs:
a) secure the use of the terms *active* and *passive*
b) know how sentences can be re-ordered by changing one to the other
c) identify examples of active and passive verbs in texts
d) experiment in transformation from active to passive and vice versa and study the impact of this on meaning

SL5　to use reading to:
a) investigate conditionals, e.g. using *if ... then, might, could, would* and their uses, e.g. in deduction, speculation, supposition
b) use these forms to construct sentences which express, e.g. possibilities, hypotheses
c) explore use of conditionals in past and future, experimenting with transformations, discussing effects, e.g. speculating about possible causes (past), reviewing a range of options and their outcomes (future)

WL3　to use independent spelling strategies, including ... applying knowledge of spelling rules and exceptions

Range:	Science fiction
Texts:	From *Living Fire*, Nicholas Fisk
Resources:	Big Book 6B pp. 12–15
	Pupil's Book 6 pp. 42–44
	Homework Book 6 p. 14
	Copymaster 13: A sudden change of scene (planning sheet)

DAY 1

Big Book pp. 12–13; Pupil's Book pp. 42–43

Shared reading

- Read the first extract once. Before rereading, discuss which parts should be read most expressively.
- Ask children what is happening in the story: a boy dreamer and his fantasy world.
- Examine the two styles of writing describing the two "worlds":
  – the real scene: What picture is Nicholas Fisk trying to build up? A homely Granny witters on, preoccupied with domestic issues.
  – the space scene: How does it contrast? You could mention fear, tension, no demonstration of feeling, the galactic issues at stake.
- Ask the children to discuss how effective they think the writing is, giving reasons.

Focused word/sentence work

- Discuss the meanings of these words: *grave, rely, gaze* (as opposed to *look*), *thermic* (Greek: *therme = heat*), *crude, sardonically* (= grimly, bitterly), *measure, irregular, fission, holocaust, Galaxy*.
- Why is *Zigger* in square brackets? It is explanatory, not belonging to the original quotation.
- How does Nicholas Fisk show that Granny witters on? He uses long sentences with commas where full stops would normally be.
- *Already his mind had completed the list of what he would need to complete the task that lay ahead.* Challenge the children to identify the element of poor writing style here – the double *complete*. Later on, Fisk very deliberately avoided repeating *uneven break*. What phrase has he used to replace it? *Irregular fission* is an exact translation!
- *– who better? –* What does the insertion of this brief phrase tell us?

Independent work

- Comprehension.

Plenary

- Discuss selected answers to the independent comprehension work, particularly sections B and C.

DAY 2

Big Book pp. 12–13; Pupil's Book p. 43

Shared reading

- Focus on comprehension question B1: the way in which the writer links the real and fantasy worlds. Point to the linked subject matter – lighting the fire/Reddiflame packet of thermic bombs – and the repetition of spoken words as the fantasy world opens up.
- From their reading, can children describe other ways in which writers handle the transition from reality to fantasy? Aladdin's magic lamp and C.S. Lewis's Narnia wardrobe are good examples.

- What other ideas do children have for changing from reality to fantasy in a story?
- Read the fantasy part of the story again. What techniques does the writer use to build up tension? Mention the fear/gravity/worry of the captain, the veiled threat of failure, the global implications, slow, deliberate movements, the clipped sentences, the non-sentences that represent Zigger's thoughts.

Focused word/sentence work

- Focus on conditional sentences. Look at the captain's truncated sentence: *If you fail ...* How might it have ended? Explain that this is a "conditional", i.e. it expresses a condition, or reservation, where the outcome is uncertain. As another example, a speeding motorist might be given a *conditional discharge*, i.e. let off *on condition* that he doesn't get caught speeding again.
- Write down children's ideas for sentence beginnings using *If*.
- Show that *if* is often followed by *then*. Ask the children to think of examples, e.g. *If you help me, then I will help you.*
- Take a very simple example (e.g. *If I see them, I will tell them*). If the tense changes, what happens? *If I saw them, I would tell them; If I had seen them, I would have told them.*
- Examine different circumstances in which conditionals are used, and point out conditional verbs such as *could, might, would*. Deduction: *If Colonel Mustard had entered the kitchen with the dagger, then Rev. Green could not have ...* Speculation: *If the television hadn't been invented, life might have been very different.* Supposition: *If that car had been coming any more quickly, we would not have had a chance.*
- A possible tie-up might be to read Rudyard Kipling's famous poem "If".

Independent work

- Children work on conditional sentences.

Plenary

- Recap on what a conditional sentence is, discussing selected answers to independent work.
- Look specifically at the wording of letters requesting something:
  Right: *I should be grateful if you would ...*
  Wrong: *I would be grateful if you could...*
- Finally, as a slight red herring, remind children that *If I were you ..., If I were queen ...,* etc., are correct, not *If I was ...*

DAY 3

Big Book pp. 12–13; Pupil's Book p. 44

Shared writing

- Recap on possible techniques or scenarios for transferring story action from the real world to a fantasy world.
- Recap on techniques for building tension in a story.
- With reference to the passage, stress the importance of planning beforehand the sequence of thought and action within a description, in order to keep a firm grip of the narrative when finally writing.

- Plan together the beginning of a story that switches from a real but mundane situation to a fantasy "life-or-death" scene. Explain the phrase *life-or-death* as necessary.
- Choose a child from the class as the "star" in the hero role, perhaps linking the setting in some way with another subject being studied.
- Copymaster 13 provides a framework for planning that could be used here as an OHP transparency.
- The writing should build up to the climax only. (The resolution follows on day 4.) Keep a record of the story in order to write its conclusion on day 4.

Focused word/sentence work

- Find this sequence of opposites within the passage: *irregular, uneven, uncontrolled.* Suggest other words from which opposites can be formed by adding a prefix.
- Examine words such as *illegible, immeasurable, innumerable, irresponsible.* What rule is at work here?
- Go through the passage together, enjoy providing opposites for **any** words that lend themselves to this (e.g. *came/went; there/here; see to/neglect; afraid/unafraid*). Look particularly for those that use a prefix to form an opposite.

Independent work

- Ask the children to write about themselves being suddenly shifted from an ordinary scene into a tense, exciting "life-or-death" situation.
- Less able children could have the option of writing a story with the same plot as the shared writing, but starring themselves.
- Children can use Copymaster 13 to help plan this piece of writing.

Plenary

- Read selected examples of independent work, inviting children to comment on how successfully others have transferred from reality to fantasy, and on the techniques used to build suspense.

DAY 4

Big Book pp. 12–15; Pupil's Book p. 44

Shared reading

- Ask children to read the second extract. Ask them to read it again, aiming to achieve maximum suspense and expression. Are there any further techniques beyond those identified in the first extract that the writer uses to build tension?
- Point out that *So Zigger didn't* is the actual end of the story. Explain the meaning of the phrase *anti-climax*, linking this with the word *climactic* in the passage.

Shared writing

- If time permits, complete the class story that you began on day 3. If time is tight, make a list of suggestions for how it could end.

Focused word/sentence work

- Examine the paragraph beginning *Zigger said nothing.* List what information is being communicated to the reader (e.g. the captain's eyes were blue-grey, the spacesuit was blue-grey; the captain's eyes were bright, the visor was bright).

- Point out that the writing is extra-effective in two ways:
  1. It gives information interestingly and gently – without saying *His eyes were bright. His helmet visor was bright. His helmet was under his arm.*
  2. It links one sentence or idea to another in a smoothly flowing whole.

- Experiment together with a simple description, say, of the classroom, showing how information can be integrated in a pleasing and non-cumbersome way. It might be a good idea to list the points before you start and try different ways of linking them, for example:
  The sky was a thundery grey outside the classroom window, matching Mrs X's expression as she stormed in.
  David's face turned as white as the ice cream he was eating.
  It left his chocolatey mouth in a hurry and disappeared into his already bulging pockets.

- If time allows, you could point out *narrow-eyed* as an example of economy of words. Think of other possible examples in the piece: Gran could be *domestic-minded*; the captain could be *grave-voiced*.

- If further time is available, ask what the flame growing triumphantly is an example of: personification, since a flame can never be triumphant!

Independent work

- Children complete the "life-or-death" story begun on day 3.

Plenary

- Read one or two selected examples of independent work, inviting constructive criticism.

- Write a scene-setting description giving information as seamlessly as possible. One way is to extract the facts from the beginning of a book that you know and compare your efforts with those of the author. Alternatively you could choose your own facts to link, e.g.
  The day was breezy.
  The sky was blue with clouds.
  Small boats were bobbing offshore.
  A large ferry was on the horizon.
  Some children were playing rounders.
  Some parents were joining in.
  Others were in deckchairs on the beach.

DAY 5

Big Book pp. 12–15; Pupil's Book p. 44

Shared reading

- Quickly and briefly list each stage of Zigger's thoughts and actions through the paragraph in the first extract beginning *It's up to you*. The main point to make is that in writing it is important to put oneself in the place of the characters and, even in a fantasy story, to work through a scene very carefully making sure it is believable. Professional writers often say aloud the speeches they are writing for their characters.

Focused word/sentence work

- Have fun trying to change suitable subject–verb–object sentences from the first extract from active to passive verbs. E.g. *The room was entered by Gran and Zigger was seen kneeling there by her; "The fire must be seen to by you"; Nothing was said by Zigger. The steady gaze of the captain was returned by him.*

- What changes have to be made to accommodate the passive verbs? How would the impact of the story have been affected if the author had used passive verbs? Is the meaning changed in any of the sentences?

- Reinforce the point that passive verbs tend to weaken the impact of writing; e.g. in an advert, compare: *You will be amazed by new Daz* to *New Daz will amaze you.*

Independent work

- Children work on the different sounds of *ea*; on adding *-es* to form plurals; on opposites with certain types of prefix (e.g. *illegal, irregular*); and on using a dictionary to find word origins (a class dictionary may be needed).

Plenary

- Discuss selected samples of the "life-or-death" stories, particularly with regard to how carefully the scene has been set and the plot developed.

Consolidation and extension

- Ask children to write their own flashback story.

- Ask children to create artwork based on a flashback or reality-to-fantasy theme: the same place transformed. They should write accompanying exciting descriptions of what has taken place.

Homework

- Page 14 of the Homework Book focuses on various spelling rules: *-es* plurals; *-ally* endings; opposites with unusual prefixes.

Unit 14 Poems of Different Forms

Key Learning Objectives

TL3 to recognise how poets manipulate words:
a) for their quality of sound, e.g. rhythm, rhyme, assonance
b) for their connotations
c) for their multiple layers of meaning, e.g. through figurative language, ambiguity

TL4 to investigate humorous verse; ... how poets play with meanings ... where the appeal lies

TL5 to analyse how messages, moods, feelings and attitudes are conveyed in poetry

TL6 to read and interpret poems in which meanings are implied or multi-layered; to discuss, interpret challenging poems with others

WL2 to use known spellings as a basis for spelling other words with similar patterns or related meanings

WL3 to use independent spelling strategies, including:
a) building up spellings by syllabic parts, using known prefixes, suffixes and common letter strings

b) applying knowledge of spelling rules and exceptions
c) building words from other known words, and from awareness of the meaning or derivations of words

WL4 to revise and consolidate work from previous four terms with particular emphasis on:
a) learning and inventing spelling rules
b) inventing and using mnemonics for irregular or difficult spellings
c) unstressed vowel spellings in polysyllabic words

WL5 to extend work on word origins and derivations from previous term. Use personal reading, a range of dictionaries and previous knowledge to investigate words with common prefixes, suffixes, word roots

WL6 collect and explain the meanings and origins of proverbs – referring to dictionaries of proverbs and other reference sources

---

Range: Different poetic forms

Texts: "Overheard on a Saltmarsh", Harold Monro
"Arithmetic", Gavin Ewart
"The Little Man with Wooden Hair", Kenneth Patchen
"View of Rabbit", Mark Richard
Trout Haiku, Onitsura, translated by Harold G. Henderson
"Tanka Tanka", John McIlwain
"Poem on the Devonshire Grave of William H. Pedrick"

Resources: Big Book 6B pp. 16–20
Pupil's Book 6 pp. 45–47
Homework Book 6 p. 15
Copymaster 14: Planning a haiku/Planning a tanka
Etymological dictionaries
"Kennings", Linda Whish and "A View of a Horse", Rebecca Sturt, in *The Poetry Book for Primary Schools*, edited by A. Wilson and S. Hughes
Does It Have To Rhyme? and *What Rhymes with Secret?*, Sandy Brownjohn

---

Preparation

- It might pay to have a preliminary look at the background to kennings, haiku and tanka from the notes below.
- The two books by Sandy Brownjohn listed above are useful background reading for the day 2 plenary work.

DAY 1

Big Book p. 16; Pupil's Book pp. 45–46

Shared reading

- Read "Overheard on a Saltmarsh" together, at first minimising the differentiation between the nymph's and the goblin's words.
- Ask the children what is unusual about the poem. (It is a conversation.)
- Therefore how could they read it more effectively? They might use high and low voices; the goblin could be harsh and guttural, the nymph smooth and serene. Using the acting talent available, read it again as expressively as possible.

- Summarise the "plot" briefly. Discuss pupils' visions of the setting and the characters. What do they think a nymph is, or looks like? It is a mythological divine spirit in the form of a beautiful young woman. What does a goblin look like? There is plenty of scope for development here – describing contrasting appearances, attitudes, habitat, diet, etc. This could be linked to work on haiku and kennings later in the unit.
- Discuss pupils' reactions to the poem. How would they describe the goblin's character? Ought we to be sorry for him to any degree? Why?
- How does the poet use words to create the mood and the contrast in characters? Point to the monosyllabic words for the goblin, gentle smooth words for the nymph, e.g. *Hush, I stole them out of the moon.*
- Where does this pattern break down? When the goblin says: *they are better than ...*
- Note the lyrical images that the goblin uses to describe how lovely the beads are; also the assonance (*winds that sing*); also the introduction of rhyme for the only time. What is the poet seeking to achieve by using these techniques in the goblin's speech?

- What does the goblin's use of the phrase *man's fair daughter* tell us?
- How does the poet use repetition for effect? *Better* occurs three times; *No* four.

Focused word work

- *nymph*: *y* is being used here as a short vowel. Ask children to find examples of other words which use *y* as the main vowel (e.g. *sympathy, mystery, hysterical, rhythm, myth*). They should use dictionaries as necessary. Contrast words that use *y* as a long vowel, e.g. *rhyme, try, by*.
- *what, why*: Question words generally begin with *wh-*. Ask the children to identify the others: *where, when, which, who*. What other words begin with *wh-*? Discuss the difference between *whether* and *weather*.
- *night*: What prefixes can be added? E.g. *overnight, fortnight, goodnight*. Discuss *benighted* (overcome or marooned by darkness). The *be-* prefix is used when the subject becomes the victim of an outside force, e.g. *bedazzled, beset, bewildered, becalmed, bemused, befuddled*.
- *deep*: What suffixes can be added? E.g. *deeper, deepest, deeply*. Discuss *deepen*. The suffix *-en* is used in connection with increasing the quality described by the root adjective or noun, e.g. *lengthen, shorten, weaken, strengthen, moisten*. What other words use the *-en* suffix? Note that *-en* can also be a prefix with the same function, e.g. *enrich, enlarge, enfold, enfeeble*.
- *better*: Point out that this is the comparative adjective of *good*. Recap on positive, comparative, superlative. It is the comparative adverb of *well*. What are the equivalents for *bad*? *Better* ends in an unstressed *-er*. So do *water* and *daughter*. What other words end in *-er*? What exceptions are there to this? Mention *doctor, author, editor, councillor*.

Independent work

- Comprehension.

Plenary

- Recap on selected answers to comprehension, focusing particularly on the answers to sections B and C.
- If time remains, you could reread the poem together, discussing what other ideas children have for "conversation" poems.

DAY 2

Big Book pp. 17–18; Pupil's Book p. 46

Shared reading

- Read the poem "Arithmetic" together. What mood does it convey? How would children describe their feelings for the girl? Why?
- Discuss the meaning of *dunce* and *rec*.
- Is this a rhyming poem? What effect does rhyming two lines at the end have? It seems to give the poem a very final, tired, resigned feel. *I do what's required* has a tremendously stoical quality to it.
- Why is the poem called "Arithmetic"? Why does the word have a double significance in the poem?
- What adjectives would describe the girl? Is she really a dunce?

- Is this a fantasy poem? If necessary, make the point that this story is being acted out today in thousands of households. How do the children think things will go when mother gets home? What other unsung acts of bravery or courage can they think of? You could suggest people tending for sick relatives, looking after handicapped children.

Focused sentence work

- From the poem, introduce the proverb *All work and no play makes Jack a dull boy*.
- Complete these other work proverbs: *Many hands* (make light work); *Too many cooks* (spoil the broth). What do they mean? What is curious about them? (They appear to contradict one another.)
- Finish these proverbs, and explain their meaning: *Slow and steady* (wins the race); *Empty vessels* (make the most sound); *Make hay while* (the sun shines).
- What is a proverb? It is a condensed, rhythmic expression of practical wisdom.
- Ask children to complete these proverbs, and explain them. Do they agree with them? *Spare the rod and* (spoil the child). *Pride comes before* (a fall).

Independent work

- Children work on unscrambling, interpreting and completing proverbs.

Plenary

- Spend five minutes looking at selected answers to the independent work on proverbs.
- In the last five minutes, have fun reading "The Little Man with Wooden Hair". Note that poems don't always have to rhyme or be realistic to be effective. Exactly how and why does the man get his hair cut? (Presumably the driver brakes with shock at the outburst and the man's head jerks through the back window!) Note how all the necessary information is subtly introduced.

DAY 3

Big Book p. 19; Pupil's Book p. 47

Shared reading

- Read "View of Rabbit" by Mark Richard. You might also read Rebecca Sturt's kenning, "A View of a Horse".
- From these, establish what a kenning is, i.e. an oblique and unusual, slightly cryptic way of looking at a familiar object, using pairs of words. It is almost a riddle. Kennings derive from Old Norse. Linda Whish cites three useful examples:
  From Old Norse: *seal's field* = the sea
  From Old English: *skull splitter* = a sword
  From North American Indian: *fire water* = alcohol

Shared writing

- Write a kenning about a well-known object, e.g. a chair, a lesson, a car.
- To tap the children's imagination, brainstorm ideas from different approaches. Think of it in anthropomorphic terms (i.e. as a live being). What does it remind you of? What are its uses or its defects? Linda Whish suggests thinking of a line relating the subject to each of your senses.

- Having written these down, work on them together for maximum interest and expressiveness. You could perhaps put the most cryptic clues first, the most obvious last.

Focused word/sentence work

- Word combinations in kennings can be of several types. Use these examples from the Whish article, asking children to identify the parts of speech used:
  swan road = a river (noun + noun)
  black dot = a tadpole (adjective + noun)
  ring giver = a king (noun + noun from a verb [or gerund])
- Name a suitable subject and ask for pairs of words using these specified combinations.
- Develop this by using three-word combinations including the object described, e.g. *youth-stealing time; light-swallowing night; chocolatey eater baby; brilliant shining sun.*

Independent work

- Children write a kenning about an animal, using the sensory approach.

Plenary

- Read out the children's kennings, inviting positive comments, and writing up on the board or OHP the most effective lines. Analyse why they are effective, mentioning the parts of speech involved.

DAY 4

Big Book p. 19; Pupil's Book p. 47

Shared reading

- Read the trout haiku together. Then perhaps these (the first by an English boy, Peter Kelso, aged 12; the second by the celebrated Japanese poet Basho, translated by Harold G. Henderson):

  Bee Haiku
  The bee is a merchant.
  He trades among
  flower planets.

  Sudden Shower
  Not even a hat –
  and cold rain falling on me?
  Tut-tut! think of that!

- Ask children to suggest what, in broad terms, a haiku is. Brownjohn describes them as *snapshots which capture a moment and feeling.* If possible they can *comment in a wider sense about life or the spirit of the subject.* Originally haiku were not poems for the reader, but poems for the writer, an object of meditation, drawing back the curtain on essential truth. Their key elements are simplicity, directness and profundity. Each has its dominant mood – isolation, poverty, impermanence, mystery. The principle of "less is more" operates. A perfect haiku has 17 syllables, ideally broken into a 5 + 7 + 5 construction. In purist terms, Haiku should never be titled, although Brownjohn feels a title is useful but, if used, should always add something to the haiku. Although later a Japanese form, haiku originated in the Golden Age of China – T'ang through to Sung dynasty, AD 618–1279, one of the most cultivated eras in history. Poetry and painting were seen as two of many ways to the

realisation of truth. This was the state of enlightenment, knowledge of which made possible a fulfilled life and an acceptance of its limitations. Poems were meant to put the reader in touch with the Absolute. The poets were not poets as such but had had experiences which they felt only a poem could express. A Zen statement: *When a feeling reaches its highest pitch, we remain silent – even 17 syllables may be too many!*

Shared writing

- Write a haiku. Beyond the idea of three lines, don't worry about the exact form. Write short lines and make every word count. As with a kenning, everyday objects, animals and people make suitable subjects.

Focused word work

- Explore the nature of the haiku by reducing a poem to its bare essentials. Examine the Ezra Pound poem "In a Station of the Metro":

  The apparition of these faces in the crowd
  Petals on a wet, black bough.

  Which words could be omitted to distil the poem to its essence? Perhaps we need only:

  Faces in the metro –
  Petals
  On a wet black bough.

- Introduce day 5's focused word work on derivations of words, giving an interesting example. One possibility is *groggy*: this comes from *grog*, the mixture of rum and water once issued in the Navy. This in turn comes from *Old Grogram*, a nickname for the admiral who first ordered the rum to be watered down. He was called this because of his grogram overcoat, *grogram* itself deriving from the French *grosgrain*, meaning coarsely woven.
- Ask children to use a dictionary to find one word with an interesting derivation, and be prepared to explain this on day 5. The *Collins Shorter School Dictionary* lists words with interesting derivations on page 436.

Independent work

- Children write a haiku. Copymaster 14 can help them with this.

Plenary

- Read the haiku written independently, inviting constructive comment, and perhaps writing up the best examples. Now might be the time to mention the perfect construction of 5 + 7 + 5.
- Make Brownjohn's point: *Choosing words carefully to express as much as possible should be carried over into all writing.*

DAY 5

Big Book p. 20; Pupil's Book p. 47

Shared reading

- Read the poem "Tanka Tanka", which explains just what a tanka is. How do the beginning and end link? If appropriate, explain the concept of the pun, i.e the use of the same-sounding word to have two different meanings. (*Pun my word, I ought to be booked for jokes like this. I deserve a long sentence. Perhaps we ought to bring this to a full stop ... etc. ad nauseam!*)

- Note that a tanka is simpler than a haiku in its overall concept but is stricter in form, with 5 lines of 31 syllables: 5,7,5,7,7. Here is another example to read, by Christian Tatteresfield:

> Across I travel,
> Desolate and cold it is.
> My shadow follows.
> Just whistling to pass the time –
> it helps when you're so lonely.

Shared writing

- Write a tanka together, perhaps taking a first 5-syllable line suggested by a child. This could be anything, but a suggested starting point might be something they do at a time of strong emotion: perhaps when alone, upset, thoughtful or happy.

Focused word work

- Ask two or three children to talk about the derivation of the words they studied on day 4.
- Talk about and demonstrate how dictionaries are used to find the origins of words: e.g. *kenning* from Old English *cennan*, *to know* (from Germanic); *secret* from Latin *secretus*. Other words with interesting origins to investigate might include: *balaclava, bungalow, shampoo, berserk, robot, pyjamas, smack, marathon, tyrannosaurus*.

Independent work

- Children write their own tanka, starting with a 5-syllable line as in the shared writing work. Copymaster 14 can help them get started.

Plenary

- Read the "Poem on the Devonshire Grave of William H. Pedrick". Is it good poetry? Ask children to give their reasons. You might point out that, as was often the way then, Mr Pedrick senior lost his wife and two children all in the same year, yet lived for another 50 years.
- Where else do you see poetry used? In cards, in the personal ads of newspapers, in advertising.

Consolidation and extension

- Learn together at least one of the poems in the Big Book. (One good way is to write it on OHP transparency or board, and eliminate first the end words of each line, then the penultimate words and so on, each time reciting the complete poem together.)
- Collect and discuss examples of other poems with unusual forms.
- Ask children to write a renga – a series of linked haiku. The second takes its subject from something touched on in the first, the third from the second, and so on. The final haiku (Brownjohn makes it the seventh) has to draw together the themes of the other six. One effective "cheat" is to write the seventh haiku first!
- The NLS document also mentions cinquains, which you may like to try, given time! Brownjohn has a brief but useful chapter on these. They are an English form of tanka, 5 lines and 22 syllables, 2,4,6,8,2.

Homework

- Page 15 of the Homework Book focuses on the formation of opposites with various prefixes, and on word origins.

Unit 15 · Reporting

Key Learning Objectives

TL15	to recognise how arguments are constructed
TL16	to identify the features of balanced written arguments
TL18	to construct effective arguments: a) developing a point logically and effectively b) supporting and illustrating points persuasively c) anticipating possible objections
TL19	to write a balanced report of a controversial issue: a) summarising fairly the competing views b) analysing strengths and weaknesses of different positions
SL1	to investigate further the use of active and passive verbs: ... consider how the passive voice can conceal the agent of a sentence
SL4	to revise work on contracting sentences: ... note-making
WL4	to revise and consolidate work from previous four terms with particular emphasis on: a) learning and inventing spelling rules b) inventing and using mnemonics for irregular or difficult spellings
WL5	to extend work on word origins and derivations from previous term
WL8	to build a bank of useful terms and phrases for argument, e.g. *similarly, whereas*

Range:	Discussion texts
Texts:	"Are supermarkets a blessing or a curse?" from *The Week* "Zulema Menem" from the *Sunday Telegraph*
Resources:	Big Book 6B pp. 21–26 Pupil's Book 6 pp. 48–50 Homework Book 6 p. 16 Copymaster 15: Zulema Menem

DAY 1

Big Book pp. 21–24; Pupil's Book pp. 48–49

Shared reading

- Read the first extract together.

- Discuss the meaning of: *overpricing*; *"pile it high, sell it cheap"*; *retailing*; *Retail Price Maintenance*; *use of market power*; *profit*; *monopoly*; *consumer*; *return on capital*; *ratepayer*.

- Examine each section. Justify its place in the development of the argument, perhaps by trying it somewhere else, to see if a different structure works.

- Examine the main headings. What does their informal style tell you about the origin of the piece? This is a serious magazine, but not a textbook. What are the advantages of headings like *And did prices drop?* They are clear, short and to the point.

- How does the writer try to prove the points he is making? Stress the importance of evidence and examples in making a case.

- Explain that essays are more formal. Translate some headings into essay language, e.g. *... and so allow for lower prices. However, prices did not drop, because ...* (This activity is developed on day 2.)

- A more labour-intensive approach to examining the structure of the supermarket piece would be to photocopy each section separately for groups of children, jumble them up, and ask them to put them in logical order, justifying their decisions.

Focused word work

- Discuss the meanings of these words:
 principle = underlying thought (compare with *principal* = main, chief). Discuss a possible mnemonic for remembering the difference, e.g. *A principle is a rule* (ends in the same way); *Al is the principal*; *the prince is a pal of mine* (a prince being an important person).
 aisles: a transfer from ancient (church) architecture to modern usage
 unleashed a spate: Note the use of two subtle metaphors (*spate* = flood).
 eightfold: and *tenfold, threefold*, etc.
 revolutionary: Point out the hidden metaphor.
 facilities
 picketing: French *piquet* = pointed stake; the derivative link is the idea of erecting a fence or barrier. Note that *-et* words are almost certainly French in origin.
 depot: This actually is a French word, with a silent *t*; cf. *chalet, bidet, beret, bouquet*. Other directly cribbed words include *café, garage, compere, brochure*.
 nutritious: from Latin *nutrire* = to nourish
 dominance: from Latin *dominus* = master
 benefit: from Latin *bene* = well; compare *benefactor, benevolent, benign*
 monopoly: from Greek *monos* = alone; cf. *monotonous, monologue, monochrome*
 economy: from Greek *oikos* = house, *nemo* = manage
 decline: from Latin *de* = away from; *clinare* = to bend
 stringent: from Latin *stringere* = to draw tight

Independent work

- Children do a SATs-style comprehension test. This could be done as a full-length 45 minute test or as two 20 minute sessions.

Plenary

- Go through the first part of the comprehension test in detail. (Question 11 might be a suitable stopping point if you have split the test between two days.)

DAY 2

Shared reading

- Read the first passage again, section by section, looking at how the discussion/explanation is put together, briefly listing main points as you go, e.g.:

  1 Origins (always a good starting point)
  2 Original justification of lower prices
  3 Lower prices?
  4 Yes, lower prices eventually – therefore expansion
  5 But ... closed down small shops, too powerful
  6 Power of supermarkets – farmers out of business, price before quality
  7 But ... customer gets good price?
  8 No – not passed on to customer – UK supermarkets dearer than Europe
  9 Balancing argument – supermarkets reply that they are not being unfair
  10 Power used to damage environment. Isn't this inevitable?
  11 No – local authorities and central government also to blame

- Looking for examples in the text, emphasise that it is important to: make one point follow on from another; put both sides of the argument; support what you say with evidence; anticipate what opponents may say.

- Point out that, despite its seriousness, this article has a more journalistic approach than you would find in most books. What evidence is there of this? Note that each point is given a heading, the style is informal, there is very direct posing of questions, many contractions (*don't, isn't*, etc.) are used, it lacks full details of references, uses active verb sentences.

Focused sentence work

- Practise translating informal to formal. Examine how in a formal essay the same points might be expressed:

  Is the criticism justified? might become *It is therefore necessary to consider whether this criticism is justified.*

  And did prices drop? Not at first ... might become *There was no immediate decrease in prices because ...*

- Take some other informal headings or sentences, asking children how they would integrate them into a more formal essay. This might mean simply rephrasing them or, more likely, wholesale alteration to a more formal structure, eliminating the headings. Examine the way impersonal language is necessary, and point out that passive verb sentences are used to give writing "weight" or to conceal the agent. Work through the piece, showing how it would be changed to make it more formal.

Independent work

- Children continue with the SATs-length comprehension exercise.

- Alternatively, ask them to write down in note form a list of the good and bad points about television in preparation for tomorrow's shared writing.

Plenary

- Use this session to revise any items of the comprehension test that caused difficulty, and revise if necessary.

DAY 3

Shared writing

- Plan together the writing of a discussion text (advantages and disadvantages) on whether television is a blessing or a curse. Emphasise the importance of being even handed, however strong one's own feelings.

- Start by asking what the general elements of any discussion text should be.

- At each stage, without pre-empting children's thinking too much, ask for ideas on the various stages of the text.

  1 Introduction: Perhaps a brief history of television, or some statement about how the argument about television is constantly raised. TV was invented in the 1920s. The first public transmissions were in the UK, Germany and America in the 1930s. In Britain the huge wooden receivers with tiny 9-in screens were confined to a few thousand households around London. The war put a stop to broadcasts for some years, but they began again in the late 1940s and by the mid-1950s TV became a serious challenge to the cinema, which declined dramatically. (There were 340,000 UK sets in 1950, 15 million in 1968.) Radio was relegated to the second source of home entertainment. Independent TV began in 1955, BBC 2 in the mid-1960s, Channel 4 in the 1980s and Channel 5 in the late 1990s. Colour came to the USA in 1953, to the UK in 1967. Cable and satellite TV has grown enormously since the late 1980s; now many homes have between 30 and 300 channels.

  2 Points for TV: e.g. educational value. Evidence?

  3 Points against: e.g. violence. Evidence?

  4 Conclusion: Suggest that one does not have to come down on either side if there is no easy answer. Stress that if one has a personal opinion this must be clearly stated as such.

  You could mention the old motto in writing a history essay: "Tell 'em what you're going to tell 'em, tell 'em, then tell 'em what you've told 'em"!

Focused word/sentence work

- Work on terms often used in constructing an argument. (Perhaps it needs to be explained that "argument" in an academic sense is different from a punch-up in the playground!)
  Lists: *Firstly, ... secondly, ... thirdly, ... , finally or in conclusion*
  Extra points: *In addition, furthermore, moreover, similarly, in the same way*
  Logical development: *Therefore, it follows that, so, thus, consequently, from this we can conclude that*
  Comparison: *Whereas, while, however, nevertheless*
  Ways of expressing an argument: *To state, to argue, to make the point, it might be said, one might say, it would seem*
  Other useful terms: *i.e.* (Latin *id est* = that is), *e.g.* (Latin *exempli gratia* = for example)

Independent work

- Children write a discussion text: Is television a blessing or a curse?

Plenary

- Discuss selected pieces of children's independent work, picking out examples of the above phrases in action; also look for balanced viewpoints, good use of examples.

DAY 4

Big Book pp. 25–26; Pupil's Book p. 50

Shared reading

- Read the extract on Zulema Menem.
- Ask the children what similarities they notice with the piece on supermarkets. They are both chattily informal, use headings, one point leads to another.
- Introduce the phrase *tongue-in-cheek*. What does this mean? How does this quality show itself in the article? E.g. *The Queen may not have realised how privileged she was ...; ... Argentina is changing ...*
- Note how neatly the article is tied up at the end. The last paragraph makes its own point, but links it with the main theme of the piece. Many newspaper articles do this, and it is a satisfying way to construct a piece of writing.

Focused word and sentence work

- Introduce Copymaster 15. Explain that the children are going to use their notes to write a short essay, using the notes alone. The notes must be concise but contain all necessary details.
- Make notes on the piece together, but also with children writing as individuals, preparatory to shared writing. You need to keep your own notes to help children whose notes are weak. Emphasise:
  - Clear organisation. Urge children to assess the structure of the piece before you begin, so that you have the appropriate headings and hierarchies of sections.
  - The use of numbers, letters, capital letters and/or underlinings to make the hierarchy of sections clear. Numbers or letters could be replaced by bullet points, but it can be useful in revision for exams to know that there are a given number of points to remember under this heading.
  - Neatness without wasting time on being meticulous. Speed is almost as important as clarity.
  - Omission of wasted words, so leave out *a, the,* etc.
  - The use of abbreviations, but only if you are certain you will understand them on re-reading.
- Remind children that they are going to have to work from their notes on day 5. The notes could eventually be displayed.

Independent work

- Children continue writing their discussion text about television.

Plenary

- Discuss selected pieces of children's independent work, picking out examples of appropriate phrases in action, balanced viewpoints, good use of examples, etc.

DAY 5

Big Book pp. 25–26; Pupil's Book p. 50

Shared writing

- Look again at your collective notes on Zulema Menem, using them to reinforce the principles of good note-taking outlined on day 4.
- From the notes, rewrite the piece in a more formal and factual style.

Focused word work

- Check on children's understanding of the following words: *president, hectic, privileged, commentators* (in a journalistic sense), *sartorial* (Latin *sartor* = tailor), *sensitive* (meaning tricky).
- Find *-tion* endings in the Menem passage: *invitation, modernisation, distraction.* A *-tion* ending guarantees that the word is a noun. What other *-tion* words can children think of? The *-tion* ending also guarantees a Latin origin. E.g. Latin: *invitatio* becomes *invitation*; Latin: *tractus* (= dragging) gives us *traction*. What other words come from *tractus? Attract, tractor, detract, contract* (as in shrink).
- Discuss *-cial* endings. These come from roots with a *c* in them: *special* (from *species*), *crucial* (Latin *crux – crucis* = a cross), *commercial* (from *commerce*), *glacial* (from glacier).

Independent work

- Children use a dictionary to explore words ending in *-ary.*

Plenary

- Discuss the notes on the Zulema Menem article. In particular identify what main points should have been made under the headings. Check expression for necessary communication with economy of words.

Consolidation and extension

- Hold a debate on an issue of interest. Use all the formal conventions, i.e. strict politeness, only speak through the chair, etc. This is more fun and more educational.
- Display work on an issue, separating the arguments on the wall.
- Ask children to plan and conduct interviews and surveys among parents and other adults on issues such as supermarkets. These could be taped.

Homework

- Page 16 of the Homework Book focuses on *-ful* endings, and "consonant *y* changes to *i*".

Unit 16

Clockwork or All Wound Up

Key Learning Objectives

TL1	to understand aspects of narrative structures, e.g.: ... how authors handle time; ... how the passing of time is conveyed to the reader
TL2	to analyse how individual paragraphs are structured in writing, e.g. comments sequenced to follow the shifting thoughts of the writer, examples listed to justify a point and reiterated to give it force
TL8	to analyse the success of texts and writers in evoking particular responses in the reader
TL10	to use different genres as models to write, e.g. short extracts, sequels, additional episodes, alternative endings, using appropriate conventions, language
TL11	to write own story using, e.g. flashbacks or a story written within a story to convey the passing of time
TL12	to study in depth one genre and produce an extended piece of writing
SL5	to use reading to: a) investigate conditionals, e.g. using *if ... then, might, could, would* and their uses, e.g. in deduction, speculation, supposition b) use these forms to construct sentences which express, e.g. possibilities, hypotheses c) explore use of conditionals in past and future, experimenting with transformations, discussing effects, e.g. speculating about possible causes (past), reviewing a range of options and their outcomes (future)
WL2	to use known spellings as a basis for spelling other words with similar patterns or related meanings; ... building words from other known words, and from awareness of the meaning or derivations of words; ... using dictionaries and IT spell-checks
WL5	to extend work on word origins and derivations from previous term. Use personal reading, a range of dictionaries and previous knowledge to investigate words with common prefixes, suffixes, word roots

Range:	Longer-established stories and novels from more than one genre
Text:	From *Clockwork or All Wound Up*, Philip Pullman
Resources:	Big Book 6B pp. 27–31 Pupil's Book 6 pp. 51–53 Homework Book 6 p. 17

DAY I

Big Book pp. 27–29; Pupil's Book pp. 51–52

Shared reading

- These extracts give only a flavour of a very cleverly constructed story about a clockmaker's apprentice, Karl. An ancient tradition demands that each year the apprentice makes a figure for the town's elaborate clock. Karl has failed to carry out this duty, and on the eve of the figure's scheduled unveiling he sits morosely in the town's inn. Fritz is a writer who frequently regales the inn's customers with his stories. The story he has in his head at present is doubly disturbing. It has come to him in a dream and concerns Karl and his duty. What frightens him more is that the dream was interrupted, and therefore the outcome of the story, as he sets out to tell it, remains unknown – even to him. The clockwork mechanism of the tale is set in motion.

- *Clockwork* is a highly original fantasy. One unusual feature is the way the author conducts a detached commentary on the action in boxes set aside from the main text. The aim of this, one feels, is to emphasise the inevitability and helplessness of the players, and the author, as the mechanism of the story ticks on from one dark event to another.

- Set the scene for the children, then read the story together.

- Where is the story set? How do they know?

- What is the writer's aim in this part of the story? He is building up suspense, setting the dark mood of the story, for later things go seriously wrong for Karl. As always, the writer's general aim is to make the reader want to read on.

- How does Pullman achieve his aims? He describes the expectancy of the audience in the story, creates a slow build-up – Fritz doesn't just launch into the story – tells of Fritz's nervousness and private fears, gets us thinking about what is going to happen to Karl tomorrow.

- What sort of stories does Karl usually tell? How is this communicated?

- How does the writer let us know that the story is going to be a troubled one?

- There are at least two reasons why Pullman's book is called *Clockwork*. What do the children think they are?

Focused word/sentence work

- Discuss the meanings of these words and phrases: *sing for your supper, optimist, Burgomaster* (the mayor of a Dutch or Flemish town), *theme, to make someone's hair stand on end.*

- Who is speaking? Note how a dialogue can be maintained without always identifying the speaker. The best written dialogue has as few interruptions as possible, so long as the reader knows who is speaking.

- Remind children of the usual punctuation for lists, e.g. *Tom, Dick and Harry* (item 1; comma; item 2; and; item 3). Why doesn't the author follow the usual convention (why does he put an extra *and* in)? This achieves a steady measured rhythm of narration. Why should he want to achieve a measured rhythm?

- *"I've got a feeling it's going to be more horrible than anything we could imagine,"* said old Johann the woodcutter. How would Johann have said this? What would he have been feeling? A certain relish, presumably. How can we tell? He's making no move to escape!

- *But after all, it wasn't about Karl. The subject was really quite different.* Who does this line come from? Fritz. What is the writer trying to convey? Fritz's private anxious thoughts. Note the technique here. The author doesn't say *Fritz thought to himself,* he just gives us the thoughts and lets us imagine where they are coming from.

Independent work

- Comprehension.

Plenary

- Discuss selected answers to the children's independent comprehension work.

DAY 2

Big Book pp. 27–29; Pupil's Book pp. 52–53

Shared reading

- Reread the first extract. Although the author does not specifically describe the scene, a clear picture emerges from the writing. Ask the children to describe it as they see it, and discuss the likely locations of the main characters as the scene is acted out.

- The author communicates Fritz's nervousness in several ways. Discuss what these are.

- How does the author try to involve the reader in the story? By talking directly to them. Where in the passage does he do this? How does the writer achieve a confidential tone when he talks to the reader? He employs conversational speech, e.g. *to tell the truth, as I said just now,* and contractions, e.g. *hadn't.* What effect might this have on the reader's level of interest and enjoyment?

Focused word work

- Focus on unstressed syllables: Find the word *horrible* in the passage. Draw attention to the unstressed last syllable, and the fact that the *le* ending sounding *ul* is very common.

- What other words ending in *-ble* do the children know? E.g. *syllable, trouble, terrible, probable, tremble, gobble.* As appropriate, you could mention the additional point for these and the words below that when the present participle is formed, e.g. *trembling,* the *e* is omitted.

- Ask children to suggest and list five words ending in *-dle* (e.g. *handle, middle*), *-gle* (*mangle, wriggle*), *-cle* (*uncle, carbuncle*), *-fle* (*raffle, rifle*), *-kle* (*ankle, sparkle*), *-ple* (*people, simple*), *-tle* (*little, castle*), and one for *-xle* (*axle*).

- As preparation for the independent work, supply these beginnings of words that end in *-le.* Ask children to complete the spelling, and say what the present participle would be: *fid-* (*fiddle, fiddling*); *bab-* (*babble, babbling*); *set-*; *hag-*; *tack-*. Remind children of the need to double the central consonant in many cases.

Independent work

- Children work on *-le* endings.

Plenary

- Go through the answers to the independent work on *-le* endings, making sure that the concepts of adverbs and present participles are understood.

DAY 3

Big Book pp. 27–29; Pupil's Book p. 53

Shared writing

- Look at the first extract again. Find places where the author shares with us what Fritz is thinking. What is he afraid of? How does what he is saying differ from what he is saying to Herr Ringelmann?

- Ask for ideas about a situation where someone is thinking one thing and saying another, e.g. when making up excuses for not doing something; when asked to comment on something one doesn't like; a shop assistant, waiter, etc., trying to be polite to an awkward customer.

- Choose the best idea, and write **two** short dialogues together, interspersed with the person's thoughts. For clarity, put the thoughts in brackets. The first dialogue should include just one person's thoughts. The second should include **both** people's thoughts, e.g.:
"Mandy, it's about time you got up, darling!"
(The little brat's been there half an hour too long, already.)
"Just coming, Mum!"
(After I've had another ten minutes under the duvet, that is.)

- Write down further suggestions for independent writing of the same sort, as a bank of ideas for children who might need inspiration. If a child is finding sustaining one conversation difficult, suggest they write more than one.

Focused word work

- Draw attention to all the contractions in the piece (e.g. *where's*). Ask children to find the others and give their expanded meaning.

- *He's* can mean two different things. What are they?

- If appropriate, make the point that *it's* with an apostrophe means *it is,* but the possessive *its* meaning *of it* does not have an apostrophe to avoid confusion.

- Make a list of other common contractions, and secure knowledge of what they are short for, e.g. *I'm, you're.*

Independent work

- Children write a dialogue that includes unexpressed thoughts.

Plenary

- Discuss the dialogues written during independent work.

Shared reading

- Read the second extract.

- What might the canvas-covered figure be? It is a figure for the clock referred to in the previous extract.

- How is the suspense built up here? Mention the cold, dark, sleeplessness, the background of unsettled thoughts; the gloomy setting; the reference to a previous frightening story, mention of the devil, the slow unwinding of the scene; each sentence builds upon the last; the reader knows about the figure, but Gretl does not – rather like the classic pantomime "Behind you!" scene; the fact that the figure moves softly and slowly is all the more menacing.

- Why does the writer use the separate box, *OH NO! ...*? This is a device to talk separately to the reader, implying that the story has an unstoppable "clockwork" life of its own. Explain that the boxes run right through the story, and are used by the author to comment on the action or explain something fully where it wouldn't fit into the main narrative. This is something they might like to try in their own writing.

Focused word/sentence work

- Ask children to identify interjections in the two extracts. Remind them that interjections have no grammatical function. What others can they think of?

- Mention that conditionals were discussed in Unit 13. What are conditional sentences? Remind children that they concern uncertain outcomes, and use key words such as *if, might, could, would*.

- Both extracts concern very uncertain outcomes. Invent questions that would lead to past and future conditional sentences as answers. What might have caused the statue to move? What would have happened if Gretl hadn't mentioned the devil? What do you think will happen to poor Gretl? What might Fritz have been worried about? Then ask the children to answer these questions using conditional phrases. Extend this to questions, discussions, hypotheses from other areas of study.

Independent work

- Children continue with their writing from day 3.

Plenary

- Recap on what conditional sentences are. Discuss how *I will* turns into *I would, I shall – I should, I can – I could, I was – I would have, I may – I might have*, etc.

- If time permits, recap on interjections.

Shared writing

- Decide on a suitable subject, then write a paragraph together, building up suspense.

Focused sentence work

- Pose some questions to the children, inviting conditional answers, which must be precise and grammatical. e.g. *Suggest three things that could happen if ...; If you had got up late this morning ...* Experiment by changing the tense of these questions and answers from past to future, and vice versa.

- Introduce the independent work on conditionals as necessary.

Independent work

- Children complete the ends and beginnings of conditional sentences.

- Children practise using contractions.

Plenary

- Read selected examples of work on conditional sentences from the independent work, discussing their grammatical correctness.

- Remind children of the following common mistakes in conditional sentences:

  May I go out to play? is correct. *Can I go out ...* is wrong. You may be physically able to go out (you *can*), but you don't necessarily have permission (you *may*).

  In letters we put *I should be grateful if you would send me ...* not *I would be grateful if you could ...*

Consolidation and extension

- This is perhaps an appropriate time to introduce the in-depth study of a particular genre, as required under NLS objective TL12.

- Ask children to act out dialogues, interspersed with theatrical asides, representing secret thoughts.

- Discuss situations in which children (and you!) have been afraid, perhaps because they have failed to do something they should have done.

Homework

- Page 17 of the Homework Book focuses on parts of speech from a common root, common prefixes and suffixes, and word origins.

Unit 17 — Humorous Poems

Key Learning Objectives

TL3   to recognise how poets manipulate words:
a) for their quality of sound, e.g. rhythm, rhyme, assonance
b) for their connotations
c) for their multiple layers of meaning, e.g. through figurative language, ambiguity

TL4   to investigate humorous verse:
a) how poets play with meanings
b) nonsense words and how meaning can be made of them
c) where the appeal lies

Range:	Humorous poems
Texts:	"The Charge of the Mouse Brigade", Bernard Stone
	"The Scorpion", Hilaire Belloc
	"The Fly", Ogden Nash
	"Well, Hardly Ever", Anon
	"All Things Dull and Ugly", Monty Python
	"OIC", Anon
	"There Was a Young Lady from Ickenham", Anon
	"The Walrus", Michael Flanders
	From "Give Up Slimming, Mum", Kit Wright
Resources:	Big Book 6B pp. 32–36
	Pupil's Book 6 pp. 54–56
	Homework Book 6 p. 18
	Copymaster 16: Jabberwocky
	Copymaster 17: An animal that can talk

Preparation

- Shared and independent writing take place on days 2, 3, 4 and 5. These provide SATs-type tests.
- Children will need Copymaster 17 on day 2.
- You will need a collection of puns and similes for day 1; limericks for day 3; and humorous poems for day 5.

DAY 1

Big Book pp. 32–34; Pupil's Book pp. 54–56

Shared reading

- Read "The Charge of the Mouse Brigade".
- Ask the children what poem this is based on. You may also wish to reread Tennyson's poem (in Unit 4) for comparison.
- Explain the concept of parody. Can **any** piece of writing, film, etc., be parodied? When is parody possible? The best target is a very identifiable and predictable format, often one that people make fun of already.
- What are the rules of parody, i.e. how do you make it work successfully? In this case the rhythm and some of the important words had to be exactly the same; the subject must be obviously a humorous one.
- Read "The Scorpion" and "The Fly".

- The humour in these two poems isn't side-splitting. Ask the children to try to describe why they are nonetheless amusing. Hilaire Belloc (1870–1953) and Ogden Nash (1902–71) were writers of humorous verse in the traditional way, using gentle humour based on observation of life's oddities.
- What sort of poem is "Well, Hardly Ever"? (Nonsense) What pun is central to the punch line? Reinforce the meaning of *pun* with a few more examples:

    Q: Why did the chicken cross the road?
    A: Because it was a Rhode Island Red.

    It was a miserable wedding. Even the cake was in tiers.

- What is the Monty Python poem a parody of? Why is it funny? It matches the original well and is such a contrast in its mood.

Focused word/sentence work

- In "The Charge of the Mouse Brigade", what does *ravage* mean (*devastate, plunder*)? Note the use of *fishy* and *catty*; these are not used according to their literal meanings, but they sound suitably derogatory about the cats. What is *Cheddar*? Why is it so called?
- Ask children to spot the simile in the scorpion poem: *as black as soot*. What other common similes can they remember? What is a *brute*? Ask someone to look up its origin.
- Examine how the Monty Python poem mirrors "All Things Bright and Beautiful" so exactly.

Independent work

- Comprehension.

Plenary

- Read and have fun with the poems again as you wish.
- Recap on the meanings of parody, pun and simile. How is a simile different from a metaphor?

DAY 2

Pupil's Book p. 56

Shared writing

- Prepare for independent writing on a SATs-type basis: *Write a short story about an animal that can talk.*
- Ask children to make a list of the basic questions that have to be answered in the planning of a story. You can refer to Copymaster 17. Children may wish to suggest additional headings that would aid planning.

Focused sentence work

- Together choose an animal and start to plan a story along the lines suggested. You may have less able children who, for this first attempt at a SATs-type exercise, need to use the group idea as a basis. Ideally, though, children should develop their own idea in the independent work.

Independent work

- The children should be given 20 minutes to plan a story about a talking animal with the help of Copymaster 17.

Plenary

- Ask children to share their story ideas, inviting constructive criticism.

DAY 3

Big Book p. 35; Pupil's Book p. 56

Shared reading

- Why is the poem "OIC" amusing? Which number jokes work best? Why is that? You might suggest these:
  – (dash) *off a line, 6 so long, 42ude.*

- What sort of poem is the Ickenham one? What are the rules of a limerick? What is the metre and rhyme scheme? 5 lines: AABBA. Why is it amusing? It depends very much on the last line having a punch.

Focused word/sentence work

- Discuss these word meanings: *fortitude* (courage in pain or adversity); *disconsolate* (downcast, miserable).

- Talk about the ampersand (&) sign. When is it usually correct to use it? In business names, e.g. Dombey & Son; it is not correct to use it in most other forms of English. Explain how a squiggle replaces *and* in note taking (as an ampersand is too complicated).

- Examine the metre of "OIC", which is very common in doggerel verse. What nursery rhyme do the children know that matches it ("Mary had a little lamb")? If time permits, compose a collective nonsense poem to the same rhythm. Any 7- or 8-syllable line will start you off.

Independent work

- Children continue with their day 2 writing.

Plenary

- Share with the children the old chestnut *YYUR, YYUB, ICUR, YY4ME.* Another poem in the same vein is Michael Rosen's "You Tell Me" from the anthology of the same name.

DAY 4

Big Book p. 36; Pupil's Book p. 56

Shared reading

- What type of poem is "The Walrus"? What are the nonsense bits? There are several quirks in this: the double meaning of *lives on*, the absurd idea of taking the wife (or anybody!) to the tundra, the play on *tundra* and *undra*.

- Why is the extract from "Give Up Slimming, Mum" effective? Point to the simple, childlike rhythm and the satisfying rhyme at the end. If possible, try to read the whole poem, from the excellent collection, *Rabbiting On*, by Kit Wright.

Focused word work

- Look at these word meanings: *unsuspecting, tundra.*

- Why is the Kit Wright poem set out in the way it is? Talk about concrete poems, i.e. poems whose shape reflects the subject matter.

- Look at the word *floes*, meaning huge chunks of ice. How else can a word sounding the same be spelled? Discuss the part of speech and meaning of the word *flows*. Introduce the word *homophone*, from Greek *homos* = same; *phone* (pronounced *fo-nee*) = sound, and explain that these are words which sound the same but are spelled differently. What other examples can children think of? Examples are *right, write; to, two, too; cereal, serial; hour, our; heir, air; knead, need.* This is a cue for puns once more: *Bakers are only in that trade because they knead the dough!* Collect other examples.

- Introduce *homographs*, from Greek *graphe* (pronounced *graff-ee*) = writing – words which are spelled the same but have more than one meaning and may be pronounced differently (e.g. *tear* = to rip, *tear* = droplet of water; *blow; saw; light; bow; fast*). Collect other examples.

- Note that homographs and homophones are collectively called homonyms, from Greek *onoma* = name.

Independent work

- Children continue with their day 2 writing.

Plenary

- Ask children to find examples of homonyms within the poems: *claws/clause; mouse; rode; catty; fishy; fly; bar; wash*, etc.

- Sample further limericks.

DAY 5

Pupil's Book p. 56

Shared reading

- Read "Jabberwocky" together from Copymaster 16. Without looking for exact synonyms, think what pictures the different nonsense words conjure up. Children could make neat notes on the sheet prior to discussion.

- If time permits, another poem you might wish to read and discuss is Eve Merriam's "Mean Song":

  > Snickles and pode,
  > Ribble and grodes;
  > That's what I wish you.
  > A nox in the groot,
  > A root in the stoot,
  > And a gock in the forbeshaw, too.

  > Keep out of sight
  > For fear that I might
  > Glom you a gravely snave.
  > Don't show your face
  > Around any place
  > Or you'll get one flack snack in the bave.

Focused word/sentence work

- Discuss the children's animal stories, picking out and writing up good examples of word and sentence use.

Independent work

- Children write out, in their best handwriting, as much as they can of the animal story they have written.

Plenary

- Look at selected examples of the children's finished stories, commenting on handwriting and general quality of presentation.

- Remind them of the mnemonic for good handwriting, whatever the style: *same size*, *straight sticks* and *solid shapes*:

  Same size: Level writing, with the three zones – upper, lower and middle – all aligned consistently between one word and the next, and one line and the next.
  Straight sticks: The ascenders and descenders should be aligned throughout.
  Solid shapes: Rounded letters must have a uniformity of shape, and be formed in the correct direction.

- Have a round-up of terms discussed during the week (e.g. *pun*, *simile*, *homophone*, *homograph*, *ampersand*).

Consolidation and extension

- Ask children to learn one of the poems together or individually.

- Discuss and read examples of favourite humorous poems, getting children to explain why they like them.

- Ask children to read as many humorous poems as they can, attempting to classify the source of the humour in each case.

Homework

- Page 18 of the Homework Book focuses on sentence making.

Unit 18 Official Documents

Key Learning Objectives

TL17 to read and understand examples of official language and its characteristic features

TL18 to construct effective arguments:
a) developing a point logically and effectively
b) supporting and illustrating points persuasively
c) anticipating possible objections
d) harnessing the known views, interests and feelings of the audience
e) tailoring the writing to formal presentation where appropriate

TL20 to discuss the way standard English varies in different contexts, e.g. why legal language is necessarily highly formalised

SL2 to understand features of formal official language through, e.g.
a) collecting and analysing examples, discussing when and why they are used
b) noting the conventions of the language, e.g. use of the impersonal voice, imperative verbs, formal vocabulary
c) collecting typical words and expressions

Range:	Non-fiction texts
Texts:	From "The Prevention of Head Lice" (DOH pamphlet) Specimen last will and testament
Resources:	Big Book 6B pp. 37–40 Pupil's Book 6 pp. 57–59 Homework Book 6 p. 19 Copymaster 18: A person who makes me laugh (interview planning sheet)

DAY 1

Big Book pp. 37–38; Pupil's Book pp. 57–58

Shared reading

- Before you read the first extract, ask what the main aim of a pamphlet on head lice would be. To achieve this, what main points would the writers have to make? They would need to explain how to recognise lice, how they behave, how they spread, when problems are likely, how to treat them. What would be the best order?

- Now read the extract and compare prior thoughts with the actual pamphlet. Do you agree with the way the pamphlet's information is organised?

- What wrong ideas do the writers have to anticipate and argue against? They refute the ideas that lice a) always itch, b) only feed on dirty heads, c) only live in long hair. Point out that explanatory or persuasive texts need to anticipate problems.

- Why are *nits* and *lotions or rinses* in brackets? Brackets are often used to flag up anything which may not be understood or which is subsequently referred to by that name.

Focused word/sentence work

- The time allocated for this can instead be given over to the reading test, allowing a straight 45 minutes for that. To compensate, the equivalent session on day 2 should be longer.

Independent work

- Children do a SATs-type reading test.

Plenary

- Discuss the format of the reading test, and in particular the way in which questions were required to be answered. Without going into the answers in any depth, identify and clear up any difficulties or misunderstandings that children may have had.

DAY 2

Big Book pp. 37–38; Pupil's Book p. 59

Shared reading

- Reread the first extract, without children having sight of it. Leave out words as you go. Ask children to supply the missing words and then spell them. Without being the same, this activity is in some ways preparatory to a SATs-style spelling test.

Focused word and sentence work

- Go through the reading test, discussing answers and allowing children to mark their own work. Encourage them to share confusions and difficulties, as well as successes!

- Introduce the independent work, emphasising what bad writing style it would be if every fact were in a single sentence.

Independent work

- Children practise putting facts into complex sentences: breaking down and building up.

Plenary

- Go through selected examples of the independent work, particularly looking at how effectively children have joined facts together in sentences.

- Ask children to remember, in an appropriate order, the main points made by the article on head lice. Write these down as you go. Consider why each section, fact, has been put where it is.

DAY 3

Big Book pp. 37–38; Pupil's Book p. 59

Shared reading

- Look at the paragraph *Detection and Prevention* in the first extract. What voice, active or passive, is it written in? Explain that this is often the tone of official documents. But is it as helpful to the person reading it as it could be? Rewrite it together, making it as user-friendly as possible. Examine the impact achieved by using active verbs and the second person (e.g. *If you discover ...*).

- Explain that this paragraph came first in the original pamphlet (the *Facts* were on a separate flap). What problems might this have caused?

Focused sentence work

- Note the grammatical mistake in the third bulleted point. It should read: *one in ten primary school children **is** affected.*

- Link this with frequent mistakes regarding the word *none*. *None* means *not one*, so we should write *None of the people **was** hurt*, or *None of us **is** going*.

- Look at the *Facts* section. Explain that there were no diagrams in the original pamphlet. What could be done to increase its impact? It might be possible to prioritise facts, picking out certain ones using bold type, omitting others or putting them as subsidiary points. What diagrams might help? The first point might be rewritten as: ***Head lice are small and very hard to find.** They may not even itch*, with an accompanying diagram of a match head and a head louse to the same scale.

- In preparation for independent work, rewrite the first two facts together, discussing ideas for better presentation. Explain the meaning of *bullet points*. Why would these be better than 1, 2, 3 or a, b, c?

Independent work

- As a change from the test set-up, children could work in pairs on this activity.

- Ask them to rewrite the rest of the *Facts* in a user-friendly way, leaving out unnecessary words and underlining the main point in each statement.

Plenary

- *Clean hair is no protection.* What message might this be sending out? How could it be phrased better?

- Discuss the meaning of *whereupon*. Is it a user-friendly word? How could it be replaced?

DAY 4

Pupil's Book p. 59

Shared writing

- In preparation for a second piece of SATs-type independent writing, go through the instructions in the Pupil's Book, and discuss the sort of people that children might wish to interview.

- Ask them to justify their choice of interviewee in a complete and grammatical sentence.

- Together decide on a real person that most people in the class find funny, having made it clear that they cannot use the person you have used as an example. Think of one question to ask this person.

- Explain how to use the planning sheet on Copymaster 18, pointing out that the notes must be brief, must take no more than 15 minutes to jot down, and will not be marked. Discuss how the sample question can be edited down into a brief note.

Focused sentence work

- Prepare together a list of useful questions for your sample person. For each question, ask children to write down the key elements in the box at the base of their

planning sheet: *Where did you ...? What first gave you the idea of ...? When did ...? Who ...? Why was ...? How did ...? When was ...?*

Independent work

- Children do the writing test – an interview with a person who makes me laugh – using Copymaster 18 to help them. 15 minutes should be allowed for the planning, followed by two 20-minute sessions, one today and one on day 5.

Plenary

- Ask children to read out some of their questions and answers, and invite constructive criticism.

DAY 5

Big Book pp. 39–40; Pupil's Book p. 59

Shared reading

- Before you read the second extract, ask what the main aim of a will is.

- What sort of things does a will have to make clear? Bring out the key points: a) who is to look after the estate, and b) who is to benefit from it, but explain that there are also other things which need to be made clear.

- Now read the extract and compare prior thoughts with the actual document.

- Go through the will and establish why each section is there. Explain that the wife, by reason of old age, is no longer able to look after her own affairs.

Focused word work

- Explain these word meanings: *revoke, declare, hereinafter, Messrs* (also what solicitors are), *trustees, executors* (those who carry out the wishes), *testamentary, discretion, to survive someone, my said wife* (i.e. no other wife he may have had), *thereof*.

- Why is the date in words? Why is it necessary to put down everything in such minute detail?

Independent work

- Children continue with writing about an interview.

Plenary

- Ask children to read out some of their interview writing, and invite constructive criticism.

Consolidation and extension

- Investigate the mechanics of flow diagrams with yes or no options at every turn. Ask children to invent some themselves for simple processes, e.g. making a cup of tea.

- Discuss head lice from a health point of view.

- Make a display of instructions, on one theme (e.g. safety in the playground, road safety) or several.

Homework

- Page 19 of the Homework Book focuses on using an etymological dictionary.

Unit 19

Ancient Romans, Ancient Greeks

Key Learning Objectives

TL1   to understand aspects of narrative structures, e.g.:
  a) how chapters in a book (or paragraphs in a short story or chapter) are linked together
  b) how authors handle time, e.g. flashbacks, stories within stories, dreams
  c) how the passing of time is conveyed to the reader

TL2   to analyse how individual paragraphs are structured in writing, e.g. comments sequenced to follow the shifting thoughts of the writer, examples listed to justify a point and reiterated to give it force

TL7   identify key features of different types of literary text

TL18   to construct effective arguments:
  a) developing a point logically and effectively
  b) supporting and illustrating points persuasively

SL4   to revise work on contracting sentences:
  a) summary
  b) note-making

WL5   to extend work on word origins and derivations from previous term

WL7   to understand that the meanings of words change over time

Range:	Longer-established stories and novels from more than one genre: historical novels; non-chronological reports
Texts:	From *Eagle's Honour*, Rosemary Sutcliff From *Everyday Life in Ancient Greece*, C.E. Robinson
Resources:	Big Book 6B pp. 41–44 Pupil's Book 6 pp. 60–62 Homework Book 6 p. 20 Copymaster 19: A glossary of terms

DAY 1

Big Book pp. 41–42; Pupil's Book pp. 60–61

Shared reading

- The setting of the first extract is Britain in the 2nd century AD. The extract represents a flashback within this period. Aracos, the main character, now a horse trainer and supplier to the occupying Roman forces on the Welsh borders, meets up with soldiers in a tavern. Eventually it comes out that he was once an auxiliary with the Roman legions and through his bravery came by the Corona Civica, a circlet of oak leaves, the highest award. The battle then was against the Picts, the wild, blue-painted warriors from north of Hadrian's Wall, i.e. the modern Scotland. The extract is concerned with the battle.

- Before you read the extract, discuss the special "problems" of a historical novelist: the need for thorough knowledge and research; the need to establish period. How would they establish a sense of period? List some ideas: dialogue; description of surroundings, artefacts, etc.; use of key words; possibly a different style and pace of narrative.

- Give the background to the extract.

- Now read the extract. Look for evidence that this is a historical novel.

- Why is the mist a useful "tool" of the author? It increases mystery, and somehow emphasises the surprise that comes from the lack of inter-communication in those times – there were no walkie-talkies or mobile phones!

- Why do novelists often use a central character to describe a scene, often someone young, inexperienced, newly arrived or new to a situation?

Focused word/sentence work

- It is suggested that you give over the time allocated for word and sentence work to the reading test instead, allowing a straight 45 minutes for that. To compensate, the word/sentence work session on day 2 should be longer.

Independent work

- Children take a SATs-type reading test.

Plenary

- Without looking too much at detailed answers, discuss the mechanics of answering the questions. Invite children to say what they found difficult and what they found easy.

DAY 2

Big Book pp. 41–42; Pupil's Book p. 62

Shared reading

- Today this might follow the focused word and sentence work.

- Read the first passage together. Suggest that children (in pairs, if you wish) take notes on the following word meanings, as they will be needing them shortly to prepare a glossary: *interminable* (Latin *terminus* = end), *taut*, *column*, *chariots*, *Legionaries* (a Roman legion was the basic unit of invasion and subsquent control of an area; had 5,000 heavy infantry + 5,000 auxiliaries), *Cretan* (from Crete), *Asturian* (?from Asturias, a once-independent kingdom of Spain), *Tungrian* (?from Tungria), *team*, *chaos* (a direct take from the Greek *khaos*; note that *-os* is a standard Greek ending), *impetus* (from the same Latin word, meaning *attack*; *-us* is a standard Latin ending), *yoke-pole* (linking pole between the horses of a chariot), *cavalry*, *pilum* (javelin).

- Give children four or five minutes (perhaps working in pairs) to work out a summary of the passage in as few words as possible. Read out and discuss these. This exercise covers some of the same ground as the reading test.

Focused word/sentence work

- Go through the reading test, discussing answers and allowing children to mark their own work. Encourage them to share confusions and difficulties as well as successes!

Independent work

- Using a dictionary, and the notes they have taken, children prepare a glossary of the terms listed in the Pupil's Book. Alternatively Copymaster 19 could be used.

Plenary

- Go through the children's independent work on a glossary of terms, recapping on the origins of words, particularly *chaos* and *impetus*.

- What words come from these Greek words? *Arithmos* = a number; *biblos* = a book; *hippos* = a horse; *idios* = private, isolated; *hypnos* = sleep; *pseudos* = false.

- What words come from these Latin words? *Altus* = high; *caballus* = horse; *curvus* = bent; *firmus* = strong; *gratus* = pleasing; *magnus* = great; *manus* = hand.

DAY 3

Big Book pp. 41–42; Pupil's Book p. 62

Shared writing

- Explain that, in their independent work over the next two days, children will be expected to review the first extract, analysing its style and commenting on its effectiveness. Discuss and list the structure that such a piece of writing should have.

Focused word and sentence work

- Point out that there are all sorts of hidden metaphors and similes in the extract – some (e.g. *swept, wing* and *head*) that we take for granted. Which can they find? Are they metaphors or similes? Discuss what idea each is trying to communicate. You could mention these: *flurry, ripple, touch on the taut strings of a harp, snarling, crowed, swept, raining down, wheeling about, skirts, cut in, ragged, to wake with the dawn, slid, wing, head.*

Independent work

- Children comment on the style of Rosemary Sutcliff's description of the battle.

Plenary

- Discuss selected examples of the reviews, inviting constructive comment.

DAY 4

Big Book pp. 41–42; Pupil's Book p. 62

Shared reading

- How does the style of writing in the first extract compare with, say, a modern battle book or the sergeant's account of the Charge of the Light Brigade (Unit 3)? Bring out the point that Rosemary Sutcliff has a very literary style, packed with impressions and images. Why is it important that a historical writer in particular should "paint pictures" with words?

- What indication is there of time passing in the piece? Note waiting, the rising of the sun. Show how the writer uses this. Stress the importance of keeping the reader in touch with the time scale.

Focused word/sentence work

- Examine the way the action is built up to a climax – waiting, noise before the action, mention of nerves, adding to the noise ... Which verbs in the action are most dramatic? Where is the climax? Note how it relaxes for a moment with the mention of the mist, then builds again.

- Look for examples of a) where the next sentence builds on the previous one by exploiting a verbal link (e.g. *And now, to the shouting ...*), and b) where the content of a sentence is interrupted by a sudden development (e.g. *And then far ahead, a flurry ...*).

- Examine how potentially over-long sentences are broken up by punctuation, particularly the semi-colon.

Independent work

- Children continue with their review.

Plenary

- Give time to further reading and discussion of the children's independent work.

- If time is available, ask children to remind you of some of the images in the passage, particularly the ones they liked best.

DAY 5

Big Book pp. 43–44; Pupil's Book p. 62

Shared reading

- Before you read the second extract, explain that it is a non-fiction description of Greek warriors in the few hundred years before the Sutcliff extract. In what ways might a) the description, b) the warfare be the same or different?

- Now read the extract. Examine how each sentence in an explanatory text leads on to the next. Stress the importance of linking paragraphs, and particularly sentences.

- Explain what footnotes are, how and why we use them.

- Introduce the independent work. Emphasise to children that they are not writing a **diary** of that one day. When they spent the money is unimportant. The aim is to give clear statements with logical explanations, trying to link each point with the next in some way. Explain that you are shortly going to look at how to link sentences effectively.

Focused word/sentence work

- Discuss these words: *combats, at close quarters, impenetrable.*

- What is the difference between *heavy armed* and *heavily armed*?

- Explain that in an explanatory text it is important that each sentence and paragraph follows clearly and logically from the last (unless a new section is beginning). Look for examples of linking words and phrases:

They were and *These fought* pick up naturally from the previous subject.

On the other hand expresses a linked but balancing argument.

Thus equipped: *Thus* = In this way.

So long as the line ...: Notice how the word *line* picks up on its use in the previous sentence. It is important that the reader can follow the flow of the text.

we are told: Note the passive use of a verb; the agent is concealed, as it is unimportant in this context to name the source of the information.

some miles' distance: Note the use of the apostrophe; cf. *a few minutes' time*.

Independent work

- The children try a piece of explanatory writing.

Plenary

- Discuss selected examples of the independent work, particularly with regard to the clarity of statement and the flow of the text. Highlight examples of good linking.

Consolidation and extension

- Discuss how words change in meaning over time: for example *sincere* literally means *without wax* (Latin *sine cera*) – a letter written honestly did not need sealing! NLS quotes *nice, presently* and *without*. You could add: *drawing room* (where ladies withdrew to), *gay, crash, donkey, vegetable, to rubbish, couch potato* and many others.

- Ask children to look at, or make, a simple map of Roman Britain, learn some names of cities and identify major Roman roads.

- Discuss children's favourite period in history. When would they most like to travel back to in time?

Homework

- Page 20 of the Homework Book focuses on homophones and homographs.

Unit 20   Grandfather Singh

Key Learning Objectives

TL1   to understand aspects of narrative structures, e.g.:
a) how chapters in a book (or paragraphs in a short story or chapter) are linked together
b) how authors handle time, e.g. flashbacks, stories within stories, dreams
c) how the passing of time is conveyed to the reader

TL2   to analyse how individual paragraphs are structured in writing, e.g. comments sequenced to follow the shifting thoughts of the writer, examples listed to justify a point and reiterated to give it force

TL10   to use different genres as models to write, e.g. short extracts, sequels, additional episodes, alternative endings, using appropriate conventions, language

WL2   to use known spellings as a basis for spelling other words with similar patterns or related meanings

WL4   to revise and consolidate work from previous four terms with particular emphasis on:
a) learning and inventing spelling rules
b) inventing and using mnemonics for irregular or difficult spellings
c) unstressed vowel spellings in polysyllabic words

Range:	Longer-established stories and novels from more than one genre: domestic ethnic fiction
Texts:	From *Grandfather Singh Stories*, Pratima Mitchell
Resources:	Big Book 6B pp. 45–48 Pupil's Book 6 pp. 63–65 Homework Book 6 p. 21 Copymaster 20: A farewell letter (spelling test)

Preparation

• Tell children that on day 3 they will be asked to choose a relative to write about. It might therefore be useful to have some basic details about their past history, and also to think about how they might be described.

DAY 1

Big Book pp. 45–47; Pupil's Book pp 63–64

Shared reading

• Before you read the first extract, introduce it. What is an *allotment*?

• Grandfather Singh is an Indian. He finds two travellers occupying his new shed. How would he be expected to react?

• Now read the extract.

• How does Grandfather Singh's reaction compare with what the children anticipated?

• How does a modern domestic story differ in style from, say, a historical novel? Mention the narrative language, the speech, possibly the pace, the fact that less effort is needed to establish setting and time. Ask the children to find examples of the points.

• *He did like them.* Examine how the writer develops this theme, giving reasons, examples, and a climax – an invitation to a meal.

Focused word/sentence work

• Look at these word meanings: *plot* (a homograph: piece of land, cunning plan, story of a play, etc.), *committee*, *chapattis* (flat, thin cakes of unleavened bread), *Vahe Guru* (Dear God), the Western meaning of the word *guru* (an Indian mystic, a personal teacher with a mysterious knowledge and teaching ability), *appalled*, *addressing*, *alcoholic*, *scandal*.

• Ask the children to identify the contractions in the piece: *you've, won't*, etc. Discuss what they are short for and why the apostrophe is where it is. Point out that in dialogue *would've, should've*, etc., are spelled as they are and not *would of, should of*, etc., because they are contractions of *would have, should have*, etc. Many contractions that are common in speech, such as *should've*, are not used in written English unless it is very informal.

• *months*: Point out the *u* sound in an *o* word. What other words operate like that? *Monday, monkey, wonderful, front*, etc.

Independent work

• Comprehension.

Plenary

• Go through the answers to the comprehension exercise.

• Remind children about the description of a relative on days 3 and 4 (see **Preparation** above).

DAY 2

Big Book pp. 45–47; Pupil's Book p. 64

Shared reading

• Read the first extract again.

• What difficulties would an author writing about the interaction of people from differing ethnic backgrounds have? There is a potential problem in being realistic, yet not doing anything to cause or reinforce racial prejudice.

• So why is Grandmother's attitude important in a book like this? Her prejudice gives the book necessary realism; it also allows for character development to take place.

• Look at the way the author switches scene between the shed and home, i.e. straight into *Grandmother was appalled*. Why is this effective? Why wasn't it done more slowly, e.g. with a description of the journey home? It achieves much better pace, keeping the reader focused on the important issues of the story – comparable to cutting unnecessary bits out of a film or TV programme.

- Examine the handling of speech in the extract. Note the problem in writing about a conversation – what to put into speech, what to summarise. Why should we not put everything in?

Focused word/sentence work

- *Travel – travelling*; *chat – chatted*; *shrug – shrugged*; *commit – committee*: what is the rule? If you extend most words that end with a single vowel and a single consonant, you must double the consonant. What would these words sound like if we didn't double the consonant? E.g. *chated* to rhyme with *hated*; *shruged* to rhyme with *deluged*. Can the children find another word in the passage which follows the same rule (*appal – appalled*)? Think of other examples from elsewhere. Make it very clear that the rule does not apply to other formations, e.g. double vowel + single consonant: *bargain – bargaining*; or single vowel + double consonant: *roll – rolling*. Other exceptions include words like *listen – listening*, *foster – fostering*, where doubling the consonant would change the sound wrongly.

- Look at *hippies*. How do we spell one *hippy*? Almost always the rule to form the plural is "consonant *y* changes to *i*". What other word in the extract operates in the same way (*worry – worries*)? Think of other examples: *happy – happiness*. Point out that this rule does not work for vowel + *y*, e.g. *key – keys*; *donkey – donkeys*.

- Find verbs ending in *e* in the passage (e.g. *make*, *come*, *have*). Notice what happens if you add *-ing*: *making*, *coming*, *having*. What is the rule? "Knock off the *e*, add *ing*." Very rare exceptions include *singe – singeing* and *whinge – whingeing*.

Independent work

- Children work on the above spelling rules.

Plenary

- Go through the independent spelling work.
- Remind children about the description of a relative on days 3 and 4.

DAY 3

Pupil's Book p. 65

Shared writing, incorporating focused sentence work

- Prepare for a SATs-style writing test – a description of a person in your family. Ask children what basic questions have to be answered in planning a description of someone. Write a clear list of these for reference on day 4 during the test. For example:

  1 Background: approximate age, career so far, etc.; situation now.
  2 What the person looks like.
  3 What they say.
  4 Interesting events concerning them.
  5 What the person means to you.

- Discuss the options that are open in the way that facts are organised. For instance, you could start with 2 or 3, going back later to 1, or you could start with 5.

- Choose someone that you all know (e.g. a famous person or a popular teacher) and plan a description of that person, using the headings you have decided upon. Particularly important is deciding how to begin in an interesting and imaginative way.

Independent work

- The children should be given 20 minutes to plan their description of a person they know.
- Remind them to write clear notes which can be used on day 4.

Plenary

- Share ideas. Ask children who they have chosen and why. What interesting events concerning their people have they chosen? Stress the importance of including lively speech or interesting happenings at some point in their description.

DAY 4

Pupil's Book p. 65

Shared writing

- Without referring to any of your class or children's notes, discuss how they are going to organise their sections in an interesting way.
- How is their writing going to start? How will it end?

Independent work

- Children write a description of a person in their family. Make sure that the heading notes from day 3 are available.

Plenary

- Read selected examples of independent work, inviting constructive criticism. You may wish to concentrate solely on beginnings and/or endings.

DAY 5

Big Book pp. 47–48; Pupil's Book p. 65

Focused word work

- This is a SATs-style spelling test, based on the second extract. Each child will need Copymaster 20 and a pen or pencil as you require. Allow children either to cross out answers they wish to change or to use an eraser if they are working in pencil. Make sure that children cannot see the full version in the Big Book or Pupil's Book.

- Read the story twice – once "with pens down" to hear the words in context, the next time pausing for children to write the missing words in the spaces. The test should take no more than 15 minutes in all.

Shared reading

- Look at the passage again. Notice how the reader's expectation is built up, along with Baba's, in the first sentence. You could draw a comparison with the way this is done in film and TV.

- In what ways does time play an important part in the passage?

- Why is the letter a useful device for the author? It gives a sense of passed time, helps cover a lot of ground in a short amount of text, indicates character development – in most worthwhile stories and films the character develops over time.
- Introduce the day's independent work – a return letter from Baba (Balwinder Singh) to Mark and Juliet, written the same day. What might he want to say? Perhaps:
  1 Meeting them over the last few weeks.
  2 Their meeting Grandfather.
  3 The meal last night.
  4 The future.
  5 Mention Grandmother and Grandfather, Phil, Minnie, Zebedee.

  In this instance address, date, etc., can be omitted.

Independent work

- Children write a letter from Baba back to Mark and Juliet.

Plenary

- Go through the answers to the spelling test.

Consolidation and extension

- Ask children to discuss or write examples of various types of letters, with the appropriate conventions for greetings, signing off, etc.
- There are many possibilities here for exploring ethnic and cultural similarities and differences, and perhaps the prejudice issue.

Homework

- Page 21 of the Homework Book focuses on word contractions and the spelling rule "Knock off the *e*, add *ing*".

Unit 21 · Poems With a Purpose

Key Learning Objectives

TL3	to recognise how poets manipulate words: a) for their quality of sound, e.g. rhythm, rhyme, assonance b) for their connotations c) for their multiple layers of meaning, e.g. through figurative language, ambiguity
TL4	to investigate humorous verse; ... how poets play with meanings; ... where the appeal lies
TL5	to analyse how messages, moods, feelings and attitudes are conveyed in poetry
TL6	to read and interpret poems in which meanings are implied or multi-layered; to discuss, interpret challenging poems with others
TL9	to increase familiarity with significant poets and writers of the past
TL14	to write commentaries or summaries crediting views expressed by using expressions such as "The writer says that ..."

Range:	Various poetic forms; descriptive writing
Texts:	"After Prévert", Alan Brownjohn "I Saw a Jolly Hunter", Charles Causley "Good Hope", Benjamin Zephaniah
Resources:	Big Book 6C pp. 4–8 Pupil's Book 6 pp. 66–68 Homework Book 6 p. 22 Copymaster 21: The birth of a poem (spelling activity)

Preparation

- You will need A4 paper to make a planning sheet on day 4.

DAY 1

Big Book pp. 4–6; Pupil's Book pp. 66–67

Shared reading

- Read "After Prévert" to the children yourself, building up the early excitement, the strident announcement and the later pathos.

- Alan Brownjohn wrote this poem in the late 1950s, having recently read poetic work by Jacques Prévert, who often wrote light, surreal or fantasy poems with a message in them. This is very much in the same vein, inspired by the unremitting view of bleak rooftops from a stationary train near London Bridge.

- Ask the children to guess in what time period the poem is set. What picture does it paint of England's landscape in the future? What is it saying about the people of the future? Mention particularly the attitude to transport.

- The poet's use of repetition evokes successively excitement, significance, drama, helplessness.

- Ask the children whether the poem rhymes, or has rhythm. Do they know what we call poetry that doesn't have these elements – free verse? Would the poem be as effective if it did rhyme?

- What do they think of the poem? Ask them to comment on its message, its effectiveness, their favourite part, changes they would make, etc.

Focused word/sentence work

- Look at these word meanings: *hoardings, floodlights, neon lights, mounted policemen, jostling, remarking* (a useful word to replace *said*, but only in certain contexts, i.e. when commenting, passing some sort of opinion).

Independent work

- Comprehension.

Plenary

- Go through the children's answers to the comprehension questions, discussing particularly the concept of "message" in a piece of poetry, novel, art, etc.

DAY 2

Big Book pp. 4–6; Pupil's Book p. 67

Shared reading/writing

- Why do the children think the poet repeats *Which rabbit?* a third time? The effect is almost sneering – "as if one needed to ask".

- Examine the shifts in narration style without any obvious verbal change: the wide-eyed sightseer going to see the rabbit; the commentator (*The rabbit has gone, yes, the rabbit has gone*); the "Big Brother" (*1984*) style announcer; the rabbit itself.

- Discuss the wealth of meaning behind the word *despite* in *Despite all these people*. Who is saying the sentence? What does this say about the sightseer's attitude/understanding of rabbit behaviour? It reveals tremendous arrogance and ignorance; the sightseer is expecting the rabbit to put on a show because there is such a crowd, and cannot understand why it should be frightened and want to hide away.

Focused word work

- Administer a SATs-style spelling test. Each child will need Copymaster 21 and a pen or pencil as you require. Allow children either to cross out answers they wish to change or to use an eraser if they are working in pencil.

- Read the piece twice – once "with pens down" to hear the words in context, the next time pausing for children to write the missing words in the spaces. The test should take no more than 15 minutes in all.

- Here is the full text with the words to be spelled in bold:

The brakes squealed piercingly, and the **train** juddered to an unexpected halt. The jolt forced his **eyes** open. He turned to look through the rain-dappled carriage **window**, across countless metal rails to the monotone landscape beyond. London in winter. Slate rooftops **stretched** endlessly away into the distance under a solid blanket of cloud, the bleak skyline **punctuated** only by steeples and factory chimneys. Rainwater poured along a thousand gutters. A **thousand** drab buildings added their **smoke** to the **gloom**. Not a bird, not a blade of grass, not so much as a leafless branch in view.

As lights flickered on in the November streets below, a

sudden, chilling **thought** overtook him. Will it all be **like** this one day? When the last bulldozer has done its work, when the last brickie puts down his trowel, when the last farm tractor is left to rust in the rain? In a **hundred** years from now, where will the countryside be? He let his eyes close again and a thought emerged from the **darkness** – a rabbit, alone on a small patch of grass, amid a wasteland of barbed wire and concrete. The only rabbit in **England**.

The train jerked once more and began to **move**. He pulled a notebook and pencil from his raincoat and hastily began to **write**. "We are going to see the rabbit ..."

- Introduce the independent work. Children have to write a commentary on the poem, "After Prévert", using the third person (e.g. *The writer is describing a scene in the future. The person in the poem is going to ...*).

Independent work

- Children write a brief commentary on the poem "After Prévert", including 1) a summary, 2) an assessment of the poet's feelings, 3) comments on how the poem is written, 4) comments on the poem's effectiveness.

Plenary

- Go through the answers to the spelling test.
- Explain that the passage used in the test describes the real-life experience that prompted the poet to write the poem.

DAY 3

Big Book pp. 4–8; Pupil's Book p. 67

Shared reading

- You may wish to have children do further work on the commentaries from day 2 before introducing the new poems, i.e. to reverse the Literacy Hour on this occasion.
- Read "I Saw a Jolly Hunter". What is its message?
- How does it compare with "After Prévert" in style? Is it effective? What part, if any, does the humour play in this? Do the children think that its "jolly" style means the author believes any less in the point he is making? Point out that humour is often the best way to get a point over.
- Read the poem "Good Hope" by Benjamin Zephaniah. What is the poem's message? What different things does the poet say he believes in?
- Can the children describe the form of this poem – free verse with a strong rhythm? Would its message lend itself to a rhyming format?
- What have "I Saw a Jolly Hunter" and "Good Hope" got in common? They both express strongly felt sentiments, and make very repetitive use of a single word.

Focused word/sentence work

- Why does Charles Causley use the word *jolly* so much? He is mocking the presumed style of speech of the red-faced hunting squire.
- Where does the concept of *I believe* come from in "Good Hope"? Recall the Church creed: *I believe in one God ...* (from Latin *credo* = I believe).
- What is a *not sure*?

- Ask the children to discuss whether the writer ignores the negative things that happen in the world. Stress the importance in putting a case of anticipating counter-arguments.
- How is the poem tied up neatly at the end? Point to the almost unexpected reversal of the drummed-in rhythm of the rest of the poem.

Independent work

- Children continue with their commentaries.

Plenary

- Read selected examples of the children's commentaries, inviting constructive criticism.

DAY 4

Pupil's Book p. 68

Shared writing

- In preparation for the independent writing assignment, discuss with the children what an essay is.
- Discuss the sort of issues that they might wish to write about ("green" issues, the existence of a god, equality, hunting, corporal/capital punishment, pupil power, etc.).
- Ask them to justify their choice of topic orally, but in a complete and grammatical sentence.
- Without the children referring to the Pupil's Book, make a planning sheet together based on the ideas listed in the Pupil's Book. Write suitable headings on a sheet of A4 paper, leaving space for notes under each heading: 1 Subject chosen; 2 Reason for choice; 3 Arguments **for**; 4 Arguments **against**; 5 Conclusions – Why do "Reasons for" beat "Reasons against"? 6 Ending.

Independent work

- Using the planning sheet just created, children plan their essay. Point out that their notes must be brief, must take no more than 15 minutes to jot down, and will not be marked.

Focused sentence work

- Examine ways of rounding off an essay like the one on beliefs: *In conclusion ...; To sum up ...; It is clear to me that ...*
- Explain that the first person is allowable in this essay, but that often one would have to use a more impersonal approach: *It would seem that ...; The writer thinks ...; One ...*

Plenary

- Discuss the children's choices of subjects for their essays, sampling the arguments for and against that they have used (i.e. testing whether they have adopted a balanced approach).

DAY 5

Shared reading

- Give a brief (5 minutes or so) introduction to the second piece of independent writing, *Write an essay about something you believe in very strongly.* Go over the main planning headings, stressing the need for convincing but balanced argument and a tidy conclusion.

- It is suggested that the writing takes a straight 45 minutes, and replaces the normal structure of the Literacy Hour on this occasion.

Independent work

- Children complete their essay or commentary to display standard.

Plenary

- Read selective examples of the independent writing, particularly highlighting examples of convincing sentences, treatment of counter-arguments, neat conclusions.

Consolidation and extension

- Suggest children add their own verses to the middle of the poem "Good Hope".

- Ask children to give 5-minute talks on something they believe in or don't believe in, giving reasons. Alternatively, organise a formal debate.

- Ask children to discuss, write about or make a display on the future. What will be invented? What will be obsolete? What will be the benefits and the drawbacks?

Homework

- Page 22 of the Homework Book focuses on word series, covering various spelling rules and patterns.

Unit 22

Cardboard Characters, Predictable Plot

Key Learning Objectives

TL7	identify key features of different types of literary text, e.g. stock characters, plot structure, and how particular texts conform, develop or undermine the type, e.g. through parody
TL9	to increase familiarity with significant poets and writers of the past
TL10	to use different genres as models to write, e.g. short extracts, sequels, additional episodes, alternative endings, using appropriate conventions, language
TL11	to write own story using, e.g. flashbacks or a story written within a story to convey the passing of time
TL13	parody a literary text
SL3	to revise work on complex sentences: ... identify main clauses; ... constructing complex sentences; ... appropriate use of punctuation
SL5	to use reading to: a) investigate conditionals, e.g. using *if ... then, might, could, would* and their uses b) use these forms to construct sentences which express, e.g. possibilities, hypotheses c) explore use of conditionals in past and future, experimenting with transformations, discussing effects

Range:	Longer-established stories and novels from more than one genre: adventure
Texts:	From *Goldfinger*, Ian Fleming From *The Adventures of Sherlock Holmes*, Sir Arthur Conan Doyle
Resources:	Big Book 6C pp. 9–12 Pupil's Book 6 pp. 69–72 Homework Book 6 p. 23 Copymaster 22: Main and subordinate clauses

Preparation

- Children will need a plain sheet of A4 for planning notes on day 2.

- You may find it useful to have the Austin Powers extracts (see day 3) on an OHP transparency.

- Suggested sentences for day 4's focused sentence work on main and subordinate clauses need to be written out large or on an OHP transparency.

DAY I

Big Book pp. 9–10; Pupil's Book pp. 69–70

Shared reading

- Before you read the first extract, tell children they are going to read about M (Bond's boss) and about Goldfinger (the baddy), both face to face with Bond. Predict what they will say and do.

- Now read the extracts on M and Goldfinger. Compare the children's predictions with what you read.

- Read the other two Bond extracts. Do we know much about any Bond characters beyond a sentence or two? Explain the phrase "cardboard characters", i.e. mechanical people necessary to the action but in whose deeper thoughts and feelings we have no interest and are given no serious insight. For instance, we don't need to know where Miss Moneypenny lives – just that she always ... what? (sits at a desk and fancies James Bond in vain); likewise M – he is always ... impatient and slightly abrupt with James Bond; Q is always ... exasperated with Bond who always ... does what with the gadgets? (fools around with them). Note the use of *always* – these characters always behave predictably. Why should this be?

- Do Bond or the characters develop during the stories or the whole range of books/films? No – as soon as he wanted to grow up and get married they killed his new wife off in a car accident!

Focused word/sentence work

- Focus on these word meanings: *log; sardonic; bitten-off; amiabilities; sing* (to give information); *colonel; mien* (pronounced *meen*: look, demeanour); *divine; carat; Universal* (Universal Exports – Bond's cover organisation when on missions).

- Explain the terms "cliché" and "hackneyed". Identify in the passages any Bond cliché phrases and situations.

Independent work

- Comprehension.

Plenary

- Go through the answers to the comprehension questions.

DAY 2

Big Book pp. 9–10; Pupil's Book p. 70

Shared writing

- In preparation for a SATs-like test, plan and begin writing together a story scene in which James Bond (or an agent of your own choosing) is confronted by an arch-baddy.

- Discuss what headings need to go into a plan, e.g. setting, situation, the baddy's name and appearance, the name and appearance of the henchman, the awful fate that awaits the agent.

- Use your agreed headings to write an A4 planning sheet, but do not write more than the headings, leaving a space below each for independent planning.

- When you begin writing together, pay particular attention to the way the speech is punctuated. Encourage children to use speech in their final writing.

- Encourage children who are able to do so to invent their own scene and characters. Less able children could use the ideas developed communally.

Focused word/sentence work

- Recap on the meaning of conditional verbs, i.e. those used when the outcome is not definite: *I might go if I have time.*

- Examine the changes that take place from a definite verb to a conditional verb:

I will go → *I would go if ...;*
I can go → *I could go if ...;*
I shall be grateful → *I should be grateful if ...;*
I was → *I would have been if ...*

- Introduce *may* and *might*. Which is stronger: *I may go* or *I might go*? *May* is more positive, more probable.

- Make this conditional: *I did go to the show* → *I might have gone to the show*.

- Change Goldfinger's words from direct to indirect speech, using the correct conditional verbs.
  E.g. *Goldfinger said, "Mr Bond, if you sing, you will die painlessly."* → *Goldfinger told James Bond that if he sang, he would die painlessly.*

  1 Goldfinger said, "Mr Bond, if you do not sing, you will die slowly." →
  2 Bond replied, "I will say nothing, because I have nothing to say." →
  3 Goldfinger said, "If I hear nothing from you, I may have to use a little persuasion." →

Independent work

- Children plan a scene from a secret agent story, using the plan prepared during shared writing.

- As the story writing takes place on day 3, you may wish to collect in the notes and hand them out again on day 3.

Plenary

- Discuss children's ideas for the story, inviting constructive criticism.

- Recap on the punctuation of speech, using some sample sentences.

DAY 3

Pupil's Book p. 71

Shared reading

- You may wish to do this session after the story writing, as a bit of light relief.

- Recap on what parody is. What sort of books and films are most easily parodied?

- You may enjoy sharing these snippets from the script of the film *Austin Powers*, a parody of the Bond films, starring Mike Myers as Austin Powers **and** the baddy, Dr Evil. Mr Bigglesworth is Dr Evil's cat. Random Task is his Korean henchman (as in Oddjob!):

Dr Evil (sneeringly): Ladies and gentlemen, welcome to my underground lair. I have, gathered here before me, the world's deadliest assassins, and yet each of you has failed to kill Austin Powers. That makes me angry, and when Dr Evil gets angry, Mr Bigglesworth gets upset, and when Mr Bigglesworth gets upset, people die! [Their seats tip up and the assassins disappear to the piranha fish below.]

In this parody Dr Evil, instead of being totally free to do his evil deeds, has an awkward, normal teenage son, Scott:

Dr Evil: Gentlemen, my name is Dr Evil.
Scott (referring to Austin Powers): Why don't you just kill him?
Dr Evil: No, Scott. I have an even better idea. I'm going to place him in an easily escapable situation involving an overly elaborate and exotic death ... All right, guard, begin the unnecessarily slow-moving dipping mechanism.

Talk about the last speech. Why is it funny? What parodies have the children seen? What other books or films could easily be parodied?

Focused word/sentence work

- It is suggested that the independent writing take over this section today, so that children get a 45-minute period like that in the SATs test.

Independent work

- Using their planning notes, children write the scene from a secret agent story.

Plenary

- Read out selected examples from the children's secret agent stories, inviting constructive criticism.

DAY 4

Big Book pp. 9–10; Pupil's Book p. 71

Shared reading

- Read the first extract again as necessary.

- Talk in detail about the Bond character stereotypes. List the things that they (e.g. Bond himself, Q, the arch-baddy, the baddy's henchman) always do.

- How does M's speech compare with Goldfinger's? Why is this? M's speech is clipped, brief, whereas Goldfinger's is long-winded, with a veneer of civilisation hiding lurking cruelty. Make the point that everything (speech, appearance, habits) has to support the character stereotype. How does this differ from real life? We are all a mass of contradictions and inconsistencies, but this is not recognised in James Bond's world.

- List the things that virtually always happen in James Bond books/films.

- "... *Station H* –" Why does the writer have M cut Bond off, having asked him a question? This helps keep up the pace of the book: yesterday at Station H is unimportant to the plot, so it gets ruthlessly cut.

- Why do James Bond books adapt well to the screen? Point out that they are all action, set in exotic locations, and people enjoy predictability! What sort of books would be difficult to adapt? Ask children to give their reasons.

Focused word/sentence work

- Explain that complex sentences usually comprise main and subordinate clauses. To find the main clause, we have three stages:

  1 Find the **subject** of the sentence.
  2 Then find the **verb** that the subject controls. (Mention the **object**, but warn children there may not be one, e.g. *She ran* has no object.)
  3 Identify the **main clause**, which includes the subject and verb already found.

- Try the process together on this sentence: *Mr Bond, I love gold, particularly its texture.* Put a ring round the subject (*I*), a wavy line under the verb (*love*) and a straight line under the main clause (*I love gold*).

- Then ask the children to do this one: *The girl I shall then give to Oddjob, as I did that cat, for supper.* Subject: *I*; verb: *shall give*; main clause: *The girl I shall then give to Oddjob for supper.*

- Look at section 4 of the first extract. Identify the subjects, verbs and main clauses in the three sentences following *I love the texture* ... (*I love the texture; I love the warm tang; I love the power*).

- Now try these sentences (written out large or on OHP transparency, without the underlinings, etc.!):

  1 Smithers keeps an eye out for fishy things going on in the world of currency.

  2 Holding the steering wheel on a light rein, Bond idled along at 50, listening to the relaxed purr of the exhausts.

  3 Crouched by the wall, the agent saw Goldfinger climb the stairs and disappear down the corridor.

  4 With no sign of emotion, Oddjob, totally focused, brought his hand down on the banister, smashing it to smithereens.

  Note the difference between the next two sentences:

  5 Have you time, considering how late it is, to stop the bomb going off?

  6 "Have you time, considering how late it is, to stop the bomb going off?," asked the woman.

Independent work

- Children identify main clauses in complex sentences using either the Pupil's Book or Copymaster 22.

Plenary

- Go through the answers to the independent work.

- Reinforce the concept of main and subordinate clauses. E.g. *She answered the door when I rang the bell* – the last part is clearly subordinate to the first main idea. But introduce the fact that some complex sentences can have two main clauses, where two ideas have the same importance, e.g. *I like the shoes but I'm not so keen on the dress.*

DAY 5

Big Book pp. 11–12; Pupil's Book p. 72

Shared reading

- Before you read the second extract, discuss and describe the popular image of Sherlock Holmes and Dr Watson. Where does Holmes live? 221B Baker Street, London. What does he look like? He is tall, gaunt, cadaverous, with a large bony face. What does he say? He makes staggering deductions from apparently unimportant scraps of information, adding comments about his deductions that make them seem simple. What role does Watson play? He's an honest and reliable plodder bumbling along in Holmes's wake, guaranteed to marvel at Holmes's brilliance.

- Compare the extract with the children's preconceptions. Were they correct?

- What sort of thing always happens in Holmes stories? Somebody comes to Holmes in distress with an apparently baffling set of circumstances; Holmes accepts the case, calls in Watson and off they go in a carriage;

Holmes makes some stunning deductions; Watson is baffled; the crime is solved; everyone is amazed ... except Sherlock Holmes, who regards it all as ... *elementary, my dear Watson* (a clichéd misquote!).

Focused word/sentence work

- Do the children know the historical period Holmes lived in – late Victorian? What evidence is there that the story was written in Victorian times, not just about them? Notice the phrase *brilliantly lit* – we now probably wouldn't use the word *brilliantly* in that way; *I observe*; *into harness*; *My dear Holmes*; the old-fashioned way sentences are put together.

- What are the three dots (...) called? *Ellipsis*; plural *ellipses*. What do they indicate? (In the passage *"Quite so," he answered* ... they indicate that we have omitted the details of Holmes's deduction because of a shortage of space.)

- How does the pattern of dialogue reflect Holmes's character? Point out the short sentences – very clipped, precise, implying keen intelligence, no time for wasted words.

- Discuss these words: *spare*; *silhouette* (must be French with an ending like that); *in practice*; *to go into harness*; *to deduce*; *distinction*.

Independent work

- Children write a summary of the passage in their own words, but in the third person, trying to capture the Victorian flavour. Ask them to begin like this: *The hansom cab stopped outside 221B Baker Street, the lodging of Mr Sherlock Holmes. Dr Watson alighted, gave the cabby his pence and looked up to the first floor.*

- Less able children could just write a simple summary of the passage, say in 100 words.

Plenary

- Read selected examples of children's work, praising successful attempts to capture the Victorian flavour, and inviting suggestions as to how other Victorian elements might be introduced.

- If time permits, discuss how it might be possible to parody Sherlock Holmes. What features would you exaggerate? (This has been done, notably in the Gene Wilder film, *The Adventures of Sherlock Holmes' Smarter Brother*.)

Consolidation and extension

- Discuss other books and films that rely on stock characters and predictable plots.

- Ask children to write a short piece parodying a scene from James Bond, Sherlock Holmes, Enid Blyton or any other laughably predictable story. Inspiration for this can often be found in the softback Christmas gift books published to accompany TV comedy programmes.

Homework

- Page 23 of the Homework Book focuses on the punctuation of speech.

SCHOOL _____ CLASS _____ TEACHER _____

	Phonetics, spelling and vocabulary	Grammar and punctuation	Comprehension and composition	Texts
Continuous work **Weeks 1–5**	WL 1, 2, 3, 4	SL 3, 4		**Range** Non-chronological reports, work on the same theme by several poets, explanations linked to other National Curriculum subjects, reference texts, work on the same theme by several authors: divorce

Blocked work					
Week	**Unit**				**Titles**
1	23			TL 15, 16, 17, 18, 19, 20, 21	"Istanbul – Where East Meets West", *Independent*
2	24		SL 1	TL 2, 3, 4, 6, 11, 12, 13, 20, 21	From "The Daffodils", William Wordsworth; "Sowing", Edward Thomas; "Loveliest of Trees, the Cherry Now", A.E. Housman; From "Naming of Parts", Henry Reed; "The Poet's Garden", Roger McGough
3	25			TL 15, 16, 17, 18, 19, 20, 21, 22	From *The Guinness Book of Knowledge*
4	26			TL 15, 16, 17, 18, 19, 20, 21, 22	From *The Hutchinson Unabridged Encyclopedia*
5	27		SL 1, 2	TL 1, 6, 7, 8, 9, 12	From *The Suitcase Kid*, Jacqueline Wilson

HALF-TERMLY PLANNER

TERM 3

Year 6 • Term 3 • Weeks 6–8

SCHOOL _____   CLASS _____   TEACHER _____

	Phonetics, spelling and vocabulary	Grammar and punctuation	Comprehension and composition	Texts
Continuous work Weeks 6–8	WL 1, 2, 3, 4	SL 3, 4		**Range** Comparison of work by one significant children's author, different authors' treatment of the same theme, comparison of work by significant poets
Blocked work **Week** / **Unit**				**Titles**
6 / 28	WL 6, 7		TL 1, 5, 9, 10, 11, 12	From *Madame Doubtfire*, Anne Fine
7 / 29	WL 5, 6, 7		TL 3, 4, 5, 6, 14	From "The Lady of Shalott", Alfred, Lord Tennyson; "First Day at School", Roger McGough
8 / 30			TL 1, 5, 9, 11, 12	From *Flour Babies*, Anne Fine

Focus on Literacy Teacher's Resource Book 6 © John McIlwain, HarperCollins*Publishers* Ltd 1999

Non-chronological Reports

Key Learning Objectives

TL15 to secure understanding of the features of explanatory texts from Y5 Term 2 (complex sentences, passive voice, technical vocabulary, hypothetical language, connectives)

TL16 to identify the key features of impersonal formal language, e.g. present tense, passive voice, and discuss when and why they are used

TL17 to appraise a text quickly and effectively; to retrieve information from it; to find information quickly and evaluate its value

TL18 to secure the skills of skimming, scanning and efficient reading so that research is fast and effective

TL19 to review a range of non-fiction text types and their characteristics, discussing when a writer might choose to write in a given style and form

TL20 to secure control of impersonal writing, particularly the sustained use of the present tense and the passive voice

TL21 to divide whole texts into paragraphs, paying attention to the sequence and the links between one paragraph and the next (e.g. through the choice of appropriate connectives)

Range:	Non-chronological reports linked to other NC subjects (developing countries)
Texts:	From "Istanbul – Where East Meets West", promotional report issued with the *Independent*
Resources:	Big Book 6C pp. 13–16 Pupil's Book 6 pp. 73–75 Homework Book 6 p. 24 Copymaster 23: The killer spelling test A world map, and ideally a larger-scale one showing Istanbul's position relative to Europe and Asia

Preparation

• Because of the SATs-style reading test on day 1, the structure of day 2 is designed to redress the balance of shared activity, and may be a longer "hour" than usual!

• On day 3, in discussing how to work with complex sentences you may wish to work with the Bloggsbridge Primary School facts (listed in the Pupil's Book) on OHP, together with some alternative ways of expressing them as examples.

DAY 1

Big Book pp. 13–14; Pupil's Book pp. 73–74

Shared reading

• Before you read the first extract, discuss where Istanbul is, and its importance as gateway to Asia.

• If they were trying to interest commercial people in a city, what topics would the children write about?

Mention location, history, achievements. Would it be a good idea to ignore problems? Why not?

• Now read the extract. Discuss these words: *unique, straits, underfunding, infrastructure, public transport.*

• What is the purpose of this report? Is it unbiased? How can you tell? In fact it is a promotional report, designed to encourage businessmen to invest in the city.

• Quickly scan the basic structure of the report by looking at the paragraphs. Make a list of subject headings. What patterns emerge from this? You might note: *General introduction – history and growth – problems – positive finish.*

• In the first few paragraphs, are the verbs mainly active or passive? Give examples. Why is this? The author is trying to be upbeat and communicate in a lively way.

• Experiment with changing some sentences over to passive. Discuss the relative impact.

Focused word/sentence work, independent work

• It is suggested that, for realistic practice, the reading test should take the full 45 minutes, on this occasion subsuming focused word/sentence work and independent work.

Plenary

• Discuss the reading test in general terms, and any problems experienced with it.

• If time permits, practise, as a race (even a team event), scanning for quick retrieval of information. Questions could include:

– How old is Istanbul?
– What are the two main religions there?
– What was the population in 1975?
– What is the name of the straits?
– What is the average number of children in a classroom?
– What single word means the number of people in a place?

DAY 2

Big Book pp. 13–14; Pupil's Book p. 75

Shared reading

• Go through the answers to the reading test that can be treated in this way. Then ask children to read out their answers to the longer questions. Point out, or invite children to do so, where sentences are especially good or could be improved, with suggestions for this.

Focused word/sentence work

• Discuss these words in the first extract: *unique* (Why is it incorrect to say something is rather unique?); *financial and educational institutions*; *expertise*; *throwing up* (echoes of being sick – what might be a more formal word to use?); *welfare*.

• Look at the first sentence: *Istanbul is often described ...* Is the verb active or passive? Why is this? In this case it is irrelevant to know who has described it – a list of people would be absurd and time-wasting!

- Look at the last paragraph: *Special emphasis is being placed ..., A start has been made ...* Again the agent of the sentence is not specified and is not important.

- Examine this sentence: *It is a staggeringly beautiful city, but also one which bustles with energy.* It has a nice flow and balance, using two contrasting ideas.

- *Once known as Constantinople, the city's history ...* Why is this bad English? There is no agreement – it was not the city's history that was known as Constantinople, but the city itself. How could we correct this? Perhaps: *Once known as Constantinople, the city has a history ...* Apart from the mistake, this is again a pleasing sentence.

Shared writing

- Introduce Bloggsbridge Primary School (BPS). Some jumbled facts about it are printed in the Pupil's Book on page 75. Together, choose pairs of facts to link in well-constructed sentences, e.g. *BPS has eight classes, with eight teachers and four non-teaching assistants.*

- Then link three or more facts in well-constructed sentences, e.g. *Opened in 1936, BPS has eight classes and 250 pupils, their ages ranging from 4 to 11 years.*

Independent work

- Children identify pairs of facts that go well together.

- They write five complex sentences linking two facts from the list.

- They write sentences linking three or more facts.

Plenary

- Read selected examples of children's independent work, particularly pointing out where they have caught the right formal tone and used passive verbs effectively.

DAY 3

Big Book pp. 13–16; Pupil's Book p. 75

Shared reading

- What are the two serious problems identified in the second extract? Mention accommodation and inflation if the children do not do so. What is seen as a partial solution? EU membership.

- Practise scanning for information. Ask some sample questions about information from a variety of places in the text, expecting quick answers. For instance: How many children are there in an average Istanbul class? 70.

- Discuss these words: *tourism, conventions, excluded, European Union, commercial.*

Focused sentence work

- Focus on complex sentences. Examine the first sentence of the second extract together. What different facts are being conveyed here? How else could these same facts be organised? Experiment with different combinations.

- Find other complex sentences in either extract and look how they have been joined effectively, e.g. using words like *despite, however;* use of the present participle to add an extra clause (e.g. *Being excluded from the ...*).

Shared writing

- In preparation for independent work, write a general introduction to Bloggsbridge Primary School for the first page of the school brochure, using the facts listed in the Pupil's Book.

- Why should the brochure be written fairly formally? How should the formal nature of the document be reflected in its style? Point out that the writing should be impersonal, and passive verbs should be used where possible. Perhaps you could demonstrate how inappropriate informal writing might be: *You'll just love Bloggsbridge Primary School. We think it's a really cool place. All the kids do too. We've got bags of space and we're pretty hot on maths and stuff like that. Ben Bouncer's the Deputy Head. He's only 31 and a real laugh ...*

- Identify what the first fact might be, and discuss how to express this formally. Perhaps: *Bloggsbridge Primary School is situated near the bus station on Education Road, Bloggsbridge;* or *Bloggsbridge Primary School has been described by the* Bloggsbridge Journal *as the best in Loamshire. Situated in ... it was built in ...*

Independent work

- Children write a formal description of Bloggsbridge Primary School as an introduction to the school brochure.

Plenary

- Read selected examples of the brochure introductions, inviting constructive criticism. Pick out particularly those which have caught the appropriate style.

DAY 4

Big Book pp. 15–16; Pupil's Book p. 75

Shared reading

- Discuss the following words from the second extract: *intensify; republics; living standards; statistics; rampant inflation; privatisation; universal; investment.*

- What has been the positive result of Turkish exclusion from the EU?

- Look at the last three paragraphs of the second extract. Identify why they are separate (i.e. what theme does each have?). Then examine how they flow from one to another. Emphasise the importance of writing that has a logical structure, with identifiable links which make it easier to read and to understand.

- Examine how, in both extracts, points are made with evidence to support them, e.g. the rise in living standards.

Focused word/sentence work

- Administer the SATs-style spelling test. Each child will need Copymaster 23 and a pen or pencil as you require. Allow children either to cross out answers they wish to change or to use an eraser if they are working in pencil.

- Read the piece twice – once "with pens down" to hear the words in context, the next time pausing for children to write the missing words in the spaces. The test should take no more than 15 minutes in all.

- Here is the full text with the words to be spelled in bold:

  David got off the bus at the stop before Bloggsbridge Bus Station and turned into Education Road. As **usual** his mate Wesley was waiting at the corner, trying to **dribble** his lunch box round a tree. After six years at Bloggie they didn't need to exchange greetings. A nod and a grunt was **enough** and the two **friends** went off up the road together shoulder to shoulder.

  Normally he and Wes told jokes or punched each other or tried to trip each other up, but today David just wasn't in the mood. Today was **different**. Today was THE day. The day of the killer spelling test.

  "To get you ready for your national tests, my little angels!" Mrs Rose had **said**, rubbing her hands together with glee, a wicked grin on her face.

  It was all right for Wes and Dawinder and Angela. They **always** got full marks at spelling. David **didn't**, even when he'd tried his hardest to learn them. He **reckoned** he had written out more spellings at playtimes than they'd had hot **dinners**. "Diss-something or other", Mrs Lively, their **headteacher**, had called it at Parents' Evening.

  The shouts and squeals from the playground grew louder and school loomed out of the morning mist. Wes pushed open the **squeaky** gate and the **two** boys merged with the crowd, **receiving** the usual thumps of welcome from their pals. "Anyway," David **thought**, "at least it'll be over by playtime."

Independent work

- Children continue writing the brochure introduction.

Plenary

- Go through the spelling test, not just giving answers but looking for links with other words following similar patterns, or extending from them, e.g. *usual – usually*; *dribble – giggle – little*; *didn't – wasn't – couldn't*.

DAY 5

Big Book pp. 13–16; Pupil's Book p. 75

Shared reading

- Ask children why both extracts quote people, rather than just saying what is planned or predicted. They are adduced as evidence, giving the statements authority; also to add life to the piece – although serious, it is not a truly formal piece of writing.

- Ask children to scan both extracts in five minutes and, with a partner, list eight important points that the article is making about Istanbul, e.g. *East meets West*; *beauty*; *v. busy trade centre*; *overcrowded*; *underfunded*; *tourism important*; *inflation rampant*; *still bright future*. Discuss the choices. A good idea would be to list the main topics as they emerge and do a survey of how many people have chosen each one.

- Initiate a discussion: You are a millionaire. After reading the piece, would you a) build a hotel there? b) buy a factory there? c) invest money in a business there, e.g. by buying a hotel? Give your reasons.

Focused word/sentence work

- Examine the second sentence of the first extract. Find a) the **two** main clauses, and b) the two subordinate parts.

- Why is only *but because the city …* etc. a subordinate **clause**? Because it has a verb.

- Look at the sentence beginning *This must be viewed …* Which is the main clause? Which is the subordinate clause? When is *however* used in a sentence? When there is some reservation; it is a posh word for *but*. Is there anywhere else that *however* could be put in the sentence? It could go at the beginning, or even the end. Why did the writer put it in the middle?

- Look at the sentence beginning *Despite the concern …* Discuss other ways of making the same points in one sentence. Why is one part in parentheses?

Independent work

- Children copy out their introduction to the Bloggsbridge Primary School in their best handwriting.

- You may wish to change the piece to be copied out, as appropriate, e.g. the extract used for the spelling test on day 4.

Plenary

- Read examples of the Bloggsbridge brochure writing, inviting constructive criticism.

- This might also be a good time to demonstrate examples of good handwriting, and pick up on any common faults.

Consolidation and extension

- Ask children to list the good and bad points they could make about your own region. Again, this could make a formal debate if enough people take opposing views.

- Ask children to write a brochure about your class or school.

Homework

- Page 24 of the Homework Book focuses on the formation of nouns, verbs, adjectives and adverbs from the same root.

Unit 24 Poets and Spring

Key Learning Objectives

TL2	to discuss how linked poems relate to one another
TL3	to describe and evaluate the style of an individual poet
TL4	to comment critically on the overall impact of a poem – showing how language and themes have been developed
TL6	to look at connections and contrasts in the work of different writers
TL11	to write a brief helpful review tailored for real audiences
TL12	to compare texts in writing, drawing out: a) their different styles and preoccupations b) their strengths and weaknesses c) their different values and appeal to the reader
TL13	to write a sequence of poems linked by theme or form
TL20	to secure control of impersonal writing, particularly the sustained use of the present tense and the passive voice
TL21	to divide whole texts into paragraphs, paying attention to the sequence and the links between one paragraph and the next (e.g. through the choice of appropriate connectives)
SL1	to revise the language conventions and grammatical features of the different types of text (formal comparison)
SL3	to revise formal styles of writing: a) the impersonal voice b) the use of the passive c) management of complex sentences

Range:	Work on the same theme by several poets
Texts:	From "The Daffodils", William Wordsworth "Sowing", Edward Thomas "Loveliest of Trees, the Cherry Now", A.E. Housman From "Naming of Parts", Henry Reed "The Poet's Garden", Roger McGough
Resources:	Big Book 6C pp. 17–21 Pupil's Book 6 pp. 76–78 Homework Book 6 p. 25 Copymaster 24: Naming of Parts

DAY 1

Big Book pp. 17–19; Pupil's Book pp. 76–77

Shared reading

- Read and reread the first two verses of "The Daffodils" by Wordsworth. Can the children tell how long ago it was written? (Wordsworth lived 1770–1850.) How can they tell?

- What metaphors and similes can they find in it?

- Read and reread the poem "Sowing". What basic similarities and differences are there with "The Daffodils"? Mention time of day, subject, rhyme, style, etc.

- Is "Sowing" an older or more recent poem? How can they tell? (Edward Thomas lived 1878–1917; the poem was written between 1914 and Thomas's death in the First World War.)

- Read and reread Housman's cherry tree poem from *A Shropshire Lad*. Which of the other two Spring poems is it more like? Why? (A.E. Housman lived 1859–1936; the poem was written in 1896.)

- Which of the three poems do children like best, and why?

Focused word/sentence work, independent work

- It is suggested that, for realistic practice, the reading test should take the full 45 minutes, on this occasion incorporating focused word/sentence work and independent work.

Plenary

- Discuss question 16 of the independent work, i.e. the comparison between the three poems, examining each poem's subject matter, rhyme and rhythm. What do children think inspired the poets to write about the subject? The daffodil and cherry tree poems were clearly inspired by walking in the country.

- What other points of comparison can be made?

DAY 2

Big Book pp. 17–19; Pupil's Book p. 78

Shared reading

- Read Wordsworth's "The Daffodils" again, perhaps reading the whole poem with the other verses printed below.

- Say something of Wordsworth's importance as England's leading Romantic poet. He was Poet Laureate from 1843 until his death in 1850. He was born in the Lake District and lived there most of his life.

- Explain what Romanticism means (i.e. an emotional and spiritual response to nature, the feelings, heroes, nostalgia, etc. – not necessarily to do with romance in a Mills & Boon sense!).

- How does Wordworth show this response in "The Daffodils"?

- What words and phrases identify it as being at the latest a 19th-century poem? Mention *o'er, stretched, sprightly dance.*

- The final verses of "The Daffodils", as well as being very beautiful, illustrate how language changes with time.

> The waves beside them danced; but they
> Out-did the sparkling waves in glee:
> A poet could not but be gay,
> In such a jocund company:
> I gazed – and gazed – but little thought
> What wealth the show to me had brought:
>
> For oft, when on my couch I lie
> In vacant or in pensive mood,
> They flash upon that inward eye
> Which is the bliss of solitude;
> And then my heart with pleasure fills,
> And dances with the daffodils.

- Read "Sowing" again. Examine the meaning of each verse in turn:

Verse 1: What is *sowing*? How did it take place at the time the poem is referring to? Seeds were hand sown from a bag slung over the shoulder.

Verse 2: What does *tasted deep the hour* mean? Note the hidden metaphor.

Verse 3: How did the poet feel, and why? He was satisfied after a long, successful day's work.

Verse 4: What does *hark* mean? The word also shows that it is not too modern a poem. Would the rain have been welcome? Why? Examine *windless* – not a usual word, but it summarises the art of the poet, saying something in a very condensed and elegant way. The *kiss/tear/goodnight* element is particularly poignant. It is almost certain that "Sowing" is a nostalgic look back at pre-war experiences, written while Thomas was on active service in the First World War, not long before he was killed in action; it is also an echo (conscious or unconscious) of Foreign Secretary Edward Grey's famous 1914 quotation, *The lamps are going out all over Europe; we shall not see them lit again in our lifetime.*

- You could go on to explain that the horrific slaughter of the First World War also put an end to the 19th-century Romanticism epitomised by Wordsworth's poems.

Focused word/sentence work

- Go through the answers to the SATs-style reading test of day 1. Mention that in the real SATs the questions requiring longer answers get marks scaled up pro rata, so it is important to give them proportionately more attention.

- Introduce the independent work on using a thesaurus. Ensure that the word *synonym* is understood, and if appropriate identify and explain the example for each section.

- It may be appropriate, for some less able children, to ask them to write a simple dictionary definition instead of finding synonyms.

Independent work

- Children practise using a thesaurus.

Plenary

- Read the cherry tree poem again. Mention that A.E. Housman, the writer of the poem, was born not long after Wordsworth died, and lived until well after the First World War. Mention that this poem is Poem 2 of Housman's famous collection of 63 poems *A Shropshire Lad* published in 1896, standing squarely between the Wordsworth and Thomas poems in both style and chronology.

- In other parts of *A Shropshire Lad* Housman dwells on the subject of country lads going off to fight and die, reflecting the change of mood in Britain (the Zulu and Boer Wars taking place and the World War to come). Poem 3, "The Recruit", starts: *Leave your home behind, lad,/ And reach your friends your hand,/ And go, and luck go with you/ While Ludlow tower shall stand.*

DAY 3

Big Book pp. 17–21; Pupil's Book p. 78

Shared writing

- Read the extract from "Naming of Parts" and "The Poet's Garden". In preparation for independent writing, make notes on a comparison between two of the poems in this unit, examining subject, rhyme, metre, inspiration, things liked and disliked, the likely reaction of others.

- What other points of comparison can be made?

- Take some of the notes children have made, and talk about how they can be turned into polished writing of the appropriate style. Demonstrate the use of the impersonal voice, and passive verbs.

Focused word/sentence work

- Take isolated elements (e.g. rhyme, subject matter) at random from any two of the poems and write sentences comparing them. The main point of this is to bring out vocabulary likely to be useful in comparing two things formally: e.g. *whereas, similarly, by contrast, in contrast to, on the other hand, in the same way.* Write up examples of usage where children can refer to them.

Independent work

- Children write a comparison of two of the poems studied in this unit, preferably not the ones you compared in your collective discussion. As "Naming of Parts" and "The Poet's Garden" are not reproduced in the Pupil's Book, you may wish to make sure the Big Book is accessible.

Plenary

- Read selected examples of children's poem comparisons, inviting constructive criticism. Discuss the way the comparisons are phrased, identifying examples of polished writing, particularly good linking between sentences and paragraphs.

DAY 4

Big Book p. 21; Pupil's Book p. 78

Shared writing

- Look more closely at Roger McGough's "The Poet's Garden". What is his attitude to the garden? How does McGough very deliberately bring home his indifference to the garden?

- Why are phrases such as *particularly all right, as green as grass, studded with ... studs* ridiculous?

- Is there another message about poets and writers within the poem? Perhaps debunking pomposity?

- Is McGough a Romantic poet?! What would Wordsworth or Housman have thought about the piece?

Focused word/sentence work

- Look together at suitable ways to end the independent comparative work. Suggest a neat summary of the writer's view, perhaps stating their own preference. Write up suitable phrases such as *Overall, Finally, In conclusion, To summarise.*

Independent work

- Children continue with their poem comparisons.

Plenary

- Read selected examples of children's poem comparisons, inviting constructive criticism. Discuss the way the comments are phrased, identifying examples of polished writing, particularly appropriate endings.

- You may wish to use this parody on Wordsworth's "The Daffodils":

> I wandered lonely as a cat
> That thinks it owns both dale and hill.
> When suddenly I saw a rat
> The colour of a daffodil.
> When next I saw a penguin pass
> With scarlet chest and tartan bill,
> I just collapsed upon the grass
> And knew that I was ill.
>
> *Brian Aldiss*

DAY 5

Big Book pp. 20–21; Pupil's Book p. 78

Shared reading

- Read the extract in the Big Book from "Naming of Parts" yourself. Before doing so, say that you are now going to read it badly. After a fairly flat reading, ask for suggestions about how it should be read properly. Reread it together.

- In what circumstances do you think that the poet thought of the idea for the poem? Henry Reed was one of many conscripts called up to fight in the Second World War. In this instance he was forced to sit through rifle drill.

- What "trick" does the poet use? Why are the language and theme of the poem so effective?

- Reread the Roger McGough piece. How does it contrast with all the others? What is his aim? Humour. How does he achieve it? Through deliberately describing beauty in totally banal, not to say moronic, terms.

Focused word/sentence work

- Discuss the action of the bolt and the breech of the rifle. The breech is the long slot at the back into which bullets are put. The bolt slides up and down within it to prepare the rifle for firing.

- *You can do it quite easy*: Do children have any comments on this? Is the poet bad at grammar? If not, why did he use an incorrect word?

- Why are some of the words in italics?

- Do children think the poet understood the lecture? Did he like it? Give reasons.

- What is a pun? What is the main pun used in the poem (*easing the spring*)?

- Ask children to clarify exactly what the poet is doing in the poem. He is taking the words of the sergeant and adapting them to what he is either looking at or thinking about.

Independent work

- Children write their own poem about spring.

Plenary

- In what way do children think today's two poems complete the sequence of five poems? Suggest the

sequence: Romanticism – Romanticism (with shadows of war) – wartime nostalgia – wartime contrasts – total unromanticism.

- Go through the sequence again, looking at changing attitudes and styles. How might the poems be received by people of another age?

Consolidation and extension

- Give the children a SATs-style spelling test. Each child will need Copymaster 24 and a pen or pencil as you require. Allow children either to cross out answers they wish to change or to use an eraser.

- Read the piece twice – once "with pens down" to hear the words in context, the next time pausing for children to write the missing words in the spaces. The test should take no more than 15 minutes in all.

- Note that Copymaster 24 uses verses 1, 2 and 5 of the poem "Naming of Parts"; the Big Book reproduces verses 1, 3 and 4. Here is the full text of verses 1, 2 and 5, with the words to be spelled in bold:

> **Today** we have naming of parts. **Yesterday**
> We had daily cleaning. And **tomorrow** morning,
> We shall have what to do what after **firing**. But today,
> Today we have naming of parts. *Japonica*
> *Glistens like coral in all of the neighbouring gardens,*
> And today we have naming of parts.
>
> This is the lower sling swivel. And this
> Is the upper sling swivel, **whose** use you will see
> When you are **given** your slings. And this is the
>   piling swivel
> Which in **your** case you have not got. *The **branches***
> *Hold in the garden their silent, eloquent gestures,*
> **Which** in our case we have not got.
>
> This is the safety catch ...
>
> And this you can see is the bolt ...
>
> They call it easing the Spring: it is **perfectly** easy
> If you have any **strength** in your **thumb**: like the
>   bolt,
> And the breech, and the cocking **piece**, and the point
>   of balance,
> Which in our case we have not got; *and the almond*
>   *blossom*
> *Silent in all of the gardens and the bees going* **backwards**
>   *and forwards,*
> For today we have naming of parts.

- Read and discuss a series of linked poems on the same theme, e.g. *Old Possum's Book of Practical Cats*.

- Ask children to find and read aloud poems that they enjoy from different eras and in different styles. Perhaps you could read others by Wordsworth, Housman and McGough.

- If appropriate, children could try their hand at parody.

- Ask children to write a series of poems on the same theme.

Homework

- Page 25 of the Homework Book focuses on *al-* words, Greek and Latin prefixes, and the formation of adjectives from nouns.

Unit 25 — Explanatory Texts

Key Learning Objectives

TL15 to secure understanding of the features of explanatory texts from Y5 Term 2 (complex sentences, passive voice, technical vocabulary, hypothetical language, connectives)

TL16 to identify the key features of impersonal formal language, e.g. present tense, passive voice, and discuss when and why they are used

TL17 to appraise a text quickly and effectively; to retrieve information from it; to find information quickly and evaluate its value

TL18 to secure the skills of skimming, scanning and efficient reading so that research is fast and effective

TL19 to review a range of non-fiction text types and their characteristics, discussing when a writer might choose to write in a given style and form

TL20 to secure control of impersonal writing, particularly the sustained use of the present tense and the passive voice

TL21 to divide whole texts into paragraphs, paying attention to the sequence and the links between one paragraph and the next (e.g. through the choice of appropriate connectives)

TL22 to select the appropriate style and form to suit a specific purpose and audience, drawing on knowledge of different non-fiction text types

SL4 to secure control of complex sentences, understanding how clauses can be manipulated to achieve different effects

WL4 to revise and consolidate work from previous five terms with particular emphasis on … learning and inventing spelling rules

Range:	Explanations linked to other NC subjects
Texts:	From *The Guinness Book of Knowledge*
Resources:	Big Book 6C pp. 22–25
	Pupil's Book 6 pp. 79–82
	Homework Book 6 p. 26
	Copymaster 25: Signs, symbols and abbreviations for taking notes

Preparation

- For day 2's plenary session, have ready (perhaps on an OHP) sets of facts which can be worked on to produce effective complex sentences.

- For day 3 you will need basic information about your school (full address, staff surnames, number on roll, etc.) that all children can see easily – photocopied sheets might be helpful. You will also need an A4 blank sheet per child.

DAY 1

Big Book pp. 22–23; Pupil's Book pp. 79–80

Shared reading

- You may wish to leave the shared reading until after the SATs-style reading test.

- Read the first extract. Enjoy finding answers to factual questions as quickly as possible, e.g. What greenhouse gases are named? Where does most of the carbon dioxide come from?

- Identify and analyse two or three complex sentences. What main ideas are within? How else could they be joined up?

- Identify examples of technical vocabulary. Look how these are explained within the text as necessary.

- Find examples of passive verb sentences, e.g. *Most of the world's water is found* … Why are they passive, not active? Often there is no agent involved, or the agent is unimportant; if necessary, explain the term "agent" – the "doer" of an action.

- Count the number of occurrences of past, present and future tenses. What do you find?

Focused word/sentence work, independent work

- It is suggested that, for realistic practice, the reading test should take the full 45 minutes, subsuming focused word/sentence work and independent work.

Plenary

- Whether or not you used them earlier, look at the two sentences beginning *As energy from the sun* … and *Carbon dioxide is the most common* … These represent two major types of complex sentence: 1) one point building on another, flowing through to a conclusion; 2) a balanced sentence setting one idea against another. Explain that this pattern can also emerge in a paragraph, where ideas in separate sentences either build or contrast deliberately. Find examples of this.

- Look for other examples of these two types of complex sentence.

DAY 2

Big Book pp. 22–23; Pupil's Book p. 81

Shared reading

- Go through the answers to the SATs reading test of day 1.

Focused word/sentence work

- Discuss the purpose of footnotes: to add significant information or references which would otherwise clog up the main text. How are they flagged up in the text? Mention and spell the word *aster**is**k* itself (as distinct from Aster**ix** the Gaul, a common mispronunciation!).

- How are footnotes more commonly indicated? By means of superscripted numbers; *super* = Latin above; *sub* = Latin below. Discuss also the use of the dagger (or obelisk) † and double dagger ‡ to mark a cross-reference.

- Explain the usefulness of abbreviations and symbols in taking notes, for allowing speed while maintaining clarity. Talk about the common symbols below, using examples where necessary. Children should take detailed notes about the practical meaning and usage, for the independent work that will follow.

  p. = page; *pp.* = pages; *e.g.* = for example (Latin: *exempli gratia*); *etc.* = and the rest (Latin *et cetera*; NB pronounced *et* not *eck* cetera) *i.e.* = that is (Latin *id est*); ∴ = therefore; NB = mark well (Latin *nota bene*); the asterism *⁂*, used to draw attention to something; *c.* = about (Latin: *circa* = around, as in *circle*), # = number in USA, *arrow* → = leading to, developing from; = = is the same as, means; > = larger than; < = smaller than.

Independent work
- Explain the meaning of common signs used in note-taking. Give examples of how to use those specified. Copymaster 25 can be used.

Plenary
- Practise constructing effective complex sentences together. Start from several given facts. These could be from another present area of study. For example:

  1 Prince Albert and Queen Victoria were married in 1840. He was Queen Victoria's only significant companion. 2 He died in 1861. 3 He was 42. 4 Queen Victoria was heartbroken. She went into mourning for the next 26 years. 5 Only her Golden Jubilee in 1887 brought her out into the public eye again.

  This could become:

  Prince Albert, Victoria's only real companion since their marriage in 1840, died in 1861 aged 42. The Queen was heartbroken and went into deep and private mourning, only emerging for her Golden Jubilee in 1887.

  In this example, useful techniques to point out are: the parenthetic commas enclosing the description of Albert, and the use of the present participle (*emerging*) to add another clause to a sentence rather than creating a separate sentence.

- Ask children if the passage could be improved and condensed still further. E.g. 1) *Heartbroken, the Queen went into* ... 2) Replace *1861* with *21 years later* – it is longer but adds variety, rather than having *1840* and *1861* so close together.

- Reinforce the importance of condensing ideas, avoiding repetition and achieving a flow. Drafting (or a word processor) is essential. So is reading sentences back to yourself semi-aloud.

DAY 3
Big Book pp. 22–23; Pupil's Book p. 81

Shared writing
- Prepare for an independent SATs writing test. Explain the concept of a website (an information site on the Internet that anyone on the Net, anywhere in the world, can access).

- The idea is that your school is going to have its own website, in the hope of forging links with schools elsewhere. Children will be required to write the text for their own school website.

- Discuss the headings you will need, and prepare a planning sheet together, so that each child ends up with one. Headings might include: *General information*: e.g. *where it is, how big it is*; *People in school*; *The school's day/week* (everyday events); *Special or unusual events*; *My class*; *What I think of school*.

- Explain that notes must be very brief indeed, and that they will have only 15 minutes to prepare them. Make sure the sheets are named. Collect them in after the session, and redistribute them for the writing session on day 4. (This may also give you a chance to glance at any problems that children are having in making useful notes.)

Focused word/sentence work
- Find this sentence in the first extract: *This would happen within 200 years if the present rate of warming were to continue.* Is it correct? What seems wrong? Explain that this is the subjunctive mood, used to express wishes, conditions and other non-factual situations. Discuss what happens to the verb in these examples: *He insisted that Fred **pay** for all of us. If I **were** you ... I demand that she **leave** at once. Come what may ... Suffice it to say ... Be it hereby understood ... Heaven forbid that I should ...*

- In looking at the passage, revise these points:
  – the punctuation of lists of things
  – the reason why *CFCs* is placed in brackets
  – homophones *source/sauce, some/sum, wood/would, size/sighs, raise/raze*, etc.

Independent work
- Children make notes for independent writing.

Plenary
- Revise the meanings of the abbreviations and symbols discussed yesterday. You could also bring in the way ordinary words can be shortened in note-taking without destroying clarity, e.g. *indept* = independent; *govt* = government; *inform^n* = information. Emphasise that this shouldn't be overdone to the point where it is impossible to remember, on rereading, what your abbreviations mean.

DAY 4
Pupil's Book p. 81

Shared writing/independent work
- Discuss what style would be appropriate to writing for a website. It is important to be interesting and lively, yet impart serious information.

- After this it is suggested that on this occasion children be given a full 45 minutes to do their writing.

Focused word/sentence work, independent work
- Children take a SATs-style writing test.

Plenary
- Show how an information piece on the school might be written for a more serious publication, say an educational journal. Perhaps it would be more interesting and productive to ask children for examples of information they have given in their website piece, and "translate" them into something more formal,

showing how the present tense and the passive voice are used. For instance:

Child's version: *We have sports day in June each year. Right through the school, everyone has a house. This year on sports day we will be running for our house against people in year 6.*

Formal version: *An annual sports day is held in June. A house system is operated throughout the school, and in the sports children compete against those from other houses.*

DAY 5

Big Book pp. 22–25; Pupil's Book p. 79, p. 82

Shared reading

- Read the second extract.

- Take each heading and discuss why it is in that place in the passage (i.e. look at what would happen if it were omitted or placed elsewhere in the order).

- Why is the section on what is being done at the end? Trace the logic from one sentence to the next, looking at the way each sentence develops from the last and the vocabulary used to link one sentence with another.

Focused word/sentence work

- Discuss these words: *unstable, depletion, concerted, significant, regrettably, economy.*

- From both extracts find examples of hypothetical sentences, i.e. what **may** happen.

- Make clear, concise (introduce and explain "concise") notes together on the section "What is the ozone layer?" Emphasise these points:

1 The importance of logical structure (therefore get a clear impression of the whole thing before you start writing).
2 Clear headings, hierarchy, layout.
3 Omission of unnecessary words.
4 Use of abbreviations where the meaning is obvious, e.g. *O* for *ozone*.
5 Use of dashes, arrows, etc., instead of words where possible.

Independent work

- Children make clear, concise notes on the last section of the second extract, "What is being done about global warming?"

- If they have further time, they can make notes on a section of the first extract.

Plenary

- Taking both extracts together, identify and list the eight most important facts about global warming. If time permits, you could discuss an order of importance for them.

Consolidation and extension

- Ask children to choose a section of the first extract and make clear notes about it.

- Organise a display, class assembly, etc., on Global Warming and the things we can do to minimise it.

- Ask children to practise note-taking in other lessons. With several short sessions children should improve very quickly at this vital skill.

- Via the Internet, if you have access to it, look at examples of other websites. (Visit the Collins website at www.**fire**and**water**.com!)

Homework

- Page 26 of the Homework Book focuses on note-taking on a serious subject, perhaps something currently being studied at school.

Unit 26 Definitions

Key Learning Objectives

TL15 to secure understanding of the features of explanatory texts from Y5 Term 2 (complex sentences, passive voice, technical vocabulary, hypothetical language, connectives)

TL16 to identify the key features of impersonal formal language, e.g. present tense, passive voice, and discuss when and why they are used

TL17 to appraise a text quickly and effectively; to retrieve information from it; to find information quickly and evaluate its value

TL18 to secure the skills of skimming, scanning and efficient reading so that research is fast and effective

TL19 to review a range of non-fiction text types and their characteristics, discussing when a writer might choose to write in a given style and form

TL20 to secure control of impersonal writing, particularly the sustained use of the present tense and the passive voice

TL21 to divide whole texts into paragraphs, paying attention to the sequence and the links between one paragraph and the next (e.g. through the choice of appropriate connectives)

TL22 to select the appropriate style and form to suit a specific purpose and audience, drawing on knowledge of different non-fiction text types

WL3 to use independent spelling strategies, including:
a) building up spellings by syllabic parts, using known prefixes, suffixes and common letter strings
b) applying knowledge of spelling rules and exceptions
c) building words from other known words, and from awareness of the meaning or derivations of words
d) using dictionaries and IT spell-checks

WL4 to revise and consolidate work from previous five terms with particular emphasis on ... learning and inventing spelling rules

Range:	Reference texts
Texts:	From *The Hutchinson Unabridged Encyclopedia*
Resources:	Big Book 6C pp. 26–29
	Pupil's Book 6 pp. 83–85
	Homework Book 6 p. 27
	Copymaster 26: Dictionary definitions
	Large dictionaries
	Other reference books

Preparation

- Children will need Copymaster 26 and a dictionary on day 2. It would be helpful if several larger dictionaries were also available.
- Children will need a blank sheet of A4 paper as a planning sheet on day 3.
- Have ready examples of different types of reference books for day 5 (see relevant section below).

DAY I

Big Book pp. 26–27; Pupil's Book pp. 83–84

Shared reading

- You may wish to leave the shared reading until after the SATs-style reading test.
- Note that the *Collins English Dictionary* defines weather as "the day-to-day meteorological conditions, esp. temperature, cloudiness, and rainfall, affecting a specific place".
- Read the first extract.
- Ask the children what type of reference book it has come from – dictionary? encyclopedia? How can they tell? It is a lengthier, more technical definition than you would find in a dictionary. Define the difference between the two.
- Find examples of the use of passive verbs. Explain that this is normal for most academic or formal writing, because the "agent" of the action is either unimportant or unknown. Try turning some of your examples into active verb sentences and examine the results.

Focused word/sentence work, independent work

- It is suggested that, for realistic practice, the reading test should take the full 45 minutes, incorporating focused word/sentence work and independent work.

Plenary

- Imagine you are giving an informative talk about weather and climate on children's television. Discuss how and why you would rephrase words and phrases to put the important information across in a friendly, lively way. For example:

The weather is what the clouds, the rain, the wind, the air around us are doing at any one time in any one place, and also how this changes from one day to the next. To do their forecasting, weather forecasters need accurate information from all over the country ....

Be prepared to write, rewrite and rewrite again just a few lines in order to get the right tone. Make sure you have a record of anything completed, for use on day 3.

DAY 2

Big Book pp. 26–27; Pupil's Book p. 85

Shared reading

- Read the first extract again, then go through the answers to the reading test from day 1.

Focused word/sentence work

- Find examples of phrases that would not be found in informal writing (e.g. *Such a procedure is ...; Within the term are encompassed ...*) Translate these into informal English.
- What hypothetical sentences can you find (i.e. sentences that are supposition or possibility rather than actuality)?
- Practise scanning the piece for quick answers to factual questions, e.g. What lines join points of equal pressure on a weather map?

Independent work

- Ask children to use a dictionary to look up the meanings and etymologies of other words from the extract. Remind them that the meanings must be as used in the passage. Copymaster 26 can be used as an alternative to the Pupil's Book.

Plenary

- Continue and complete the "television" talk on weather and climate. Analyse what you have had to change to accommodate a different type of audience, e.g. simpler, less academic sentence structure and vocabulary, less use of the passive voice.

DAY 3

Big Book pp. 26–27; Pupil's Book p. 85

Shared writing

- Discuss short story writing: what to do when you don't know what to do! If you were asked to write a short story called "Frozen Up", what sort of questions might you ask yourself? Brainstorm these questions without seeking answers. Start with the questioning adverbs *Where? Who? What?* etc. Then expand them and sort them into a useful order; e.g. Where is the story set? When is it set? What sort of freezing is it going to be? Who are my main characters going to be? How will the freezing affect them? How will the story start? What will be the climax of the story? How will it end? Is there anything I can do to make the story more original and exciting, e.g. an unusual main character, an unexpected twist in the plot?

- If time permits, do the same sort of exercise for a story with a reference book theme – "Atlas Adventure", "Dictionary Danger", etc. (Why might a dictionary become dangerous? Who might be affected? etc.) The aim is not so much to produce a completed plan, but more to equip children with the resources to think imaginatively about any given topic.

Focused word/sentence work

- Discuss these words: *climatic, atmospheric, day-to-day, state* (as in *condition*; what other homographs/ homonyms are there for *state*?) *meteorologist/ meteorological, term, precipitation, conventional symbols* (map symbols that follow a convention, i.e. that are standardised and known by all), *atmospheric pressure* (the pressure of the atmosphere upon the earth), *relative to, impact of another planetary body, ozone layer, greenhouse effect.*

Independent work

- Children plan a story called "The Storm". They will need a blank sheet of A4. To prevent their disappearance you may wish to collect these and distribute them again on day 4.

Plenary

- After explaining that all ideas about to be mentioned are "copyright" and that they must not pinch someone else's storyline, discuss the ideas raised for the story "The Storm". In particular, investigate the planning process, i.e. the questions that children asked themselves in order to come up with a story. Invite constructive criticism.

DAY 4

Big Book pp. 28–29; Pupil's Book p. 85

Shared reading

- Read the second extract together.

- What sort of book has it come from? How can the children tell? Point to the obvious attempt at definition, technical language, present tense, frequent use of passive voice. What is the aim of the extract?

- Analyse the way that the piece is organised – definition, division, important reservation.

- How might you start to express the same information informally? Why is informal English not appropriate in this case?

Focused word/sentence work

- Discuss these words: *systematic, experiment, observation, deduction, phenomena* (and *phenomenon*), *material, physical, comprise, contemporary debate, precision.*

- Practise the use of dictionaries to find definitions of some of the subject names quoted in the extract (e.g. *anthropology, geology*).

Independent work

- Children begin to write the story "The Storm". Allow them 20 or so minutes today and a similar time on day 5.

Plenary

- Discuss the meanings of terms to do with written texts, such as *title, caption, extract, passage, interview, bibliography, script, dialogue, text.* What is a *sub-text*? A hidden plot beneath apparently simple dialogue or action.

DAY 5

Big Book pp. 26–29; Pupil's Book p. 85

Shared reading

- Remind children where the extracts came from (an encyclopedia).

- What are reference books? What differentiates them from other books? Mention that they are to dip in rather than read end to end.

- Make a list of other important types of reference books, with their function, e.g. atlas; gazetteer; specialist dictionaries – of biography, science, music; thesaurus; directories – telephone, business; focused reference books – bird books, cookery books, etc.; catalogues; manuals – car, DIY, etc.; *Guinness Book of Records.*

- What is the difference between a dictionary and an encyclopedia?

- What other sources of information are there? CD-ROMs, Internet, personal research.

Focused word/sentence work

- Look for and list initial letters which are "silent", i.e. spelled but not pronounced. *Knowledge.* What other silent *k* words do children know? *Psychology.* What other silent *p* words do they know? *Pneumatic*, etc.

- How many other silent letters can they find? E.g. *c* in *science, disciplines*; *h* in *chemistry, technology*.
- Examine the *-logy* suffix. What prefixes could go before it? Examples are *bio, geo, anthropo, techno*. Ask children to use dictionaries to look up the Greek origins and meanings of these words.

Independent work

- Children continue writing the story "The Storm".

Plenary

- Read selected examples of children's stories, inviting constructive criticism.
- Discuss handwriting, and remind children of the mnemonic for good handwriting, whatever the style: same size, straight sticks and solid shapes.

Consolidation and extension

- Ask children to survey the reference books at home, noting down their titles, their purpose and a sample entry from each.
- Make sure that children are aware of the range of reference books in the classroom and school libraries. See if they can identify them by sight, and know their purpose.
- Arrange a visit to a local library to look at the reference facilities there and to learn how to use catalogues, microfiches, etc.

Homework

- Page 27 of the Homework Book focuses on spelling using silent letters, and on standard prefixes and suffixes (researching origin in Greek or Latin).

Unit 27 The Suitcase Kid

Key Learning Objectives

TL1	to describe and evaluate the style of an individual writer
TL6	to look at connections and contrasts in the work of different writers
TL7	to annotate passages in detail in response to specific questions
TL8	to use a reading journal to raise and refine personal responses to a text and to prepare for discussion
TL9	to write summaries of books or parts of books, deciding on priorities relevant to purpose
TL12	to compare texts in writing, drawing out: a) their different styles and preoccupations b) their strengths and weaknesses c) their different values and appeal to reader
SL1	to revise the language conventions and grammatical features of the different types of text, such as: a) narrative (e.g. stories and novels) b) recounts (e.g. anecdotes, accounts of observations, experiences) c) instructional texts (e.g. instructions and directions) d) reports (e.g. factual writing, description) e) explanatory texts (how and why) f) persuasive texts (e.g. opinions, promotional literature) g) discursive texts (e.g. balanced arguments)
SL2	to conduct detailed language investigations
WL2	to use known spellings as a basis for spelling other words with similar patterns or related meanings
WL3	to use independent spelling strategies, including: a) building up spellings by syllabic parts, using known prefixes, suffixes and common letter strings b) applying knowledge of spelling rules and exceptions ... d) using dictionaries and IT spell-checks e) using visual skills, e.g. recognising common letter strings and checking critical features (i.e. does it look right, shape, length, etc.)
WL4	to revise and consolidate work from previous five terms with particular emphasis on ... learning and inventing spelling rules

Range:	Work on the same theme by several authors: divorce
Texts:	From *The Suitcase Kid*, Jacqueline Wilson
Resources:	Big Book 6C pp. 30–34 Pupil's Book 6 pp. 86–88 Homework Book 6 p. 28 Copymaster 27: D is for Dad Copy of *The Suitcase Kid*

Preparation

- The theme of *The Suitcase Kid* is divorce and its effect on the child – distress, anger, frustration, hostility to step-relatives. Gradually Andy becomes reconciled to the fact that things will never return to what they were, and begins to look at life positively again. *The Suitcase Kid* has been chosen for **Focus on Literacy** not only for its quality and potential for enjoyment as a class reader, but also because in line with NLS objectives TL6 and TL12 it can be compared with *Madame Doubtfire* (Unit 28), which deals with the same subject in a different but equally effective way. Short extracts do not allow adequate comparison between books; it is therefore strongly recommended that, at least for the week of this unit, you and your children spend some time reading and enjoying *The Suitcase Kid* further.

- In preparation for days 3 and 4, examine the texts suggested to see if they bring out all the features you wish to mention in line with objective SL1 (conventions and features of texts), supplementing them as you think necessary. You will definitely need some advertising copy.

- On day 5 children will need Copymaster 27. You will also need a photocopy of the second extract at Big Book size (or bigger if possible) or an OHP transparency of this text.

DAY I

Big Book pp. 30–32; Pupil's Book pp. 86–87

Shared reading

- You may wish to leave the shared reading until after the SATs-style reading test suggested for today.

- Introduce the background to the story, reinforcing the fact that Andy is a girl (Andrea), then read the first extract.

- What person is the story written in? In what person are other stories the children know (e.g. stories read to class recently) written?

- Explain that the book is unusually constructed in alphabetically titled chapters. The pattern clearly started in the author's mind because Andy shuttles between House A and House B, and the book is neatly tied up by an alphabetical reference in its last line.

- Ask children to think of words and phrases which describe the style the extract is written in, giving evidence to back up each word they choose. You might mention very naturalistic, personal, conversational.

- How does "speech" differ from narrative in its style? There are no inhibitions about repetition, sentence length, the use of "frowned-on" words (e.g. *get*, *really*), contractions (*didn't*, *it's*, etc.).

- What do children think is the main theme of the book? The child of a divorce wants to be in two places at once, or better still return to the old life.

- What other themes might someone writing about a divorcing family choose?

Focused word/sentence work, independent work

- It is suggested that, for realistic practice, the reading test should take the full 45 minutes, incorporating focused word/sentence work and independent work.

Plenary

- Discuss children's answers to questions 13, 14 and 15 of the reading test.
- Ask children this supplementary question: If you had been asked whether you wanted to read more of the book, how would you have answered? Give reasons.

DAY 2

Big Book pp. 30–32; Pupil's Book p. 88

Shared reading

- How effective do children think the author, Jacqueline Wilson, is in describing the effects of separation on a child? Do they think she describes Andy's feelings accurately? effectively? Ask for their reasons and examples.
- Recap on the main theme of the book, as discussed on day 1. Why would writing in the third person have been less effective in pursuing this theme?
- What divorce issues does the author touch on, even in this short extract? Mention the fact that the child wants to be in two places at once, each parent wants the child all the time, the parents are still acrimonious towards one another, the resentment of the "host" child to new "stepsister/ brother", the resentment of child to the "host" child, the resentment of the child towards her new "parent".

Focused word/sentence work

- Go through the answers to the reading test on day 1.
- Give a brief introduction to the independent work. Each group has a common element (phoneme, prefix, meaning, part of speech, etc.).

Independent work

- Children complete word groups according to spelling rules, etc.

Plenary

- Go through the answers to the independent work. Ones to watch:

  Section C4: *envious, victorious, notorious, previous*, etc.; not *mischievous*, which should be pronounced as spelled – *miss-chiv-us*.
  C6: Answers should all be prepositions.
  C8: Answers should all be adverbs of time.

DAY 3

Pupil's Book p. 88

Shared writing

- Imagine the headteacher is going to set the class a story to write. The drawback is that you haven't yet been told what the title is. This information should arrive at any minute, but so as not to waste time you are going to do as much of the planning as you can beforehand.

Together make a list of the important questions you must ask yourself about **any** story. Go over the "question" technique outlined for day 3 of Unit 26 (Pupil's Book p. 85).

- At this time the title ("The Big Row") could be revealed. To add to the fun, you could actually send someone to the office for the title (which you have left there in an envelope). By the time they return, explain that there is no time to plan it together and that they must do the planning themselves. Merely talk about the title (*Row* as in argument!), explaining that the story could be fact or fiction, domestic, set at school or about the wider world. Perhaps it could relate to another area of study.
- If you wish, this is an opportunity to give the children your own title appropriate to other work you are doing.

Focused word/sentence work

- Plan a story: "The Big Row".

Independent work

- Children begin to write "The Big Row".

Plenary

- Ask children to suggest differences in conventions and features between the text of a story and the way it is set out compared with other texts: e.g. no paragraph headings, few passive verbs, use of direct speech, use of contractions, informal language; there is no restriction on the way authors writes fiction – they can be as imaginative as they like.
- Do the same exercise for the texts of Unit 24 (poems), Units 3 and 4 (accounts), Unit 15 (balanced accounts) and Unit 8 (newspapers). For newspapers you may wish to mention the terms *banner headline, strapline* (subsidiary headline), *byline* (the line which says *by Fred Bloggs*).
- This exercise may well extend into future plenary sessions.

DAY 4

Big Book pp. 33–34; Pupil's Book p. 88

Shared reading

- What do all the paragraphs in the second extract represent? They are threatening questions from all those who have dealings with Andy.
- Compare the style of each speaker. Try to identify the people asking the questions.
- Why is this question chapter a very clever piece of writing? Point out that it says a lot, very effectively, about what is happening to Andy in very few lines.

Focused word/sentence work

- Analyse in detail how you have identified the speakers without any direct attribution of each question, e.g.the use of *Andrea* in Miss Maynard's and the social worker's speech, the old arithmetic (more likely to be Dad than Mum).
- Each question in the second extract means more than it says. What is the hidden "sub-text" behind each section? What overall conclusions can we draw from this brief chapter?

- Is this realistic and effective writing of speech? Ask children to give reasons and examples.
- Y6 children may not be acquainted with the "Time to go home" link with Andy Pandy. Andy Pandy was a children's TV puppet programme of the 1950s which always ended with the lullaby-like song "Time to go home".

Independent work
- Children annotate a text, working on Copymaster 27 in conjunction with the Pupil's Book.

Plenary
- Recap on the distinctive features of the texts discussed yesterday. Discuss the texts in Unit 19 (reports), Unit 18 (instructional), Unit 25 (explanatory); advertising material (promotional); text books (the Pupil's Book itself; even the Teacher's Book).

DAY 5

Big Book pp. 30–34; Pupil's Book p. 88

Shared reading
- From both extracts (and one hopes, from further experience of the book), comment on the author's style and discuss its effectiveness. Give reasons and examples at all times.
- What other books have children read recently, or are they reading now? Discuss similarities and differences in style, subject matter, etc., in comparison with *The Suitcase Kid*. Again, ask children to give reasons and examples to justify what they say.

Focused word/sentence work
- Hand out photocopies of the second extract. Discuss and demonstrate how children would answer these questions (emphasising that it is not good practice to write on real books!).

1 In the left margin write who you think is each speaker.
2 In the right margin, for each paragraph note the effect the divorce seems to be having on Andy. (You could point out that paragraph 1 mentions skipping school.)
3 In two places Andy's response (or lack of it) is indicated. Identify these and note briefly what the response is or might be. (For instance, against paragraph 1 you might write *A turns away*, *A no reply*, etc.)
4 Put a wavy line under evidence that Andy is distracted by the divorce, writing *Distracted* in the margin.
5 Put an *ADV* over one adverb, e.g. *simply*, *nowadays* (not forgetting adverbs of time, place, etc.). Put a *PP* over three present participles, e.g. *mucking*. Put a *V* over five verbs ... (and so on for nouns, adjectives, pronouns, etc., as time permits).

Independent work
- Children complete their work based on Copymaster 27.

Plenary
- Go through the answers to the text annotations.

Consolidation and extension
- Read as much of *The Suitcase Kid* to children as you can. This will enable a sustained comparison between it and *Madame Doubtfire*.
- If appropriate, the whole issue of divorce and its effects could be discussed.
- This is probably the appropriate time in the term for children to conduct the detailed language investigation required under NLS objective SL2. This could be based on the family if required, e.g. most people of older generations have a rich reservoir of family sayings and dialect words from their place of origin.

Homework
- Page 28 of the Homework Book focuses on writing questions that would provide given answers.

Unit 28 Madame Doubtfire

Key Learning Objectives

TL1	to describe and evaluate the style of an individual writer
TL5	to compare and contrast the work of a single writer
TL9	to write summaries of books or parts of books, deciding on priorities relevant to purpose
TL10	to write a brief synopsis of a text (e.g. for back cover blurb)
TL11	to write a brief helpful review tailored for real audiences
TL12	to compare texts in writing, drawing out: a) their different styles and preoccupations b) their strengths and weaknesses c) their different values and appeal to reader
WL6	to practise and extend vocabulary, e.g. through inventing word games
WL7	to experiment with language, e.g. creating new words, similes and metaphors

Range:	Comparison of work by one significant children's author; different authors' treatment of the same theme
Texts:	From *Madame Doubtfire*, Anne Fine
Resources:	Big Book 6C pp. 35–38 Pupil's Book 6 pp. 89–91 Homework Book 6 p. 29 Copymaster 28: An extended story (planning sheet) Copy of *Madame Doubtfire* Video of *Mrs Doubtfire*

Some important notes

- The NLS requirement for children to do extended written work of different sorts in Term 3 does not always sit comfortably with a day-to-day prescriptive approach to the tasks concerned. In addition, much of the comparative work between texts involves a greater depth of knowledge than can be supplied by the necessarily short extracts normally used. There may therefore be a need for a few days' reading and discussion about certain books before children are ready to undertake some of the tasks required. With this in mind, the last three units depart from the format of the rest of *Focus on Literacy*, in the following respects:
  - The extracts, together with the points to think and talk about, appear on days 1 and 2 so that children get the maximum exposure to the text as early as possible. In addition, it is hoped that you will read more of the book to children as occasions allow.
  - It is suggested that on occasion the Literacy Hour be rescheduled to allow time for planning sessions in which extended writing projects are introduced and for the extra writing needed to complete them satisfactorily. Also, having shown children the *Mrs Doubtfire* video, you may wish to schedule some time to discuss comparisons with the book.
  - For the same reason, some of the plenary sessions are left open for you to decide what is most appropriate.

- It is recommended that you read as much as possible of *Madame Doubtfire* to your class, so that children have a good basis on which to compare it with *The Suitcase Kid*, which deals with the same theme, and *The Flour Babies* (Unit 30) by the same writer. It would also enable a much fuller and more useful comparison with the film adaptation (see below).

- Because *Mrs Doubtfire*, the film version of this book, is well done, highly popular and widely available on video, the story lends itself excellently to a comparison between original and adapted work as required under the NLS guidelines. Some of the differences between the film and the book are discussed at the end of the notes for this Unit.

- NLS objective TL14 calls for the writing of an extended story, over time, on a theme identified in reading. This could be a theme from the extracts used in *Focus on Literacy*, but is likely to come from another area of in-depth study, e.g. a historical theme, or from children's own reading.

Preparation

- Have a list of stock similes ready for day 4's shared writing.

DAY 1

Big Book pp. 35–36; Pupil's Book pp. 89–90

Shared reading

- Like *The Suitcase Kid*, this book deals with the traumas of divorce, but from the father's angle rather than the child's. Most of the time Daniel's three children live with his ex-wife, Miranda. The lingering animosity between mother and father means that the atmosphere is fraught with tension, to the great distress of the children. Normally an easy-going type, Daniel, an actor, is unable to bear the lengthy separations from his children. When his wife advertises for a "daily" and childminder, he dons drag and applies. "Madame Doubtfire" gets the job and quickly establishes him/herself as a treasure. But inevitably the truth comes out …

- Introduce the background to the story, then read the first extract, which comes at the start of the book.

- Ask children to say what person this story is written in. What person was *The Suitcase Kid* written in? Which of these is the conventional narrative approach?

- Ask them to comment on the theme of the book – that the divorced father is still angry with the mother, but loves the children and wants to see more of them, no matter how desperate the means.

- What does Daniel think of his ex-wife? What evidence is there for this?

- What important information does the writer give us, without directly telling us? We gather that Dad dislikes Mum, we learn the order of the children, and the times of visits.

- How does the writer communicate that Daniel isn't sincere when he speaks nicely about his ex-wife?

Focused sentence work

- Examine closely how dialogue is handled from sentence to sentence, particularly the way the author varies the approach by:
  - putting the label *said Lydia*, etc., at different points in the speech. Note that it usually comes after the first part of the speech. Why is this?
  - putting a reaction or an action instead of *said*, etc. (e.g. *Daniel was astonished ..., Daniel peered sharply ...*).
  - using a different word instead of *said*, e.g. *remarked*.
- Is the speech natural-sounding? Ask children to give examples. How does the author achieve this?
- Introduce the independent work, explaining that they must have at least three characters in their dialogue, and that the children can be boys or girls (with real names as opposed to Child 1, 2, etc.!). The key ingredient is persuasion – characters trying to persuade other characters to do or say something.

Independent work

- Children choose three or more from these characters: mother, father, stepfather, stepmother, child 1, child 2, child 3, one other person, and write a realistic dialogue in which someone is trying to persuade another person to do something.

Plenary

- Read selected examples of children's dialogue, inviting constructive criticism, and picking up particularly on examples of imaginative and varied phrasing.

DAY 2

Big Book pp. 37–38; Pupil's Book p. 90

Shared reading

- Read the second extract.
- Ask children to think of words and phrases (e.g. *naturalistic, sensitive to feeling, descriptive, humorous, even zany*) which describe the style the extract is written in, giving evidence to back up each word they choose.
- What metaphor is sustained through several sentences? The coldness of Miranda's reaction. Trace it through each cold reference.
- Why do children think the writer features quail food in this part of the story? It adds a ludicrous touch.
- Ask children to comment on the use of humour in a scene of great emotion. Is it effective? Does it spoil it?

Focused sentence work

- Compare the humour of the second extract with the humour in *The Suitcase Kid*, e.g. in "D is for Dad" on Copymaster 27. What sort of things made children laugh in *The Suitcase Kid*? How would they describe the humour in general terms?
- Why would the zany, sardonic humour of *Madame Doubtfire* not fit in with *The Suitcase Kid*? Andy is an upset child and therefore takes herself very seriously; although Daniel is upset he still thinks wacky thoughts which are reflected in the narrative.

Planning session

- Children are to write an essay comparing *The Suitcase Kid* and *Madame Doubtfire*. Initiate a discuss of these issues:
  a) What is an essay?
  b) What is the common theme? Divorce and its effects.
  c) What common sub-themes emerge from this? You might mention animosity between ex-partners, children's distress, etc., resolution of difficulties, change of thinking, etc.
  d) In what ways is the overall treatment of the subject different in the two books? Point out the use of 1st/3rd person, child's perspective rather than father's.
  e) What are the strengths and weaknesses of each book? *The Suitcase Kid* is better at exploring the details of the child's distress; the construction of *The Suitcase Kid* is imaginative and usually effective, but is rather a straitjacket and results in one or two weak chapters such as "H is for Haiku"; *Madame Doubtfire* is very funny but slightly implausible. Ask children to give examples to support their own arguments.
  f) Do the two books have the same "messages" and values?
  g) Is the target readership different in any way? *The Suitcase Kid* seems to be aimed at a younger audience; you could point to the print size, cover, vocabulary.
  h) Do the two books have the same appeal? Ask children to give reasons for their answers.
  i) Discuss the time to be allocated to planning.

Independent work

- Children plan and write an essay comparing *The Suitcase Kid* and *Madame Doubtfire*.

Plenary

- Initiate discussion of any problems encountered during the essay planning.

DAY 3

Big Book pp. 37–38; Pupil's Book p. 91

Shared reading

- In the second extract, why does Miranda refuse Daniel's offer?
- How do children think Daniel felt about saying, *"Well, hoping really"*?
- What impression do children get of Daniel and Miranda's characters? Why were they divorced?

Shared writing

- Write a paragraph together using a sustained metaphor (e.g a cleaning lady rushing into a house and cleaning like the wind). One way to start is by collecting, in the example above, "windy" words – *to breeze along, gale, blowing*, etc. – then string them into a paragraph describing the action. Other ideas could include someone's stormy temperament or gloomy disposition.

Planning session

- Introduce the writing assignment to be planned today but written over the coming weeks – an extended story on a theme identified in children's reading.

- Discuss the following issues:
  a) Choice of theme. This may be something you wish to prescribe, or to leave to children. If the latter, discuss possible ideas.
  b) The basic ingredients of a story: beginning, middle, end, climax, character development.
  c) Other necessary qualities: a beginning which hooks the reader; readability (i.e. flow); interest (the quality that makes you want to read the next line, turn each page); balance between narrative and speech.
  d) The possibility of chapters, and how these are presented (e.g. on a new side of paper).
  e) The type of final presentation required.
  f) The time to be allocated to planning, and the desired completion date.

Independent work

- Children plan an extended story on a theme identified in their reading. Copymaster 28 could be used to aid this.

Plenary

- This session will have been shortened.
- Initiate discussion of any problems encountered during the story planning.

DAY 4

Big Book pp. 37–38; Pupil's Book p. 91

Shared writing/focused word work

- In the second extract Daniel compares the scene to being in a *Build your own story* scene. Miranda's eyes are called *cold, hard, little snowballs* (metaphor). What figure of speech would it have been if the writer had put *Miranda's eyes were like cold, hard, little snowballs*?
- Ask children the answers to some standard similes: *as hard as ...*, *as white as ...*, etc. Now invent some new similes to go with the same adjectives, e.g. *as hard as a leg of lamb from the freezer, as white as my brother's face when I pretended to be a ghost*.

Independent work

- Children continue with their extended story.

Plenary

- Your choice.

DAY 5

Pupil's Book p. 91

Shared writing

- Read three sample blurbs from book jackets (excluding *Madame Doubtfire*). Analyse what style is involved. Then, without looking at the actual one, write together a jacket blurb for *Madame Doubtfire*. Then compare it with the original.

Focused word work

- Explore some or all of these word puzzles:
  1 Palindromes (from Greek *palindromos* = running back again): e.g. *Able was I ere I saw Elba; Draw O Coward; Ten animals I slam in a net; Doc, note I dissent. A fast never prevents a fatness. I diet on cod.* What palindromic words do children know? E.g. *madam, eve, minim, sees.*
  2 Anagrams: e.g. *Daniel = nailed; Miranda = rain dam; astronomers = moon-starers; revolution = to love ruin.* Make anagrams of children's names, together and individually.
  3 Codes: Experiment with simple ones such as A = B, B = C, C = D, getting more complex as appropriate.
  4 Mention the famous pangram: *The quick brown fox jumps over the lazy dog.* It includes every letter in the alphabet.

Independent work

- Children complete, if possible, their extended story.

Plenary

- These were some of the changes when *Madame Doubtfire* was made into a film. Discuss why they were made:
  - Change in location: England to USA
  - More background: different locations, e.g. both parents at work, courtroom
  - Other characters: e.g. brother and partner, mother-in-law
  - Shows more rounded characters: D at work, D loves M, M vulnerable at work and home, much more sensitive than in book
  - Different origin of the name *Doubtfire*: from a newspaper headline
  - Different dialogue almost entirely: e.g. *It was the drink that killed him. He was run over by a Guinness truck.*
  - A lot of visual slapstick with the changeover between man and woman, not possible in the book
  - D and M's boyfriend meet
  - Different way of discovering Mrs D is Dad
  - Different showdown scene: no nude modelling, restaurant instead
  - Daniel as Mrs D on television
- Was it a good adaptation? In this writer's view, yes. Although so much was changed, the film script added a great deal that was either funny or rounded out the characters, and was faithful to the spirit of the original. At least it didn't have a corny Hollywood ending in which M and D get back together.

Consolidation and extension

- Encourage children to look further into word puzzles and games. There are many good books on the market.
- Crosswords, in particular, take time to get into, so to work at one via the OHP might be useful, learning the conventions of the crossword clue.
- Discuss other book/film translations and their effectiveness.

Homework

- Page 29 of the Homework Book focuses on word puzzles.

Unit 29 Atmospheric Poems

Key Learning Objectives

TL3	to describe and evaluate the style of an individual poet
TL4	to comment critically on the overall impact of a poem – showing how language and themes have been developed
TL5	to compare and contrast the work of a single writer
TL6	to look at connections and contrasts in the work of different writers
TL14	to write an extended story, worked on over time on a theme identified in reading
WL5	to invent words using known roots, prefixes and suffixes
WL6	to practise and extend vocabulary, e.g. through inventing word games such as puns, riddles, crosswords
WL7	to experiment with language, e.g. creating new words, similes and metaphors

Range:	Comparison of work by significant poets
Texts:	From "The Lady of Shalott", Alfred, Lord Tennyson
	"First Day at School", Roger McGough
Resources:	Big Book 6C pp. 39–43
	Pupil's Book 6 pp. 92–93
	Homework Book 6 p. 30
	Copymaster 29: Crossword
	Full version of "The Lady of Shalott"

Preparation

- Throughout the week the independent work consists of writing the extended story planned during Unit 28. The aim should be to have this finished by day 5, because other work awaits in Unit 30. It may therefore be necessary to devote a considerable time beyond the Literacy Hour to finishing the stories to display standard, and also to sharing them with the rest of the class.

- To read together other poems by Roger McGough and Alfred, Lord Tennyson would be useful in assessing the style of each poet.

- You may wish to have the poem "The Eagle" by Tennyson on OHP transparency for day 2.

- Have the riddle on an OHP transparency or written on a board for day 3.

- Collect a few interesting objects that children could suggest new names for on day 4.

- Have a list of common prefixes and suffixes suitable for inventing words ready for day 5.

DAY 1

Big Book pp. 39–41; Pupil's Book pp. 92–93

Shared reading/writing

- Victorian poets and painters were entranced by the romantic legends of King Arthur, Guinevere and the Knights of the Round Table. Tennyson wrote much poetry about them. Pre-Raphaelites such as Rossetti and Burne-Jones painted many pictures of them.

- Read the selected verses from "The Lady of Shalott". What atmosphere does Tennyson create (still, gentle, sad, lonely, etc.)?

- Remind children of "The Charge of the Light Brigade". How do the two poems compare in mood?

- What other similarities and differences can they identify between the two poems? The rhythm is very different; Tennyson uses repeated rhyme in both; the purposes of writing are very different.

- Do they like the poems? Why/why not? Which of the two poems do they prefer, and why?

Focused word/sentence work

- What is unusual about the rhyme scheme of "The Lady of Shalott"? AAAABCCCB; repetition of the same rhyme over several lines.

- Comment on the style of the poem – smooth, stately. How is this achieved? Mention the repeated rhyme and the long vowel sounds (*lie, rye, go, blow*, etc.)

- Discuss these words: *wold* (hill); *bower* (personal room); *greaves* (leg armour).

Independent work

- Comprehension.

Plenary

- Discuss answers to the independent comprehension work.

- Read again "The Charge of the Light Brigade" (Unit 4) and talk once more about the circumstances in which it was written.

- Then read the full version of "The Lady of Shalott".

DAY 2

Big Book pp. 39–41; Pupil's Book p. 93

Shared reading

- Read two verses from "The Lady of Shalott" (*A bow-shot from ...* and *She left the web ...*), and the last verse from "The Charge of the Light Brigade". Also read "The Eagle" by Tennyson (using an OHP transparency if possible):

The Eagle: A Fragment

He clasps the crag with crooked hands;
Close to the sun in lonely lands,
Ringed with the azure world, he stands.

The wrinkled sea beneath him crawls;
He watches from his mountain walls,
And like a thunderbolt he falls.

Alfred, Lord Tennyson

- What general features can children identify about Tennyson's style? It is rhythmic, rhyming – often a rhyme is repeated for several successive lines. It has been described as "musical and majestic". What does this mean? Do children agree? Which of the poems do they like most? least?

Focused word/sentence work

- What figures of speech can children identify in "The Eagle"? Mention alliteration; metaphor (*hands, wrinkled, walls*); simile (*like a thunderbolt*); personification (*crawls*). Make sure that all know what these terms mean.

Independent work

- Children continue writing their extended story planned in Unit 28.
- If they have finished their story, they begin writing a narrative poem.

Plenary

- Discuss children's extended stories, perhaps reading selected examples, checking for evidence of the necessary ingredients – flow, interest, dialogue handling, climaxes, etc.

DAY 3

Pupil's Book p. 93

Shared reading and writing

- Have a look at this riddle. Before solving it, identify the elements which go to make one, i.e. rhyme, pairing of connected words. The very clever ones link the words on each line with the word at the end.

  My first is in REAR but not in BACK.
  My second is in PARCEL and also in PACK.
  My third is in MINI but not in SMALL.
  My fourth is in LANKY but not in TALL.
  My fifth is in BENCH but not in CHAIR.
  My sixth is in HORSE but not in HAIR.
  My seventh is in WOMAN but not in her FORM.
  My whole can be the result of a storm.

  (Answer: RAINBOW)

- Now make up a riddle together, starting with the answer and working backwards.

Focused word work

- What is a pun? A play on words that relies on a word having two meanings:

  My wife came here from the West Indies. Jamaica? *No, she came of her own accord.*

  Did you hear about the chap who stole a lorry load of elastic bands? He was put away for a long stretch.

  Adhesive advert: Our word is your bond.

  Outside the factory making mole wrenches: Every mole that leaves us is a wrench.

  You could also cite some of the crude attempts at puns in tabloid headlines.

- Try some punning round the class. The art is to keep a vaguely logical thread of conversation going with a pun sub-text on a theme, e.g. *Keep the thread of conversation going without pinning your hopes too high or being needled if the children don't get the point or the*

results are only sew-sew! Children's names make a good starting point.

Independent work

- Children continue writing their extended story and/or narrative poem.

Plenary

- If time permits, have another crack at punning. *A good yolk could be eggsactly what you need.* Cue *chickening out, batteries flat, a free range of subjects*, etc. etc. ad nauseam.

DAY 4

Big Book pp. 42–43; Pupil's Book p. 93

Shared reading

- Read "First Day at School".
- Ask children to identify the overall theme of the poem – the fears and mistaken ideas of a small child stepping into the big strange world of school.
- Is home really so far away? Why does it seem so?
- Does the poem strike a chord with children by bringing back any recollections?
- How effective is the poem? How does it achieve this? Point out the very realistic baby talk as if it were the actual thoughts of a 5-year-old, the transparent fear running through it, repetition, childish misconceptions.
- Ask children to look up the word *misconceptions*, to list as many misconceptions as they can in two minutes, then compare notes.
- Compare the poem with other McGough poems children know. What is similar?
- What is different about this poem? It is deeper in thought than some, making a serious point in a humorous way.

Focused word/sentence work

- What invented words can children find in the poem? They should spot *millionbillionwillion, lessin, glassrooms, lellowwellies*. Ask them to invent new names for some well-known items: e.g. fridge = *winter box*; slug = *slimewander*; TV remote control = *zapper*; to splatter, etc. = *to marmalise, discumknockerate, spiflicate*).
- Invite children to invent some metaphors for a 4-year-old child starting school, e.g. *an island of tearful loneliness*. Do the same for an 11-year-old starting at secondary school (e.g. *a small fish in a big pond, a tiny pebble amongst boulders*).
- Together invent some similes for *small beside large*, or vice versa, e.g. *like a Goliath beside David, like a tank beside a tricycle*. Convert these into metaphors, e.g. *There he stood, a tank beside my tricycle* ... Which works better – simile or metaphor?

Independent work

- Children continue writing their extended story or narrative poem.

Plenary

- Begin to sample the extended stories written during the week, inviting constructive criticism. Clearly, as with the writing of the stories, this may need further time beyond the Literacy Hour.

DAY 5

Big Book pp. 42–43; Pupil's Book p. 93

Shared reading

- Read "First Day at School" again. What is the child's impression of bigger children? Does the school seem any different in size now than it did then?

- In this context, talk about the meaning of the words *subjective* and *objective* (related, of course, to the subject and object in a sentence).

- Read the Roger McGough poems in Units 9 and 24. How would children describe his style? Assess it against criteria such as humour, naturalism, rhyme, metre, choice of subject.

Focused word/sentence work

- Discuss well-known prefixes and suffixes that lend themselves to inventing new words, e.g. *ambi-* = both, giving *ambifootstrous* = able to kick with both feet; *-logy* = study/practice of, giving *laziology* = skiving; *trans-* = across, giving *transgrassing* = going across someone's lawn; *-phobe* = hater of, *post-* = after, giving *postophobe* = teacher who hates people arriving after school has started.

- Look at these word squares:

```
O R A L
M A R E
E V E N
N E A T
```

```
S A T O R
A R E P O
T E N E T
O P E R A
R O T A S
```

which means in Latin: *The sower Arepo guides wheels with care.*

- The answer to this one is a square puzzle. Try starting from the second clue.

  The name of an insect my first,
  My second no doubt you possess,
  My third is my second transposed,
  And my fourth is a shelter, I guess.

```
G N A T
N A M E
A M E N
T E N T
```

Independent work

- Children continue writing their extended story or narrative poem.

Plenary

- Introduce children to this comic alphabet. Explain some and see if they can get the rest.

  A is for 'orses
  B for mutton
  ... yourself (C)
  ... vescence (F)
  ... leather (L)
  ... sis (M)
  ... the rainbow (O)
  ... the bus (Q)
  ... mo (R)
  ... two (T)
  ... me (U)
  ... breakfast (X)

- Try another sort of word puzzle: e.g. *MAUD = mad about you; EV EN = break even; CAR JACK TON = jack-in-a-box; NOOS = back soon; 02EMOH = nothing to write home about.*

Consolidation and extension

- Play some oral word games, including old favourites like Just a Minute.

- Do more work on crossword puzzle clues and the "secret" language they use.

- Look for external sites in which to display children's recent written work – the local pub, the supermarket, the church.

Homework

- Page 30 of the Homework Book focuses on crosswords, as does Copymaster 29.

Unit 30 Flour Babies

Key Learning Objectives

TL1	to describe and evaluate the style of an individual writer
TL5	to compare and contrast the work of a single writer
TL9	to write summaries of books or parts of books, deciding on priorities relevant to purpose
TL11	to write a brief helpful review tailored for real audiences
TL12	to compare texts in writing, drawing out: a) their different styles and preoccupations b) their strengths and weaknesses c) their different values and appeal to reader

Range:	Comparison of work by one significant children's author
Text:	From *Flour Babies*, Anne Fine
Resources:	Big Book 6C pp. 44–47 Pupil's Book 6 pp. 94–95 Homework Book 6 p. 31 Copymaster 30: Books by Anne Fine Copy of *Flour Babies*

Preparation

- Arrange for a suitable outlet for the book reviews which children will produce for homework. This could be reading aloud to another class or an assembly, or the display of finished reviews somewhere where other children in the school can read them. They could even be e-mailed to children of a twinned school.

- It is recommended that you read as much as possible of *Flour Babies* to your class, so that children have a good basis on which to compare it with *Madame Doubtfire* by the same writer. In any case, because valid comparisons between the two cannot be drawn until children have become more familiar with the books, the written comparative work only begins on day 3. There is also some shuffling of Literacy Hour sessions on days 3, 4 and 5 to allow enough time for necessary shared introductory work and the independent writing that follows.

DAY 1

Big Book pp. 44–45; Pupil's Book pp. 94–95

Shared reading

- As well as providing a useful contrast and comparison with *Madame Doubtfire*, *Flour Babies* is looking forward to secondary school, and thus is appropriate to this time of the school year. Like *The Suitcase Kid*, it also concerns a child coming to terms with parental separation. Again it is highly recommended as a "class read".

- The first extract comes at the start of the book. What information does the author get over, without telling us directly? We glean that Mr Cartright was large, the class was 4C, 4C weren't very bright, the project was going to last for three weeks, and it was to be about something domestic in character.

- How many differences from *Madame Doubtfire* can children identify straight away? Ask them to provide evidence for their suggestions. They might mention that the setting is school rather than domestic, the age group is different, a single boy is the subject rather than a family, and the subject is of a different intelligence level – less articulate.

- What similarities do they notice? Both books have a present-day setting, naturalistic dialogue, subtle introduction of information, interplay of adult and children.

- Why does the writer give *Time* a capital *T*? To signify the importance of the draw for the project.

- Why does the writer bring Simon in separately from the rest of the class? As in a film or stage show, this draws attention to a lead character in a most effective way.

- Discuss these words: *latent, clerical error.*

Focused word/sentence work

- In what different ways does Anne Fine get across the importance of the vote? *Time ...*; the effect of Mr Cartright's vote threat on a noisy class.

- What are all the speeches about: *"Hi, nit-face!"* etc.? They are the greetings of classmates.

- Who says *"Get a brain, Simon Martin"*?

- *Simon Martin ... Martin Simon ... Of course.* What does this sentence represent? These are Mr Cartright's thoughts. Notice that the author doesn't actually tell us this; good writing often credits the reader with imagination. What do the ellipses mean here?

- *It was almost Time ...* Why does Anne Fine use an ellipsis here, rather than a full stop? To add suspense – a lingering expectation.

- Introduce the independent work. Ask how Mr Cartright might have been feeling, and encourage children to put this across in their writing.

Independent work

- Children write a summary of the events described in the first extract from Mr Cartright's point of view.

Plenary

- Read selected examples of children's independent work, particularly looking for those who have successfully imagined what Mr Cartright might have been thinking and expressed it appropriately.

DAY 2

Big Book pp. 44–45; Pupil's Book pp. 94–95

Shared writing

- Write together a summary of the events in the first extract as if you were a school inspector sitting at the back of the class. What might his/her attitude be to the class and to Mr Cartright's method of dealing with them? Include an explanation of the circumstances leading up to the extract, i.e. the vote that was impending, and its purpose. How should the language use change? It should become more formal, impersonal and "passive" where possible.

Focused word/sentence work

- Examine how speech is handled in the extract. What seems to be the rule for where the speech is placed in a sentence? It is almost invariably at the start. Recap on the reason for this – maintaining pace and interest. If a "label" has to be attached to the speech telling us who says it and how, where is this usually placed? It comes after a few words of the speech.

- Note that none of the string of pupils' speeches has a "label". Why is this? Again this is for pace, but also because who said it is unimportant. A writer should not get bogged down in unnecessary detail.

- *Another roar of laughter.* Is this a sentence? Why not? Does it matter? Why has the author chosen not to say, e.g. *There was another roar of laughter,* or *Another roar of laughter greeted this?* Make the point that pace in writing is important, as is economy of words. Mention the golden rule: Never use a long word where a short one would do.

- Point out the phrase *Not for nothing was he called ...* What does it mean? He was called Old Carthorse for very good reason – he was large! This use of the negatived opposite is a common figure of speech called litotes (pronounced *lie-toh-tees*). Think of other examples, e.g. *How are you?* Not bad!; *It is not unreasonable to ask ...; It was not unusual to ...*

- Introduce the independent work. Discuss: a) What would the pupils be thinking about before and after Simon's entry? How would their expression differ from Mr Cartright's or the school inspector's? b)What would Simon have been thinking before and after entry? What might he have been a bit mystified about? The silence before his entry and why this should be.

Independent work

- Children write a summary of the events described in the first extract either from Simon Martin's point of view or from the point of view of one of the other people in the class.

Plenary

- Read selected examples of children's independent work, particularly looking for those who have successfully imagined what pupils might have been thinking, and expressed it appropriately.

- Ask who has read other books of Anne Fine's. Mention that in plenary session tomorrow you would like them to give a brief introduction to the book and an opinion on it. If they are able to bring a copy, and read brief examples of the text, so much the better. (If no child has read further Anne Fine books, choose children to talk about other appropriate books.)

DAY 3

Big Book pp. 46–47; Pupil's Book p. 95

Shared reading

- Introduce the second extract by explaining what the flour babies were and what the purpose of the project was.

- Ask in what way *Flour Babies* shares the same theme as *Madame Doubtfire.* What was Simon worried about?

- Look back at the description of Simon in the first extract. What was he like then? How might he have changed? What was the purpose of the first description? It helps emphasise the later mellowing of his character.

- What would children say Anne Fine's strengths as a writer seem to be? Has she any apparent weaknesses?

Shared writing

- Pre-plan the independent writing task. Ask for ideas on how such a comparison should be organised, with reference to a brief summary of subject, style, characterisation (explain this term), strengths, weaknesses, likely appeal to readers, personal reactions and preferences.

- Ask children how they are going to support what they say. Stress the use of relevant examples, and the need to write a good conclusion.

Independent work

- Children plan a comparison of *Flour Babies* and *Madame Doubtfire* (and if appropriate, other books written by Anne Fine). Copymaster 30 may be useful.

Plenary

- Discuss other books by Anne Fine (or if necessary, other authors) that children may have read, asking them to give a brief summary of the plot and an evaluation of the book, perhaps reading very brief extracts of parts they enjoyed.

DAY 4

Big Book pp. 44–47; Pupil's Book p. 95

Shared reading

- Write together a piece describing and evaluating Anne Fine's writing (or alternatively any other author of whom the children have read to an appropriate extent). Ask children to suggest what ingredients ought to go into such a piece (e.g. typical subjects, style, characterisation, dialogue, comparisons with other authors).

Focused word/sentence work

- Referring to the independent work, revisit useful words and phrases for linking comparing sentences: *while, whereas, similarly, in the same way, in contrast to, nevertheless, on the other hand,* etc.

- Point out the sentence in the second extract beginning *Slipping from the desk ...* What three pieces of information does it convey? Which is the main clause? Explain that this is a classic three-clause sentence, with the main idea in the middle and additional information at front and back – any more would be overloaded, less would have been too short (since simpler sentences come before and after it). Stress the importance of varied sentence length in good writing.

- Which person is the first part of the second extract written in? What about the part beginning *DAY 4?* Examine the differences between Simon's "own" writing and that of the author in the narrative. Does the author put Simon's words realistically? If so, how does she achieve it? Look at sentence length, vocabulary, use of contractions. Where does the extract go back into the third person?

Independent work

- Children continue with their comparison between *Flour Babies*, *Madame Doubtfire*, etc.

Plenary

- This session could be given over to more independent writing time, or alternatively you could give other children a chance to describe books they have read in a systematic way, as in the day 3 plenary session.

DAY 5

Pupil's Book p. 95

Shared writing

- Plan together how to go about the homework task, which is to write a book review of any book children have read and enjoyed. Explain that this review is going to be read (or heard) by a wider audience. Give details of this, asking children to bear this in mind at all times.

- The key thing is that the review must be practical and helpful, genuinely "selling" the book to those who read the review. With this in mind, children of average and higher-than-average ability ought to choose a book that is not too widely known by others.

- Discuss the elements of a good book review, particularly bearing in mind the ideas set out in the Homework Book, i.e. brief summary of plot, description of characters, characterisation, favourite parts, strengths, weaknesses, personal opinion with reasons, conclusion.

Independent work

- Children continue with the comparison between *Flour Babies*, *Madame Doubtfire*, etc.

Plenary

- Read selected examples of the children's independent work, inviting constructive criticism and particularly praising those which have achieved the right balance and approriate comparative phraseology.

Consolidation and extension

- Ask children to discuss/write about secondary school – their existing knowledge of it, hopes, fears, etc.

- Ask children to discuss/write about caring for a younger brother or sister – the pleasure and the pain.

- Compile a class anthology of book reviews, or perhaps share your book recommendations with other classes.

Homework

- Page 31 of the Homework Book focuses on planning a book review.

 **Copymasters**

**Copymaster 1
Unit 1**

Describing an event

Use this sheet to plan your description. Write notes, not full sentences.

Details of the scene before the event

_____
_____
_____

Details of people there before the event

_____
_____
_____

How did the event start? How did people react?

_____
_____
_____
_____

What happened as the event proceeded? Remember to include what was said.

_____
_____
_____
_____

How did things reach a climax?

_____
_____
_____
_____

What happened in the end? How did you or other people feel?

_____
_____
_____
_____

A good sentence to end with:

_____
_____

Focus on Literacy Teacher's Resource Book 6 © John McIlwain, HarperCollins*Publishers* Ltd 1999

Name _____

**Copymaster 2
Unit 2**

Play scripts

Write a short play script for one scene of a story
you are reading. Use no more than three characters.

Title of your play _____

from (title of book): _____ **Author**: _____

Characters (names with a very brief description for each):

_____
_____
_____

Scene 1

Setting (brief description):

_____
_____
_____

Time – past (give details), present or future (give details):

_____
_____

Focus on Literacy Teacher's Resource Book 6 © John McIlwain, HarperCollins*Publishers* Ltd 1999

Copymaster 3
Unit 3

Journal of a Russian gunner

Use this sheet to plan your account. Write brief, clear notes, not full sentences.

Where were the guns?

_____

Where were you?

_____

Where were the English cavalry?

_____

What did you think when the cavalry started to advance?

_____

What did you say?

_____

What did the gunners near you say?

_____

What was happening as the cavalry approached?

_____

What happened as the cavalry passed through? How did you feel? Were you hurt?

_____

_____

What was the scene after the battle was over?

_____

_____

What did you think then

... about yourself?

_____

... about the slaughter of the cavalry?

_____

When and where are you writing this journal?

_____

What are your thoughts now as you look back to the Charge?

_____

_____

_____

Focus on Literacy Teacher's Resource Book 6 © John McIlwain, HarperCollins*Publishers* Ltd 1999

Comparing accounts

Compare the two accounts of the Charge of the Light Brigade (George Loy Smith's and Alfred, Lord Tennyson's). Use this sheet to help you.

1. How do the two accounts differ in their form and appearance?

_____

2. What person are the accounts written in (1st, 2nd, 3rd, etc.)?

Smith's: _____ Tennyson's: _____

3. What was Smith's aim in writing his account?

_____

4. What are the main things that Smith writes about? List three.

_____

_____

_____

5. What was Tennyson's aim in writing his poem?

_____

6. What are the main things that Tennyson writes about? List three.

_____

_____

_____

7. Look at your answers to questions 4 and 6. Write a sentence comparing the contents of the two accounts. Construct it like this: Smith writes about ... whereas Tennyson writes about ...

_____

_____

_____

8. Which of the two accounts is more critical? Why is this?

_____

_____

9. In your opinion, which of the two accounts, if either, is more successful? Give reasons for your views.

_____

_____

_____

_____

_____

Copymaster 5
Unit 5

Planning a biography

Use this sheet to plan a biography. Write brief, clear notes, **not** full sentences.

Full name of the person you are writing about: _____

When was he/she born? _____

Where was he/she born? _____

What job(s) did their father/mother have?

_____

Other details of childhood background, e.g. type of house, rich or poor, friends

_____

_____

What education did they have? e.g. schools, colleges
How well did they do?

_____

_____

How did their career develop?

_____

_____

_____

_____

Other details, e.g. character, reasons for success or failure

_____

_____

_____

_____

_____

_____

_____

_____

_____

What are your sources of information? e.g. books, CDs, Internet. Give details. If possible, use at least two sources.

_____

_____

Focus on Literacy Teacher's Resource Book 6 © John McIlwain, HarperCollins*Publishers* Ltd 1999

Creating a glossary

A **glossary** is an alphabetical list of terms or words and their meanings in a specific subject or text.

Make a glossary of terms related to the extract from *Macbeth*.

Use a colon (:) between each term and its definition. The first has been done for you.

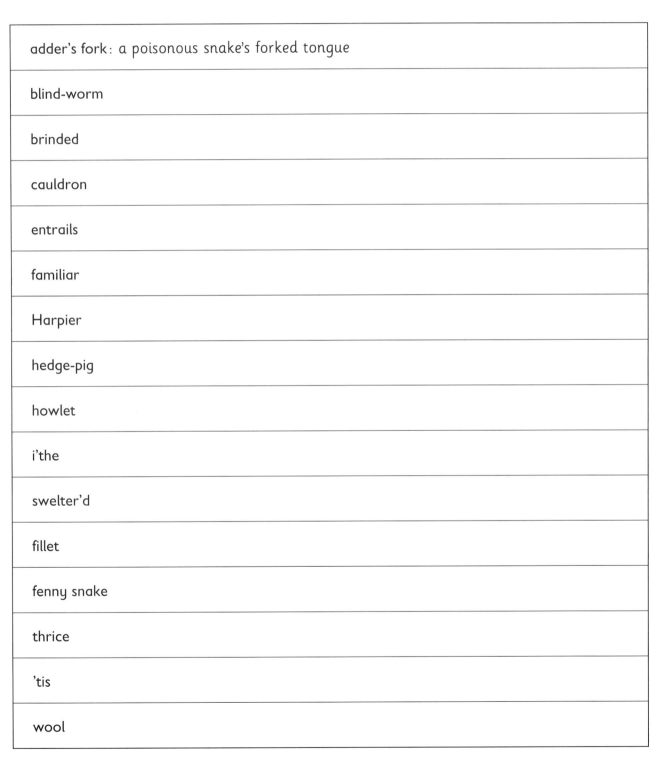

adder's fork: a poisonous snake's forked tongue
blind-worm
brinded
cauldron
entrails
familiar
Harpier
hedge-pig
howlet
i'the
swelter'd
fillet
fenny snake
thrice
'tis
wool

If you have further time, find out and write down what other words in the passage mean.

Focus on Literacy Teacher's Resource Book 6 © John McIlwain, HarperCollins*Publishers* Ltd 1999

Name _____

The Seven Ages of Man

Use this sheet to prepare for your retelling of the speech from *As You Like It*.
Under each heading write two or three sentences.

Introduction

Shakespeare compares our lives to

1. The infant

   – in a nurse's arms

   – making whimpering noises

   – being sick

2. The schoolboy

3.

4.

5.

6.

7.

Focus on Literacy Teacher's Resource Book 6 © John McIlwain, HarperCollins*Publishers* Ltd 1999

Name _____

Copymaster 8
Unit 8

A newspaper report

Use these sections to make notes for your report.
Use the other side of the sheet to write a rough version of the full story.

1. Main events of story – brief notes only

2. Background details – brief notes only

3. What may happen next – brief notes only

4. Details of eyewitnesses – names, ages, other information

5. Quotes from eyewitnesses

6. Ideas for headline

7. Summary of story for introductory paragraph

Focus on Literacy Teacher's Resource Book 6 © John McIlwain, HarperCollins*Publishers* Ltd 1999

**Copymaster 9
Unit 9**

Personification

Write down verbs for human actions that might go under each of these headings.

Sounds: verbal (e.g. shout, whisper)

Sounds: non-verbal (e.g. moan)

Ways of looking (e.g. stare)

Ways of moving (e.g. crawl)

Ways of not moving (e.g. sit)

Ways of using the mouth (e.g. munch, kiss)

Ways of responding (e.g. hesitate, get angry)

Ways of dealing with others (e.g. speak to, shake hands with)

Focus on Literacy Teacher's Resource Book 6 © John McIlwain, HarperCollins*Publishers* Ltd 1999

Copymaster 10
Unit 10

Our region

Write brief notes under the following headings.

Name of region _____

Location (where it is, related to the rest of the country)

Main features (e.g. rivers, hill ranges, mountains, cities)

Brief history of the area

Scenic places in the region (name three to five)

Interesting historical places (three to five)

Any things that visitors might not like

General information about where to stay

Ideas for an exciting introduction

**Copymaster 11
Unit 11**

Changing moods

Location 1 _____

Mood 1 _____

Adjectives and verbs which reflect the mood

Details of the scene (which reflect the mood you want to describe)

Mood 2 _____

Adjectives and verbs which reflect the changed mood

Details of the scene (which reflect the changed mood)

Location 2 _____

Mood 1 _____

Adjectives and verbs which reflect the mood

Details of the scene (which reflect the mood you want to describe)

Mood 2 _____

Adjectives and verbs which reflect the changed mood

Details of the scene (which reflect the changed mood)

Focus on Literacy Teacher's Resource Book 6 © John McIlwain, HarperCollins*Publishers* Ltd 1999

**Copymaster 12
Unit 12**

Good King Wenceslas –
the page's story

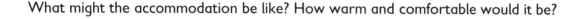

Imagine you are Good King Wenceslas's servant.
Make brief notes under these headings.

Background information

Where might you live in the castle?

What might the accommodation be like? How warm and comfortable would it be?

What might your outdoor clothes be like?

How does your master King Wenceslas treat you?

Details of the journey

What did you think of the idea? (Remember your clothing!)

What did you have to do before the journey?

How did you feel after getting the logs, etc.?

What was your opinion of the weather? Did this differ from the king's view?

What were you like at walking?

What happened to you on the journey?

How did the old man react when you gave him the gifts?

When and how did you return to the castle?

Plan the ending of your account.

Copymaster 13
Unit 13

A sudden change of scene

General plan

1 Who is going to change scene?   2 What are the two main scenes?   3 How does the character change from Scene 1 to Scene 2?   4 How are you going to emphasise the difference between Scenes 1 and 2?

Background details about main character

Scene 1

1 Describe the scene.   2 What is your character doing in it?   3 What is being said?

Transition

What happens to make the change of scene? What does your character feel about it? What is said or thought?

Scene 2

1 Describe the scene.   2 What is your character doing in it?   3 What is being said? (Make sure that everything is different.)

What happens next?

Focus on Literacy Teacher's Resource Book 6 © John McIlwain, HarperCollins*Publishers* Ltd 1999

Planning a haiku

Choose an everyday object: _____

Answer these questions about it, **but try to think of your object in a different way from usual**. Leave out any answers which are not relevant to your object.

1. What does it look like?

_____

2. What does it feel like?

_____

3. What does it sound like?

_____

4. What does it smell like?

_____

5. What use does it have?

_____

6. How does it move?

_____

7. What do you think about it?

_____

My two best ideas are numbers _____ and _____.

Now turn over the sheet and work with your ideas to make a haiku. Don't be afraid to write it and rewrite it several times.

Planning a tanka

Tankas have 5 lines of 5, 7, 5, 7, 7 syllables.

1. Write a 5-syllable line about being happy:

_____

2. Write a 5-syllable line about being sad:

_____

3. Write a 5-syllable line about being angry:

_____

4. Write a 5-syllable line about being alone:

_____

The one I am going to use is number _____.

Copymaster 15
Unit 15

Zulema Menem

Use this sheet to help you write a set of notes on Zulema Menem.
Good notes should be tidy and have a very clear structure.

1. Background

a) _____

_____

b) _____

_____

c) _____

_____

2. Father and daughter

a) _____

_____

b) _____

_____

3. Zulema and shopping

a) _____

_____

b) _____

_____

c) _____

_____

4. Father and daughter in London

a) _____

_____

b) _____

_____

c) _____

_____

Jabberwocky

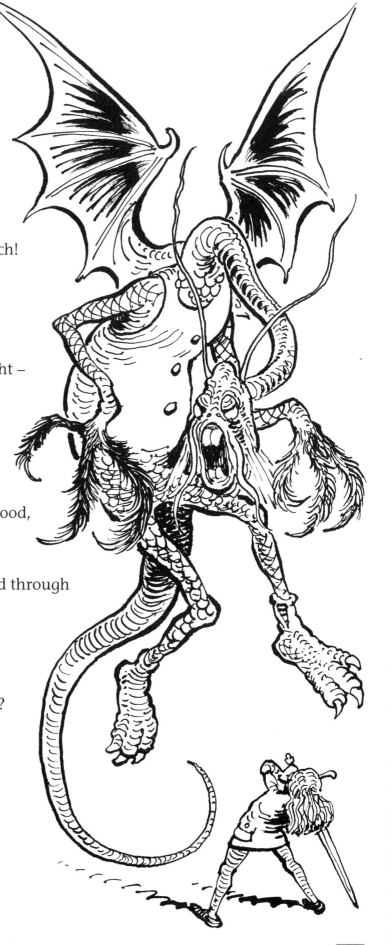

'Twas brillig and the slithy toves
Did gyre and gimble in the wabe;
All mimsy were the borogoves,
And the mome raths outgrabe.

"Beware the Jabberwock, my son!
The jaws that bite, the claws that catch!
Beware the jubjub bird, and shun
The frumious Bandersnatch!"

He too his vorpal sword in hand:
Long time the manxome foe he sought –
So rested he by the Tumtum tree,
And stood awhile in thought.

And as in uffish thought he stood,
The Jabberwock, with eyes of flame,
Came whiffling through the tulgey wood,
And burbled as it came!

One, two! One, two! And through and through
The vorpal blade went snicker-snack!
He left it dead, and with its head
He went galumphing back.

"And hast thou slain the Jabberwock?
Come to my arms, my beamish boy!
O frabjous day! Callooh! Callay!"
He chortled in his joy.

'Twas brillig and the slithy toves
Did gyre and gimble in the wabe;
All mimsy were the borogoves,
And the mome raths outgrabe.

Lewis Carroll

**Copymaster 17
Unit 17**

An animal that can talk

Remember to plan these things: ☑

Setting (where and when your story happens) ❑

Main *animal* (e.g. What animal is it? What is it like?) ❑

Other characters ❑

How the story *begins* ❑

What *happens* ❑

Speech bubble: COME ALONG, JOHNNY — TIME FOR WALKIES!

This space is for **very brief notes** to help you plan your ideas. Your notes will not be marked.

Focus on Literacy Teacher's Resource Book 6 © John McIlwain, HarperCollins*Publishers* Ltd 1999

A person who makes me laugh

This interview planning sheet is for very brief notes to help you plan your ideas. Your notes will not be marked.

· ·

Write your useful phrases here.

A glossary of terms

Use your notes or a dictionary to write definitions for these terms:

cavalry _____

_____

chaos _____

_____

chariot _____

_____

column _____

_____

Cretan _____

_____

impetus _____

_____

interminable _____

_____

javelin _____

_____

legionary _____

_____

pilum _____

_____

taut _____

_____

yoke-pole _____

_____

Focus on Literacy Teacher's Resource Book 6 © John McIlwain, HarperCollins*Publishers* Ltd 1999

A farewell letter

I was glad to say yes _____ it would give me the chance of seeing Juliet and

Mark for the last time.

But _____ had already gone. There was an envelope addressed to Mr Singh

stuck in the door frame. Grandfather _____ it and as he read a smile appeared

on his face.

"Where've they gone, Grandfather? What _____ it say?"

He handed the _____ to me to read.

Dear Mr Singh,

It's dawn and we want to be on the road before the early-birds get to

_____ allotments. We thought about _____ you said last

_____ and you may have a point. We've decided to go

_____ _____ and look up our parents and see how things

stand. Mark and I _____ start making plans for what we want to

do. I want to see if I can get a place at college and train to be a teacher.

We both want to _____ you for everything _____ done

for us. It was great having that time to think in your allotment shed. Please

thank Phil and Baba and Minnie for their friendship and your daughter and

wife for the wonderful meal last night. We'll be in touch and let you

_____ what happens to us.

With best _____

Mark and Juliet

P.S. There's a tin of sardines for Zebedee on the shelf. _____ give

him a cuddle from us.

Name _____

The birth of a poem

The brakes squealed piercingly, and the _____ juddered to an

unexpected halt. The jolt forced his _____ open. He turned to

look through the rain-dappled carriage _____, across countless

metal rails to the monotone landscape beyond. London in winter. Slate

rooftops _____ endlessly away into the distance under a solid

blanket of cloud, the bleak skyline _____ only by steeples

and factory chimneys. Rainwater poured along a thousand gutters.

A _____ drab buildings added their _____ to the

_____. Not a bird, not a blade of grass, not so much as a

leafless branch in view.

    As lights flickered on in the November streets below, a sudden,

chilling _____ overtook him. Will it all be _____ this

one day? When the last bulldozer has done its work, when the last

brickie puts down his trowel, when the last farm tractor is left to rust in

the rain? In a _____ years from now,

where will the countryside be? He let his

eyes close again and a thought emerged

from the _____ – a rabbit,

alone on a small patch of grass, amid

a wasteland of barbed wire and concrete.

The only rabbit in _____.

    The train jerked once more and began to _____. He pulled

a notebook and pencil from his raincoat and hastily began to

_____. "We are going to see the rabbit ..."

Focus on Literacy Teacher's Resource Book 6 © John McIlwain, HarperCollins*Publishers* Ltd 1999

Main and subordinate clauses

The subject controls the main verb. It often comes first, but not always!

A Find the subject of each sentence. Put a ring round the word.
The first one has been done for you.

1. As the car door was opened for him, (James Bond) stepped out.

2. Behind his huge desk, M puffed away at a pipe.

3. Are you listening to me?

4. "Are you listening to me?" said Goldfinger.

5. Behind the tree, wearing a man's overcoat, stood a woman with a gun.

B Put a ring round the subject of each sentence.
Then put a wavy line under the main verb.
The first one has been done for you.

1. "I think your golf is better than mine," (Goldfinger) muttered.

2. Keeping check on the door, Bond photographed the plans in the safe.

3. Rubbing his forehead wearily, Q turned back towards his office.

4. "007, do you know what you have started?" said M, looking out of the window.

5. Its paintwork gleaming, the sports car was wheeled from the garage by the mechanics.

6. From his armchair, Goldfinger motioned lazily at the pool of deadly piranha fish, then pressed the button.

C Now underline the main clauses.
The first one has been done for you.

1. An evil gleam in his eye, (Goldfinger) set the bomb ticking.

2. Q gave the exploding torch to Bond, who immediately began to juggle with it.

3. Oddjob, with his lethal hat ready to throw, moved slowly forward.

4. The sun was setting as Bond drove up to the club.

5. M put his pipe, still smoking, on his desk.

6. Like an expert, Bond slung the car, an Aston Martin DB4, smoothly round the hairpin bends.

The killer spelling test

David got off the bus at the stop before Bloggsbridge Bus Station and turned

into Education Road. As _____ his mate Wesley was waiting at the

corner, trying to _____ his lunch box round a tree. After six years at

Bloggie they didn't need to exchange greetings. A nod and a grunt was

_____ and the two _____ went off up the road together

shoulder to shoulder.

　　Normally he and Wes told jokes or punched each other or tried to trip each

other up, but today David just wasn't in the mood. Today was _____.

Today was THE day. The day of the killer spelling test.

　　"To get you ready for your national tests, my little angels!"

Mrs Rose had _____, rubbing her hands together

with glee, a wicked grin on her face.

　　It was all right for Wes and Dawinder and Angela.

They _____ got full marks at spelling. David

_____, even when he'd tried his hardest to learn

them. He _____ he had written out more spellings

at playtimes than they'd had hot _____.

"Diss-something or other", Mrs Lively, their _____,

had called it at Parents' Evening.

　　The shouts and squeals from the playground grew louder and school loomed

out of the morning mist. Wes pushed open the _____ gate and the

_____ boys merged with the crowd, _____ the usual thumps

of welcome from their pals. "Anyway," David _____, "at least it'll be

over by playtime."

Focus on Literacy Teacher's Resource Book 6 © John McIlwain, HarperCollins*Publishers* Ltd 1999

Naming of Parts

_____ we have naming of parts. _____

We had daily cleaning. And _____ morning,

We shall have what to do after _____. But today,

Today we have naming of parts. *Japonica*

_____ like coral in all of the neighbouring gardens,

And today we have naming of parts.

This is the lower sling swivel. And this

Is the upper sling swivel, _____ use you will see

When you are _____ your slings. And this is the piling swivel

Which in _____ case you have not got. *The* _____

Hold in the garden their silent, eloquent gestures,

_____ in our case we have not got.

This is the safety catch ...

And this you can see is the bolt ...

They call it easing the Spring: it is _____ easy

If you have any _____ in your _____: like the bolt,

And the breech, and the cocking _____, and the point of balance,

Which in our case we have not got; *and the almond blossom*

Silent in all of the gardens and the bees going _____ and forwards,

For today we have naming of parts.

Henry Reed

Focus on Literacy Teacher's Resource Book 6 © John McIlwain, HarperCollins*Publishers* Ltd 1999

Signs, symbols and abbreviations for taking notes

These signs, symbols and abbreviations will help you take notes quickly and clearly.

A Write down the meaning of these symbols. One has been done for you.

c.   _about_ _____

p.   _____

i.e. _____

e.g. _____

etc. _____

NB   _____

=   _____

>   _____

<   _____

∴   _____

pp.   _____

_____

B Give examples to show how you could use these signs. One has been done for you.

c.   _about. He died in c.1937._ _____

i.e. _____

e.g. _____

etc. _____

NB   _____

∴   _____

Focus on Literacy Teacher's Resource Book 6 © John McIlwain, HarperCollins*Publishers* Ltd 1999

Copymaster 26
Unit 26

Dictionary definitions

A Use a dictionary to find the meanings of the words below *as they occur in the passage*. Write what part of speech they are, then a definition.
The first one has been done for you.

Try to open the dictionary as near the right place as possible. Use the guide words at the top of the page to help you. They tell you the first and last words on a page. If the word is not in your dictionary, look in a larger one.

scatter Verb: to throw or drop things all over an area

predict _____

station _____

equal _____

surface _____

B Do the same with these words, but add the origin of the word if you can.

compile Verb: to put together several items in a book, report, etc. Latin compilare: to pile together

primary _____
_____

element _____
_____

limited _____
_____

analyse _____
_____

C Do the same as section B with these. You may need to use a larger dictionary.

variation _____
_____

depletion _____
_____

visibility _____
_____

term _____
_____

determine _____
_____

encompass _____
_____

Focus on Literacy Teacher's Resource Book 6 © John McIlwain, HarperCollins*Publishers* Ltd 1999

Name _____

D is for Dad

Dad came to collect me on Friday evening. I got so excited and fidgety before he came that I couldn't even sit still to watch *Neighbours*. I couldn't wait for him to get here – and yet when he tooted his car horn I suddenly clutched Mum and didn't want to go after all. It's always like that. Dad doesn't come to the front door any more. Dad and Mum still row a lot if they're together for long. And once Dad and the baboon nearly had a fight. They both had their fists in the air and circled round each other. Mum yelled but they didn't take any notice of her. I kept tugging at Dad but he just brushed my hand away. It was Katie who stopped them fighting.

"Oh please stop, Daddy, you're scaring me," she squeaked, blinking the famous blue eyes.

I can't stick Katie.

There's one really good thing. My Dad can't stand her either.

"I had another fight with Katie," I told Dad when we were driving over to his place.

"And who won?"

"*I* did."

Dad chuckled. "Good for you, Andy. She's a spoilt little brat if ever I saw one."

"Uncle Bill said I was spoilt the other day," I said.

Focus on Literacy Teacher's Resource Book 6 © John McIlwain, HarperCollins*Publishers* Ltd 1999

Name _____

Copymaster 28
Unit 28

An extended story

Good stories must have: a beginning, a middle, an end, at least one climax, character development, a beginning which hooks the reader, readability (i.e. flow), interest (the quality that makes you want to read the next line, turn each page), and balance between narrative and speech.

Plan your extended story with the help of these headings.

Subject or theme

Characters

How it starts

What happens

How it ends

The climax will be

How the main character(s) will develop

Focus on Literacy Teacher's Resource Book 6 © John McIlwain, HarperCollins*Publishers* Ltd 1999

Crossword

TAKE PART IN A RACE →		PIGS LIVE HERE ↴ BRIGHT BOY'S NAME ↓	↴	FEMALE SHEEP ↴	↴	TV COMMERCIAL ↓		CHICKENS GROW FROM IT ↴
				WHAT A DOG MIGHT DO WITH ITS TAIL →				GO IN ↓
A SORT OF CASTLE IT COMES BEFORE JUNE →				THE BORDER OF SOMETHING →				
↴			IT KEEPS US COOL IN SUMMER ↓	↴ MOST PEOPLE HAVE ONE			GIRL'S NAME (ANAGRAM OF USE) ↓	
JAMES BOND WAS ONE	MANY TREES TOGETHER →							
					REGRET (ANAGRAM OF ERU) →			
↴ BOILED WATER (ANAGRAM OF MATES)	MORE TIDY →							

Focus on Literacy Teacher's Resource Book 6 © John McIlwain, HarperCollins*Publishers* Ltd 1999

Copymaster 30
Unit 30

Books by Anne Fine

Use this sheet to plan your comparison between two of Anne Fine's books. Make fairly brief notes, using the other side of the sheet if you need it.

Summary of subject

Mme D	FB

Style

Mme D	FB

Characterisation

Mme D	FB

Likely appeal to readers

Mme D	FB

Strengths

Mme D	FB

Weaknesses

Mme D	FB

My opinion of:

Mme D	FB

Other points

Mme D	FB

My preference

Conclusion

Focus on Literacy Teacher's Resource Book 6 © John McIlwain, HarperCollins*Publishers* Ltd 1999

Focus on Literacy 6

Achievement Award

Awarded to _____

For _____

Signed _____   Date _____

School _____

Focus on Literacy 6

Achievement Award

Awarded to _____

For _____

Signed _____   Date _____

School _____

Focus on Literacy Teacher's Resource Book 6 © John McIlwain, HarperCollins*Publishers* Ltd 1999

NAME _____   CLASS _____

Year 6 • Term 1

Word level work: phonics, spelling, vocabulary

Objective	Comment
Spelling strategies	
1 Identifying own misspelt words	
2 Using known spellings to spell other words	
3 Using independent strategies	
Spelling conventions and rules	
4 Patterns for unstressed vowels in polysyllabics	
5 Using roots, prefixes, suffixes to support spelling	
6 Connectives: meanings and spellings	
Vocabulary extension	
7 Words changing over time	
8 Origins of proper names	
9 New words to language	
10 Etymological dictionary: use and function	

Sentence level work: grammar and punctuation

Objective	Comment
Grammatical awareness	
1 Word classes Re-expressing sentences Construction of complex sentences Conventions of Standard English Adapting texts	
2 Active and passive: transforming sentences	
3 Active and passive: change of meaning	
Sentence construction and punctuation	
4 Investigating connecting words and phrases	
5 Forming, evaluating, understanding complex sentences	
6 Colons, semi-colons, parentheses, etc.	

Text level work: comprehension and composition

Objective	Comment
Fiction and poetry	
Reading comprehension	
1 Compare novel/play with film/TV version	
2 Viewpoint in a novel	
3 Personal responses to literature	
4 Familiarity with established authors	
5 Shared discussion about literature	
Writing composition	
6 Manipulate narrative perspective	
7 Plan plot, characters, structure of own writing	
8 Summarise passage, etc., in a given number of words	
9 Prepare section of story as script	
10 Write poems using active verbs and personification	
Non-fiction	
Reading comprehension	
11 Distinguish between biography and autobiography	
12 Comment critically on non-fiction	
13 Understand features of non-chronological reports	
Writing composition	
14 Biographical and autobiographical writing	
15 Understand journalistic style	
16 Write in journalistic style	
17 Write non-chronological reports	
18 Use IT in writing	

   Focus on Literacy Teacher's Resource Book 6 © John McIlwain, HarperCollins*Publishers* Ltd 1999

NAME _____   CLASS _____

Year 6 • Term 2

Word level work: phonics, spelling, vocabulary

Objective	Comment
Spelling strategies	
1 Identifying own misspelt words	
2 Using known spellings to spell other words	
3 Using independent strategies	
Spelling conventions and rules	

4   Spelling rules
     Mnemonics
     Patterns for unstressed vowels in polysyllabics	

5 Word origins and derivations	
Vocabulary extension	
6 Proverbs	
7 Change of meanings over time	
8 Phrases for argument	

Sentence level work: grammar and punctuation

Objective	Comment
Grammatical awareness	
1 Active and passive verbs	
2 Formal official language	
Sentence construction and punctuation	
3 Complex sentences	
4 Contracting sentences	
5 Conditionals: investigating and using	

Text level work: comprehension and composition

Objective	Comment
Fiction and poetry	
Reading comprehension	
1 Narrative structure	
2 Structure of paragraphs	
3 Poetry: manipulation of words	
4 Humorous verse	
5 Messages, moods, etc., in poetry	
6 Interpret challenging poems	
7 Key features of text types	
8 Analyse success of texts in provoking response	
9 Increased familiarity with past writers and poets	
Writing composition	
10 Use different genres as models	
11 Write using flashbacks, etc.	
12 Study one genre, writing extended piece	
13 Parody a literary text	
14 Summaries or commentaries	
Non-fiction	
Reading composition	
15 Understand construction of arguments	
16 Identify features of balanced arguments	
17 Official language	
Writing composition	
18 Construct effective arguments	
19 Write balanced report	
20 Discuss variations in Standard English	

   Focus on Literacy Teacher's Resource Book 6 © John McIlwain, HarperCollins*Publishers* Ltd 1999

NAME _____   CLASS _____

Year 6 • Term 3

Word level work: phonics, spelling, vocabulary

Objective	Comment
Spelling strategies	
1 Identifying own misspelt words	
2 Using known spellings to spell other words	
3 Using independent strategies	
Spelling conventions and rules	
4 Spelling rules Mnemonics Patterns for unstressed vowels in polysyllabics	
Vocabulary extension	
5 Invent words using known prefixes	
6 Practise and extend vocabulary	
7 Experiment with language	

Sentence level work: grammar and punctuation

Objective	Comment
Grammatical awareness	
1 Conventions and features of different texts	
2 Detailed language investigations	
Sentence construction and punctuation	
3 Formal styles of writing	
4 Complex sentences	

Text level work: comprehension and composition

Objective	Comment
Fiction and poetry	
Reading comprehension	
1 Describe and evaluate style of one writer	
2 Linked poems	
3 Describe and evaluate style of one poet	
4 Comment on impact of a poem	
5 Compare and contrast work of one writer	
6 Connections and contrasts between writers	
Writing composition	
7 Annotate passages	
8 Use reading journal	
9 Write summaries	
10 Write synopsis	
11 Write review	
12 Compare texts	
13 Write sequence of poems linked by theme or form	
14 Write extended story from reading	
Non-fiction	
Reading comprehension	
15 Understand explanatory texts	
16 Identify features of formal language	
17 Appraise, retrieve information from text	
18 Skimming, scanning, etc.	
19 Review range of non-fiction texts	
Writing comprehension	
20 Impersonal writing	
21 Use paragraphs effectively	
22 Write in appropriate style and form	

   Focus on Literacy Teacher's Resource Book 6 © John McIlwain, HarperCollins*Publishers* Ltd 1999

Appendices

NLS and *Focus on Literacy*: overview charts

Term 1

Word level	Sentence level	Text level
1 Continuous work	1 Continuous work	1 Continuous work
2 Continuous work	2 Units 3, 11	2 Units 2, 4, 11
3 Continuous work	3 Units 3, 4	3 Units 1, 2, 3, 4, 6, 7, 9, 11
4 Units 1, 2	4 Units 1, 2, 6, 7, 8, 10, 11	4 Units 6, 7, 11
5 Units 5, 7	5 Units 1, 3, 7, 10	5 Units 1, 6, 7, 11
6 Unit 12	6 Units 1, 5, 6, 7, 9, 11	6 Units 2, 4, 6, 7, 12
7 Units 4, 6, 7, 11, 12		7 Unit 1
8 Unit 10		8 Units 1, 3, 4, 7, 10, 12
9 Units 6, 8		9 Unit 2
10 Units 4, 6, 11		10 Units 6, 9
		11 Units 4, 5
		12 Units 3, 4, 7, 8, 10
		13 Unit 10
		14 Units 3, 4, 5
		15 Unit 8
		16 Unit 8
		17 Unit 10
		18 Continuous work

Term 2

Word level	Sentence level	Text level
1 Continuous work	1 Units 13, 15	1 Units 13, 16, 19, 20
2 Continuous work	2 Unit 18	2 Units 13, 16, 19, 20
3 Continuous work	3 Unit 22	3 Units 14, 17, 21
4 Continuous work	4 Units 15, 19	4 Units 14, 17, 21
5 Continuous work	5 Units 13, 16, 22	5 Units 14, 21
6 Unit 14		6 Units 14, 21
7 Unit 19		7 Units 19, 22
8 Unit 15		8 Units 13, 16
		9 Units 21, 22
		10 Units 16, 20, 22
		11 Units 13, 16, 22
		12 Unit 16
		13 Unit 22
		14 Unit 21
		15 Unit 15
		16 Unit 15
		17 Unit 18
		18 Units 15, 18, 19
		19 Unit 15
		20 Unit 18

Term 3

Word level	Sentence level	Text level
1 Continuous work	1 Units 24, 27	1 Units 27, 28, 30
2 Continuous work	2 Unit 27	2 Unit 24
3 Continuous work	3 Continuous work	3 Units 24, 29
4 Continuous work	4 Continuous work	4 Units 24, 29
5 Unit 29		5 Units 28, 29, 30
6 Units 28, 29		6 Units 24, 27, 29
7 Units 28, 29		7 Unit 27
		8 Unit 27
		9 Units 27, 28, 30
		10 Unit 28
		11 Units 24, 28, 30
		12 Units 24, 27, 28, 30
		13 Unit 24
		14 Unit 29
		15 Units 23, 25, 26
		16 Units 23, 25, 26
		17 Units 23, 25, 26
		18 Units 25, 26
		19 Units 23, 25, 26
		20 Units 23, 24, 25, 26
		21 Units 23, 24, 25, 26
		22 Units 25, 26

Medium frequency word list

These words should be revised during Year 6.

above
across
almost
along
also
always
animals
any
around
asked
baby
balloon
before
began
being
below
better
between
birthday
both
brother
brought
can't
change
children
clothes
coming
didn't
different
does
don't
during
earth
every
eyes
father
first
follow(ing)
found
friends

garden
goes
gone
great
half
happy
head
heard
high
I'm
important
inside
jumped
knew
know
lady
leave
light
might
money
morning
mother
much
near
never
number
often
only
opened
other
outside
own
paper
place
right
round
second
show
sister
small

something
sometimes
sound
started
still
stopped
such
suddenly
sure
swimming
think
those
thought
through
today
together
told
tries
turn(ed)
under
until
upon
used
walk(ed)(ing)
watch
where
while
white
whole
why
window
without
woke(n)
word
work
world
write
year
young